Humean Moral Pluralism

Humean Moral Pluralism

Michael B. Gill

OXFORD
UNIVERSITY PRESS

OXFORD
UNIVERSITY PRESS

Great Clarendon Street, Oxford, OX2 6DP,
United Kingdom

Oxford University Press is a department of the University of Oxford.
It furthers the University's objective of excellence in research, scholarship,
and education by publishing worldwide. Oxford is a registered trade mark of
Oxford University Press in the UK and in certain other countries

The moral rights of the author have been asserted

First Edition published in 2014
Impression: 1

Published in the United States of America by Oxford University Press
198 Madison Avenue, New York, NY 10016, United States of America

British Library Cataloguing in Publication Data
Data available

Library of Congress Control Number: 2014930994

ISBN: 978-0-19-871403-3

Printed and bound by
CPI Group (UK) Ltd, Croydon, CR0 4YY

Links to third party websites are provided by Oxford in good faith and
for information only. Oxford disclaims any responsibility for the materials
contained in any third party website referenced in this work.

Acknowledgements

This book is pluralist in method as well as content. I examine historical texts, empirically grounded work in moral psychology, and intuitively supported conceptual arguments. I believe the resulting view is all the more plausible for being arrived at through a variety of approaches. Looking at the same issue through different lenses is also, to me at least, more interesting.[1]

I am deeply grateful to the many friends and colleagues who helped me in this project. Special thanks go to Shaun Nichols, Mark Timmons, and Jenann Ismael, who discussed almost every aspect of this work with me innumerable times. Their feedback made the book much better than it would otherwise have been. Their company made it immeasurably more enjoyable to work on.

I have also received significant help from all of the following: Kate Abramson, Julia Annas, Rachel Cohon, Stephen Darwall, Remy Debes, Richard Dees, Sam Fleischacker, Jerry Gaus, Ryan Hanley, James Harris, Colin Heydt, Tom Holden, Terry Horgan, Rachana Kamtekar, David Owen, Eric Schliesser, David Schmidtz, and Elizabeth Radcliffe

It used to be a relatively common practice to include in a book's acknowledgements a statement along the lines of: "Any flaws and errors herein are strictly my own, and not the responsibility of those who have helped me in the writing of this book." Such statements always struck me as irritatingly unnecessary.[2] Of course the flaws and errors are yours! But now I find myself wanting to say the same thing. For on matters outside my field of expertise I have sought guidance from friends. Yet I'm sure I've still made mistakes—of both commission and omission. So what I want to say is: those mistakes are present despite my friends' efforts. They really did their best to try to get me to do better.

To Sarah, Hannah, and Jesse: thanks for filling my life with so many different things of value.

Chapter 2 is based on my "Humean Moral Pluralism," *History of Philosophy Quarterly*, 28 (2011): 45–64.

Chapter 3 is based on my "Humean Sentimentalism and Non-Consequentialist Moral Thinking," *Hume Studies*, 37 (2011): 165–88.

Chapter 4 is based on my "Moral Pluralism in Smith and his Contemporaries," *Revue Internationale de Philosophie*, 68 (2014).

Parts of Chapter 5 are based on Michael B. Gill and Shaun Nichols, "Sentimentalist Pluralism: Moral Psychology and Philosophical Ethics," *Philosophical Topics*, 18 (2008): 143-67.

Chapter 10 is based on my "Agonizing Decisions and Moral Pluralism," in Mark Timmons (ed.), *Conduct and Character*, 317–29. Oxford: Oxford University Press.

Contents

List of Abbreviations

D   David Hume (1998b). "A Dialogue," in *An Enquiry concerning the Principles of Morals*, ed. Tom L. Beauchamp. Oxford: Oxford University Press. Numeral denotes paragraph.

E   David Hume (1751/2006). *An Enquiry concerning the Principles of Morals*, ed. Tom L. Beauchamp. Oxford: Oxford University Press. Numerals denote section and paragraph. The appendices from the *Enquiry* are referred to as "App," with the numerals following denoting appendix number and paragraph.

Essays   David Hume (1987). *Essays, Moral, Political, and Literary*, ed. Eugene F. Miller. Indianapolis: Liberty Fund.

History   David Hume (1983). *The History of England* (based on 1778 edn). Indianapolis: Liberty Fund. Numerals denote volume and page.

Letters   David Hume (1932). *The Letters of David Hume*, ed. J. Y. T. Greig, i. Oxford: Oxford University Press.

T   David Hume (1739–40/2002). *A Treatise of Human Nature*, ed. David Fate Norton and Mary J. Norton. Oxford: Oxford University Press. Numerals denote book, part, section, and paragraph.

TMS   Adam Smith (1759/1984). *The Theory of Moral Sentiments*. Indianapolis: Liberty Fund.

Introduction

Many perennial debates in moral philosophy are compelling because of how they bear on justification's end. For instance—does morality originate in reason or sentiment? If morality originates in reason, then it will be at least theoretically possible to provide a thoroughly rational justification for all our moral judgments. If morality originates in sentiment, then moral justification will end with concerns of ours that are not rationally required. The danger of a mistaken sentimentalism is giving up too soon: we might think a moral commitment of ours is as justified as it can be, when in fact it is based on something that can be shown to be irrational. The danger of a mistaken rationalism is unrealistic expectations: we might think a moral judgment is illegitimate because it cannot be shown to be fully rational, when in fact it is as justified as it can be.

Is morality universal or relative to culture? If it's universal, then if two cultures assign differing moral status to a single practice it will always be at least theoretically possible to show that one of them is wrong. If it's relative, then two cultures with differing views may both be as justified as can be. The danger of a mistaken relativism is, once again, giving up too soon: resting content with a practice that further moral scrutiny would reveal to be unjustified. The danger of a mistaken universalism is insisting on the impossible: refusing to accept the legitimacy of a practice because it fails to achieve a justificatory standard that is in fact unreachable.

Its bearing on justification's end is also what makes the debate between pluralists and their opponents compelling—and profoundly important to the first-person, deliberative life of a moral agent.

Moral pluralists hold that there is a multitude of basic moral principles that can come into conflict with each other. Their opponents hold that such conflict is impossible. If the opponents of pluralism are right, in every situation it will always be at least theoretically possible to justify a certain course of action by showing that it and only it follows from a correct application of basic moral principles. Every moral question you will ever face will have a principled answer. You will, of course, have to execute judgment to correctly apply principles to particular situations. But if you know what the relevant principles are and how they apply, the right answer will be clear. It will always be appropriate for you to aspire to completely principled moral justification.

If pluralism is true, in contrast, you may find yourself in a situation in which two principles require conflicting actions, and you may not be able to rely on any other principle for resolving the conflict. In morally fraught situations your final judgment may outstrip principled support, confronting you with an unfillable justificatory gap between general principles and particular judgments. Even after you have given the best justification for a course of action that it is possible to give, you may sometimes have to acknowledge that to follow that course will be to act in conflict with something of fundamental moral importance. Your best justification may fail to make all of the moral ends meet.

The danger of a mistaken opposition to pluralism is refusing to accept a course of action as truly justified because it conflicts with something of fundamental moral importance, when in fact the situation may be one in which conflict between things of fundamental moral importance is ineliminable. The danger of a mistaken pluralism is accepting as justified a course of action that conflicts with a fundamental moral end, when it is in fact possible to find a way to act that is consistent with everything morally fundamental.

In this book I explore a Humean pluralist view of morality. I elucidate how this view developed in the eighteenth century and argue for its continuing viability today. Let me start by explaining briefly what I mean by "pluralist" and by "Humean" and by giving a quick overview of the book as a whole.

A view of morality is *pluralist*, as I will use the term, if it holds that there is a multiplicity of ultimate moral ends (i.e. more than one), if the multiplicity of ultimate moral ends can come into conflict with each other, and if there is no invariable ordering principle for resolving all such conflicts.[1] Berys Gaut's description of the difference between "prioritarian" and "pluralist" views captures well the distinction I will be concerned with.[2] "Prioritarianism," Gaut says,

is the claim that for any action there is a rule or rules which entail that just one of the following possibilities is true of that action: that it is required, or forbidden, or permitted. We can distinguish three ways in which a theory may be prioritist. Firstly, if a theory has only one principle which can be applied to any set of actions, such as utilitarianism, it is prioritist. Secondly, a theory can be prioritist if it incorporates a multitude of principles which are ranked in such a way that for any circumstance one knows which takes precedence over the other. Rawls' theory of justice incorporates two principles, but it is prioritist since he gives a priority rule that lexically orders one over the other. Finally, a theory can be prioritist because, though it lacks a comprehensive ranking method, it claims that the principles *never* clash. (Gaut 1993, 9)

Pluralist views, in contrast, hold that there are multiple fundamental ends, that these ends can require incompatible actions, and that there is no comprehensive ranking method for resolving such conflict. As Rawls puts it,

[Pluralist] theories, then, have two features: first, they consist of a plurality of first principles which may conflict to give contrary directives in particular cases; and second, they include no explicit method, no priority rules, for weighing these principles against one another: we are simply to strike a balance by intuition, by what seems to us most nearly right. Or if there are priority rules, these are thought to be more or less trivial and of no substantial assistance in reaching a judgment. (Rawls 1971, 34; quoted by Gaut 1993, 18)[3]

I will call any prioritarian view that has only one ultimate end a "monism." A prioritarian view that affirms a multitude of ultimate ends that never conflict with each other I will call "non-conflict multiplism." A prioritarian view that affirms a multitude of ultimate ends that conflict with each other but are lexically ordered I will call "ordered conflict multiplism," or just "ordered multiplism."[4] Non-prioritarian views—i.e. views that affirm a multitude of ends that conflict with each other but deny any strict or lexical ordering—I will (following Gaut) take to be instances of "moral pluralism."[5]

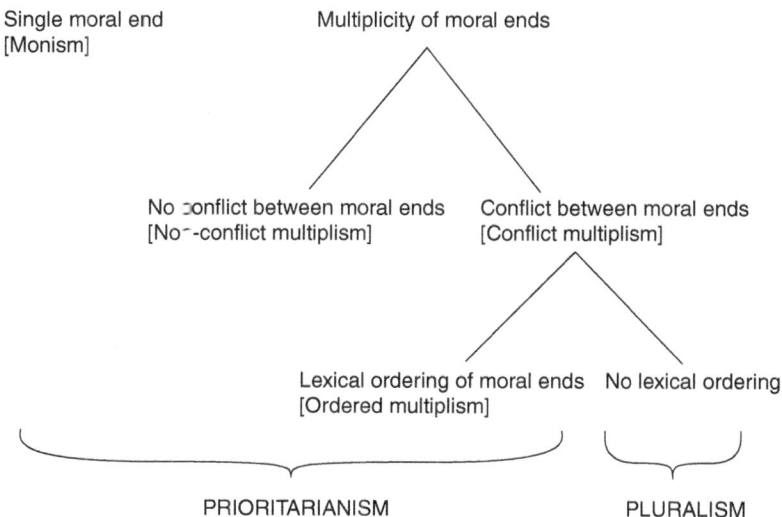

So a pluralist position on moral judgment holds that our activity of making moral judgments is best explained by attributing to us a multiplicity of potentially conflicting ultimate moral ends, and by not attributing to us an invariant ordering principle for resolving all conflicts between ultimate moral ends.

A view of morality is *Humean*, as I will use the term, if it holds that human sentiments are causally essential to the activity of human moral judgment and that there exist no mind-independent moral properties that human moral judgments track. On the Humean view, if humans did not have sentiments they would not make moral judgments, and if humans had different sentiments they would make different moral judgments. Humeanism holds that in the best causal explanation of our activity of making moral judgments sentiments play an essential role and mind-independent moral properties play no role at all.

In calling a moral view "Humean" I do not mean to say that it takes any particular position on the meaning of moral terms, on whether statements of right and wrong have a descriptive or expressive function, on whether our concept of morality commits us to moral objectivity or relativity, or the like. Humeanism as I understand it is a claim about the best causal explanation of our activity of moral judgment, not a conceptual meta-ethics. I have argued elsewhere that our moral thinking is too variable and indeterminate to support any single, determinate answer to those conceptual questions.[6]

I believe, as well, that there is no single, determinate answer to the question of whether our concept of morality is pluralist or prioritarian. There are probably some people whose moral thinking is almost entirely pluralist and other people whose moral thinking is almost entirely prioritarian. I suspect, though, that the moral thinking of most of us includes both pluralist and prioritarian strands. Part of my goal in the historical sections of this book (Chapters 1–4) is to show how these two strands were woven into eighteenth-century British moral thought— with a focus on the uneasy eighteenth-century coexistence of pluralism and prioritarian multiplisms. Chapters 5 and 6 are intended to bolster especially the *Humean* side of Humean pluralism, by showing the support that Humean sentimentalism has gained from recent work in moral psychology (Chapter 5) and Humean pluralism's superiority to the non-naturalist pluralism of Ross (Chapter 6). In Chapter 7, I explain what I take to be the most powerful reason for thinking we should retain the prioritarian aspects of our moral thinking and jettison the pluralist aspects— a reason that leads to the grand monistic theories of Kant and the utilitarians. In Chapters 8 and 9, I argue that if Humeanism is true, we in fact have better reasons to retain the pluralist aspects and reject the prioritarian. Chapter 10 is intended to bolster the *pluralist* side of Humean pluralism, by developing an argument showing the great depth of the commitment to pluralism in commonsense moral thinking.

The pluralist account of the content of morality has been traditionally perceived as belonging with non-naturalist intuitionism. Hume's sentimentalist account of morality has been traditionally perceived as not belonging with any view of morality's content at all. My goal is to explode both those perceptions: to convince you that pluralism and Humeanism belong together, and that together they make a couple of significant philosophical power.

1

Multiple Ultimate Ends, or Only One? The British Moralist Debate

If you were forced to choose one moral theory as being the most influential in Britain in the modern era, you would have to pick Bentham and Mill's utilitarianism. Much of utilitarianism's power comes from its simplicity. It places a single principle at "the foundation of morality," gives us a single "criterion of right and wrong," tells us that there is one and only ultimate "end of human action in every situation," one and only one "ultimate standard" (Mill 1861/2001, 1–3; Bentham 1823/1907, 1). This end, of course, is happiness or utility (Mill 1861/2001, 7). Bentham and Mill acknowledge that determining which particular actions to perform in real-world situations is not always a simple matter. Figuring out what will best promote utility often involves "real" and "knotty" difficulties (Mill 1861/2001, 25–6). But even if the empirical tasks involved are difficult, the monistic structure of Bentham and Mill's utilitarianism provides perfectly unitary normative guidance.

This is not what British moral theory looked like a century before. In the late seventeenth and early eighteenth centuries, the more common view was that at the base of morality were *three* ultimate ends: (1) the duty to worship God, (2) the duty to treat other people well, and (3) the duty of moderation or temperance.

A good example of this three-part picture can be found in *The Whole Duty of Man*, the most popular English devotional work between 1660 and 1711.[1] The title on the first page of the first sermon of *The Whole Duty* reads: "Of the Duty of Man by the Light of Nature, by the Light of Scripture: the three great branches of Man's Duty to God, our selves, our Neighbour" (1). The author then goes on to write, "This I find briefly contained in the words of the Apostle, *Tit.* 2.12. *That we should live soberly, righteously, and godly in this present world*; where the word, *Soberly,* contain our *duty* to our *Selves*; *Righteously,* our *duty* to our *Neighbour*; and *Godly,* our *duty* to *God*. These therefore shall be the Heads of my Discourse, our DUTY to GOD, our SELVES, and our NEIGHBOUR" (4). What then follow are extensive examinations of the specific duties that grow out of these "three great branches."

In sermons delivered in the 1660s and 1670s, Benjamin Whichcote claimed that morality was based on the same three fundamental ends: "to reverence and acknowledge the deity"; "to live in love, and bear good will towards one another [and] to deal justly, equally and fairly in all our transactions and dealings each with other"; and "to use moderation and government of ourselves, in respect of the necessaries and conveniences of this state" (Whichcote 1751, iv. 351; see also Whichcote 1751, i. 383–4). Whichcote went on to derive from these three basic duties particular rules dictating how one ought to conduct oneself in matters of worship, speech, contracts, diet, and the running of a household, including instructions on how parents are to treat their children, husbands are to treat their wives, masters their servants, and men their dogs and horses (Whichcote 1751, i. 253–5, ii. 218–19, iv. 351–61).

The same three-part picture can be found in Samuel Clarke, who maintained in 1705 that there are 'three great and principal Branches, from which all the other and smaller instances of duty do naturally flow, or may without difficulty be derived" (Clarke 1705/1738, 618). These three branches were, once again, our duties "in respect of *God*," "in respect of our *Fellow-Creatures*," and "with respect to *our selves*" (Clarke 1705/1738, 618–22).

In 1724 Gershom Carmichael said much the same: "As the basis of the natural laws we place not one fundamental precept ... but three: that God is to be worshipped; that each man should pursue his own interest without harming others; and that sociability should be cultivated. To the first of these we refer the duties which are to be performed directly toward God; to the second those duties of man toward himself which do not conflict with the interest of any other person; and to the third, all the duties of a man toward other men ..." (Carmichael 1724/2002, 1.5.12).[2]

The authors of the *Whole Duty of Man*, Whichcote, Clarke, and Carmichael, were moral multiplists. They all held that there is a multiplicity of ultimate moral ends, not just one. What was the route from this multiplist moral picture of the late seventeenth and early eighteenth centuries to Bentham and Mill's monistic utilitarianism?

As Julia Driver (2009) has shown, there were numerous utilitarian antecedents in the seventeenth and eighteenth centuries. But none laid the groundwork more clearly than Francis Hutcheson.

All of morality, Hutcheson claimed in 1726, has "one general Foundation," and that is approval of the motive to promote the welfare of humanity in general

(Hutcheson 1726/2004, 116). "Love, or Benevolence," Hutcheson writes, "is the Foundation of all apprehended Excellence in social Virtues... [T]he only way of deciding the Controversy about any disputed Practice [is] to enquire whether this Conduct, or the contrary, will most effectually promote the publick Good. The morality is immediately adjusted, when the natural Tendency, or Influence of the Action upon the universal natural Good of Mankind is agreed upon. That which produces more Good than Evil in the Whole, is acknowledg'd Good; and what does not, is counted Evil" (Hutcheson 1726/2004, 118). Or as Hutcheson's more famous formulation has it: "that action is best, which procures the greatest happiness for the greatest numbers; and that, worst, which, in like manner, occasions Misery" (Hutcheson 1726/2004, 126). While his three-part predecessors tried to show that all of our specific duties grew out of "three great and principal branches," Hutcheson claimed it was possible to produce "deductions" of all the parts of morality—including our judgments of others' actions and characters, and our notions of property and rights—from the single end of the promotion of public good (Hutcheson 1726/2004, 266, 277–8).[3]

Hutcheson acknowledged that we sometimes approve of people when they intend to promote the welfare of only a few people and not humanity as a whole. We approve of parents' love for their children, of friends' mutual concern for each other, of patriots' commitment to their country. But what makes these cases of "partial benevolence" virtuous, according to Hutcheson, is their goal of promoting human welfare, and it is always morally better to promote more human welfare rather than less. Partial benevolence is a morally lesser version of general benevolence.[4] We recognize "different Degrees of Moral Beauty," and the highest degree is a benevolence toward all humans that "controuls our kind particular Passions... or counteracts them" (Hutcheson 1726/2004, 231). The morally best thing is to try to promote the welfare of all, even in those cases in which it means sacrificing the "Happiness of certain smaller Systems of Individuals," such as those composed of one's countrymen, one's friends, and one's children (Hutcheson 1726/2004, 231). Hutcheson is rightly taken to be an early utilitarian.[5]

In arguing for benevolence's moral hegemony, Hutcheson was not principally concerned to defeat the three-part multiplism of Whichcote, Clarke, and Carmichael. His explicit goal, rather, was to defeat another kind of monism: namely, the egoist monism of Hobbes and Mandeville.[6] (Perhaps this partly explains Hutcheson's view: in his zeal to show that monistic egoism was false he traveled all the way in the opposite direction, to the conclusion that monistic altruism was true.) And Hutcheson's attack on egoism was largely successful, endorsed and advanced by many of his immediate successors. Until Bentham, however, his benevolence-monism fared considerably worse. Multiplism remained predominant. Indeed, for the next fifty years, multiplist refutations of Hutcheson became something of a philosophical staple.

In one of the first and most influential of these refutations (which we will look at in more detail), Joseph Butler maintained that Hutcheson was wrong to contend that "the whole of virtue [consisted] in singly aiming, according to the best of [one's] judgment, at promoting the happiness of mankind; and the whole of vice, in doing what [one] forsee[s], or might foresee, is likely to produce an overbalance of unhappiness in it: than which mistakes, none can be conceived more terrible" (Butler 1736/1983, 74). Hutcheson's view that general benevolence is the entirety of virtue is a terrible mistake, according to Butler, because it leads us to ignore other principles that are rightly taken to be morally ultimate. These other principles include "veracity" and "justice," as well as the "gratitude" and the "friendship" that motivate us to benefit those near and dear to us rather than promote the welfare of people in general (Butler 1736/1983, 72–4). As Butler writes, "The fact then appears to be, that we are constituted so as to condemn falsehood, unprovoked violence, injustice, and to approve of benevolence to some preferably to others, abstracted from all consideration, which conduct is likeliest to produce an overbalance of happiness or misery . . . [S]ince this is our constitution; falsehood, violence, injustice, must be vice in us, and benevolence to some preferably to others, virtue; abstracted from all consideration of the overbalance of evil or good, which they may appear likely to produce" (Butler 1736/1983, 73–4). Butler thinks we should take there to be a multiplicity of independent ultimate moral ends—justice, veracity, and the partial benevolence of friendship and gratitude among them. We ought to be morally concerned with each of these for its own sake, as an independent reason for action, and not take their normative force to be reducible to or derivable from a single utilitarian foundation.[7]

Hume emphatically endorsed this Butlerian criticism of Hutcheson's monism. In a letter to Hutcheson, Hume wrote, "I always thought you limited too much your Ideas of Virtue" (*Letters*, 47), and in the *Treatise* and *Second Enquiry* he developed an account that explicitly maintained that virtue extends beyond Hutchesonian benevolence to a number of other independent moral ends. (We'll examine Hume's view in Chapters 2 and 3).

Thomas Reid also rejected benevolence-monism. Reid contended that there are multiple "first or self-evident principles, on which all moral reasoning is grounded," rather than only one (Reid 1983, 321, 351). An "example or two will serve to illustrate this," Reid tells us, and he then mentions justice and benevolence, both of which are fundamental to moral reasoning in that to "reason about justice with a man who sees nothing to be just or unjust [about], or about benevolence with a man who sees nothing in benevolence preferable to malice, is like reasoning with a blind man about colour, or with a deaf man about sound" (Reid 1983, 321–2). Each of these ends is on the ground floor of moral reasoning. Each is justificatorily basic, not derived from any other. Justice is an ultimate principle, one that we could never arrive at through the consideration of other principles (just as a blind man could never have ideas of color). Reid goes on to give a fuller list of "first principles of morals," a list which consists of eleven items divided into three categories (Reid 1983, 352 ff.), which we'll examine later.[8]

Richard Price is another clear example of an anti-Hutchesonian multiplist.[9] In his discussion of Hutcheson's benevolence-monism, Price quotes extensively from Butler's *Dissertation*, unequivocally endorsing the "clear and decisive" anti-monistic arguments presented there (Price 1787, 219). Price also advances additional arguments against benevolence-monism, in which he turns Hutcheson's own weapons against him. Hutcheson had attacked the egoists by showing that they had to attribute to agents motives based on exceedingly complicated self-interested calculations, when in fact such calculations seem never to enter into the thoughts of many agents. But similarly, Price argues, Hutcheson's benevolence-monism must attribute to agents exceedingly complicated calculations about what will produce the greatest good for all of humanity, when in fact agents are sometimes motivated by immediate, non-calculative moral responses to things like falsehood, ingratitude, and injustice (Price 1787, 226–8). Price also argues, in a manner that anticipates the counterexampling of utilitarianism that would become common in centuries to come, that Hutcheson's benevolence-monism has the absurd implication that it would be right to torture "any number of innocent beings" if it made "a greater number of beings in a greater degree happy" (Price 1787, 268). When he is criticizing Hutcheson, Price goes out of his way to stress the multiplist character of morality:

But why must there be in the human mind approbation only of one sort of actions? Why must all moral good be reduced to one particular species of it, and kind affections, with the actions flowing from them, be represented, as alone capable of appearing to our moral faculty virtuous? Why may we not as well have an immediate relish also for truth, for candour, sincerity, piety, gratitude, and many other modes and principles of conduct? . . .[10] How unreasonable is that love of uniformity and simplicity which inclines men thus to seek them where it is so difficult to find them? It is this that, on other subjects, has often led men astray. What mistakes and extravagances in natural philosophy have been produced, by the desire of discovering one principles which shall account for all effects? (Price 1787, 228–30)

Hutcheson's error is to assume that morality must have a monistic structure.

Adam Smith is equally clear in his rejection of Hutcheson's monism. Smith devotes a chapter of his *Theory of Moral Sentiments* to "those Systems which make Virtue consist in Benevolence," and he says that "of all the patrons of this system, ancient or modern, the late Dr. Hutcheson was undoubtedly, beyond all comparison, the most acute, the most distinct, the most philosophical, and what is of the greatest consequences of all, the soberest and most judicious" (*TMS* 301). Smith acknowledges that Hutcheson's benevolence-monism "has a peculiar tendency to nourish and support in the human heart the noblest and the most agreeable of all affections" (*TMS* 303). The fact is, however, that there are also other basic moral ends—ends that explain our positive moral judgment of actions and character traits independent of any thought of their effects on public happiness. (We'll examine Smith's view in Chapter 4.)

So what happened? Before Hutcheson, the mainstream of British moral philosophy was characterized by multiplist views. After Hutcheson, multiplist views continued to thrive. Then, in the late eighteenth and nineteenth centuries, the utilitarianism of Bentham and Mill came on the scene. Why did their monistic utilitarianism begin to flourish fifty years after Hutcheson's "greatest happiness for the greatest numbers" formulation, and directly in the wake of the multiplist attacks of Butler, Hume, Reid, Price, and Smith? And is it just a coincidence that the other grand monistic theory of the modern period—Kant's—developed at the same time?

There are, I'm sure, a myriad of factors that account for the rise of modern monistic moral theorizing. I aim to advance a partial hypothesis. The key to this hypothesis—which I'll baldly state before going on to try to substantiate in the chapters to follow—is the distinction not between multiplism and monism but between prioritarianism and pluralism. Much of the moral theorizing early in the modern period assumed that morality was prioritarian. So while introspection and observation led many to think there were multiple ultimate moral ends, prioritarian assumptions shielded them from considering the possibility that these different ends could come into conflict (non-conflict multiplist view). Eventually, however, the possibility of such conflict did creep into view. And then a new, tripartite choice emerged: maintain multiple moral ends, allow that they can conflict, but maintain prioritarianism by affirming ordering principles for resolving that conflict (ordered multiplism); maintain multiple moral ends, allow that they can conflict, abandon prioritarianism (pluralism); or maintain prioritarianism by affirming one and only one ultimate end, for if there is only one end moral conflict once again becomes impossible (monism).

In the remainder of this chapter, we'll look Clarke and Butler, who are examples of non-conflict multiplists, i.e. multiplists who held prioritarian assumptions that kept them from seriously considering the possibility that different moral ends could come into conflict. In Chapters 2 through 4, we'll see how Hume and Smith (and, to a lesser extent Reid and Price) brought the possibility of moral conflict into view, and how this led them to grapple with the choice between pluralism and ordered multiplism—with pluralism eventually gaining a slight upper hand in the work of Hume and Smith. Many found the anti-prioritarian implications of pluralism unacceptable, however. But rather than try to return to non-conflict multiplism or attempt to justify ordering principles, theorists such as Kant and the utilitarians sought to maintain prioritarianism by advancing monistic views, which will be our topic in Chapter 7.

Clarke

As we've seen, Clarke holds that there are "three great and principal branches of morality," three general duties from which all other particular duties can be derived. Because of this, I classified Clarke as a multiplist, someone who holds that there are multiple ultimate moral ends.

It might be objected, however, that what Clarke says about fittingness make it more apt to take him to be a monist. Fittingness might seem to be for Clarke the single trunk out of which the three great and principal branches grow. Clarke writes:

The same necessary and eternal different Relations, that different Things bear one to another; and the same consequent Fitness or Unfitness of the Application of different things or different Relations one to another; with regard to which, the Will of God always and necessarily does determine it self, to choose to act only what is agreeable to Justice, Equity, Goodness and Truth, in order to the Welfare of the whole Universe; ought likewise constantly to determine the Wills of all subordinate rational Beings, to govern all Their Actions by the same Rules, for the Good of the Publick, in their respective Stations. That is; these eternal and necessary differences of things make it fit and reasonable for Creatures so to act; they cause it to be their Duty, or lay an Obligation upon them, so to do. (Clarke 1705/1738, 608)

On a monistic reading, what Clarke says here should be taken to imply that fitness is a principle that underlies all the moral rules—that fitness is the one ultimate moral end.

Even with this commitment to the principle of fitness, however, I think it is still more accurate to categorize Clarke as a moral multiplist. This is because Clarke thinks that fitness is that which characterizes all necessary truths, not only morality but also math, logic, and geometry. Clarke's point when talking about fitness is that certain moral principles are necessarily true in the same way those other principles are (Clarke 1705/1738, 192). But that's just to say that it's necessarily true that multiple moral principles have basic normative force, not to say that there is only one moral principle. Fitness is what characterizes all self-evident rightness, not a normative principle that serves as a basis for deriving all other principles.

Each of the moral principles is a basic reason for action, not a secondary or derived one. Fitness is a property that all moral ends possess, but it is not itself a moral end, let alone the only moral end. The fitness of a moral end is not itself a justificatory ground distinct from (or deeper than) the moral end itself. Chains of moral justification can stop at different places.[11]

But can these different moral ends imply incompatible actions? Is Clarke a non-conflict or a conflict multiplist?

Clarke never explicitly denies that conflict between ultimate ends can occur, but there are so far as I can see no passages in which he addresses the possibility of such conflicts occurring. This absence of discussion of moral conflict would be conspicuous in a work of multiplist moral philosophy written today. One of the first things a philosophical reader of today would want to know, after being told that there are several different ultimate ends, is how we should deal with cases in which different ends imply incompatible actions. Is there a priority ordering of the ends? Do some ends have normative trumping power over others? Do the ends include complex specifications that, when fully spelled out, reveal that they can never actually come into conflict? Are there some moral dilemmas that are finally irresolvable?

Why don't we find these sorts of questions raised in Clarke? It's possible that conflict between individuals' moral commitments simply was not common enough in Clarke's time and place to be salient to him. Maybe the moral life was less complex then, external circumstances being such as to dampen the eruption of morally difficult situations. Rather than pursue that idea, however (which I suspect must be either misleadingly simplistic or simply false), I want to suggest that Clarke did not discuss situations in which ultimate ends conflict because he did not think such situations could arise—because he thought any action truly implied by one ultimate end would be compatible with the actions truly implied by every other ultimate moral end. And Clarke thought this—he was a non-conflict multiplist— because his deep philosophical commitment to rationalism shielded him from a confrontation with the possibility of conflict between ultimate ends.

For Clarke, all ultimate ends are purely rational—rational in the same way the axioms of geometry, logic, and arithmetic are. As he puts it in one typical passage, the truths that constitute ultimate moral ends

are so notoriously plain and self-evident, that nothing but the extremest stupidity of Mind, corruption of Manners, or perverseness of Spirit, can possibly make any man entertain the least doubt concerning them. For a Man endued with *Reason*, to deny the Truth of these Things; is the very same thing...as if a Man that understand *Geometry* or *Arithmetick*, should deny the most obvious and known *Proportions* of *Lines* or *Numbers*, and perversely contend that the *Whole is not equal to all its parts*, or that a *Square* is not *equal to all its parts*, or that a *Square* is *not double to a triangle* of equal base and height. (Clarke 1705/1738, 609)

Ultimate moral ends are self-evident necessary truths of which we have a priori certainty, and our particular duties can be demonstrably derived from them. Now we do not expect first principles of geometry, logic, or arithmetic to come into conflict with each other. Indeed, we take such conflict to be impossible. The realm of the purely rational to which such principles belong is thoroughly harmonious. One necessary a priori truth cannot imply something that another necessary a priori truth implies the negation of. Clarke thinks the first principles of morality are necessary a priori truths and thus belong to the same thoroughly harmonious realm. Those principles, therefore, must not have conflicting implications, as allowing conflicting implications of true moral principles would be akin to affirming the truth of a contradiction. It must not be possible to demonstrably derive from self-evident principles that one has a duty to Φ and a duty not to Φ.[12]

There are two different forms non-conflict multiplism can take. A non-conflict multiplist can hold that the ultimate moral ends are all simple and non-conflicting, or that at least some of the (non-conflicting) ultimate moral ends are complex, including more or less detailed specifications and qualifications. A view of this second type can hold, for instance, that there is no ultimate moral end simply to promote human welfare but rather an ultimate end to promote human welfare unless doing so requires injustice or the breaking of a promise or the telling of a lie. This second view can hold that while the simple aim of promoting human welfare might conflict with the simple aim of not telling a lie, that incompatibility is not an instance of a conflict of ultimate moral ends because ultimate moral ends are not all that simple. When we truly understand ultimate moral ends with all their specifications and qualifications, we will see that they never require incompatible courses of action.

To which of these two versions of non-conflict multiplism does Clarke adhere? At one point, Clarke notes the difficulty of ascertaining the "bounds of right and wrong" in "some nice and perplext Cases" (Clarke 1705/1738, 611), and this might suggest the second version insofar as the difficulty in question could be equated to the difficulty of determining the full specifications and qualifications of different moral ends. But Clarke never explicitly says that moral duties have specifications or qualifications. He also maintains that the ultimate moral ends are as obvious to the human mind as the most basic truths of geometry and arithmetic, which suggests that we ought not to attribute to him the second version insofar as it takes the moral ends to involve complications that may fail to be "plain and self-evident."[13] This can push us to take Clarke's comments about its sometimes being difficult to ascertain the bounds of right and wrong to be an acknowledgement not of the difficulty of determining the specifications and qualifications of ultimate moral ends but rather of the difficulty of applying perfectly clear ultimate ends to murky real-world situations, which fits better with the first version.

The fact is, Clarke does not treat these topics in an expansive or coherent enough way to give us conclusive reasons to attribute to him one version of non-conflict multiplism rather than the other. Perhaps some interpretative principle of charity would lead us to offer to Clarke one of the two versions, but that is not an issue I will address any further. The point I wish to make is that Clarke does not allow that ultimate moral ends can ever come into conflict with each other. That Clarke does not himself advance any developed view on why such conflict will not occur seems to me a strong indication that he had deep philosophical commitments that shielded him from confronting the issue of moral conflict. Indeed, it may be that there is no clear fact of the matter as to what kind of non-conflict multiplist Clarke is. Maybe, despite what I argued above, it's not even clear that Clarke isn't a monist, with fitness being the single ultimate moral end. But on the most pressing justificatory question—whether morality is prioritarian or pluralist—Clarke's view is clear.

When merging his rationalist view of morals with his anti-voluntarist theology, Clarke writes, "As these eternal moral Obligations [note the plural] are really in perpetual Force merely from their own Nature and the abstract Reason of things; so also they are moreover the express and unalterable *Will, Command, and Law of God* to his Creatures, which he cannot but expect should in Obedience to his Supreme Authority, as well as in compliance with the Nature Reason of Things, be regularly and constantly observed through the whole Creation" (Clarke 1705/1738, 597). It may be possible to construe "perpetual force" and "constantly observed" in a manner that allows for the possibility that conflict between ultimate moral ends can sometimes make it right to act contrary to one ultimate moral end. But the fact that Clarke himself never provides any such gloss—and his deep commitment to the geometric-arithmetic-logic-like nature of ultimate moral ends—gives us good reason to stick to the more natural, on-the-surface reading, which takes Clarke to hold that ultimate moral ends can never truly come into conflict. And it was his commitment to moral rationalism that shielded him from a view of such conflict.

Of course it was just the contention that moral principles are akin to geometry, arithmetic, and logic that Hutcheson and Hume would soon submit to blistering attack. But prioritarianism among early modern multiplists was not driven by Clarke-style rationalism alone. We can see this by turning to Joseph Butler, who also affirmed prioritarianism while eschewing Clarke's rationalist commitments.

Butler

Butler begins his "Dissertation upon the Nature of Virtue" by noting that all humans make moral judgments. He then raises the question of whether those moral judgments originate in sentiment or reason alone—only to drop it. The goal of his "Dissertation," Butler tells us, is to chart which sorts of things we approve of and which sorts of things we disapprove of, not to determine the meta-ethical origin of those judgments. Butler's claims about the content of our moral judgments are supposed to be neutral on the question separating Clarke and Hutcheson. The picture of morality he develops is not supposed to depend on either Clarkean rationalism or Hutchesonian sentimentalism. As Butler famously puts it, "It is manifest, great part of common language, and of common behaviour over the world, is formed upon supposition of such a moral faculty; whether called conscience, moral reason, moral sense, or divine reason; whether considered as a sentiment of the understanding, or as a perception of the heart, or, which seems the truth, as including both" (Butler 1736/1983, 69).

What sorts of moral judgments do humans make? According to Butler, we make moral judgments based on general ultimate ends that have been "universally acknowledged" in "all ages and countries" (Butler 1736/1983, 70). And what is crucial for our purposes is that he maintains that there is a multiplicity of these ultimate ends—not just one.

Butler is particularly concerned to argue against Hutcheson's view that virtue is nothing but benevolence toward humanity as a whole. There are, according to Butler, a number of other ultimate moral ends, such as "veracity" and "justice," as well as the "gratitude" and "friendship" that motivate us to benefit those near and dear to us (our benefactors and friends) rather than promote the welfare of people in general (Butler 1736/1983, 72–4). We ought to be morally concerned with each of these ends for its own sake, as an independent reason for action, and not take its normative force to be reducible to or derivable from a single moral foundation.

Butler is, therefore, a multiplist, affirming a multiplicity of ultimate moral ends. But is he a non-conflict or a conflict multiplist?

As with Clarke's, a conspicuous feature of Butler's moral account is that it leaves issues about the possibility of conflict between ultimate ends largely unaddressed. Butler does not discuss the possibility of justice, veracity, gratitude, friendship coming into conflict with each other. He simply doesn't discuss conflict between these ultimate moral ends because he, like Clarke, assumes such conflict will never occur. And the reason Butler makes such an assumption is not hard to find: he believes that God has arranged things so that we will never face conflict between our ultimate moral ends, that God has designed us and the world in such a way that we can and should take morality to be as non-conflict multiplism describes it.[14]

Butler gives his theological reasons for non-conflict multiplism in a long footnote to the sermon "Upon the Love of our Neighbor."[15] He writes:

[A]s we are not competent judges, what is upon the whole for the good of the world; there may be other immediate ends appointed us to pursue, besides that one of doing good or producing happiness. Though the good of the creation be the only end of the Author of it, yet he may have laid us under particular obligations, which we may discern and feel ourselves under, quite distinct from a perception, that the observance or violation of them is for the happiness or misery of our fellow-creatures. And this is in fact the case. For there are certain dispositions of mind, and certain actions, which are in themselves approved or disapproved by mankind, abstracted from the consideration of their tendency to the happiness or misery of the world; approved or disapproved by reflection, by that principle within, which is the guide of life, the judge of right and wrong. Numberless instances of this kind might be mentioned... [of things that] are approved or disapproved by mankind in general, in quite another view than as conducive to the happiness or misery of the world. (Butler 1729/1983a, 66)

God is a monist, having as His single ultimate end the good or happiness of all. But God realizes that humans are incapable of accurately discerning what promotes the good or happiness of all—both because of our straightforwardly epistemic limitations (we cannot see what all the long-term consequences of an act will be) and because of our susceptibility to deceive ourselves into thinking that what best promotes our own small part must be to the benefit of humanity as a whole.[16] So He has made us multiplists, putting us under several different obligations, while at the same time structuring the world so that when we fulfill those obligations we will serve His larger purpose. He has given us a moral faculty that approves of certain action-types directly, a faculty that leads us to approve of the action-types for their own sakes and not merely as means to some single ultimate end.[17] It is thus crucial for us to take our moral job to be to live in accord with the principles of veracity, justice, friendship, gratitude, and the like.

We could say that Butler's view is that the ultimate structure of morality is monistic but that *human* morality (because of humans' flaws and limitations) is multiplist, or that there is really only one criterion of morality but that (flawed, limited) humans should use a moral decision-making procedure that includes a multiplicity of principles. Such a view would be similar to Sidgwick's "esoteric morality" (Sidgwick 1907, 489) or Williams' "Government House Utilitarianism" (Williams 1995, 166)—with God as the only cognoscente, the only Person residing in the Government House.

Butler's view implies that our ultimate moral ends will come into conflict only if God makes a mistake. For God intends for us to live by a multiplicity of different ultimate moral ends. He intends for us to take each of these ends to be an independent and inviolable reason for action. He does not intend for us to calculate when it would be right to act in accord with one moral end rather than another—and that's because He realizes that our epistemic limitations and tendency to deceptive self-serving rationalizations will often lead us to calculate incorrectly. But of course God does not make mistakes. God has successfully arranged things so that we need only always follow our moral ends in order to act as we ought, and so that we are never required to calculate when it is right to act contrary to (at least one) moral end. God has seen to it that our moral ends will never come into conflict.[18]

Butler acknowledges that what *appears* to a person to be the most beneficent action can sometimes conflict with what "veracity and justice" require (Butler 1736/1983, 74). In such cases, Butler makes clear, one ought to give priority to veracity and justice. We ought to "endeavor to promote the good of mankind [only] in any ways... not contrary to veracity and justice." The correct human response to any perceived conflict between benevolence, on the one hand, and justice or veracity, on the other, is to give strict priority to the latter. Thus, from our flawed, limited perspective, morality can appear to be prioritarian not in the sense of there never occurring any conflict between moral principles but rather in the sense of there being a strict ranking for resolving such conflict. (Butler never considers what we should do when justice conflicts with veracity, but he may have thought that a proper understanding of those two principles will show that they never conflict.) Butler also thinks, however, that in fact actions contrary to veracity and justice never *really* promote the good of mankind. As he says when discussing the relationship between duties to self and duties to others, "These ends do indeed perfectly coincide; and to aim at public and private good are so far from being inconsistent that they mutually promote each other" (Butler 1729/1983b, 26). When people think an action that violates some other duty is justified because it promotes the public good, it's "almost always" because their thoughts are clouded by "ambition, the spirit of party, or some indirect principled, concealed perhaps in great measure from persons themselves"—i.e. by the tendency to self-serving rationalizations. So actually the principles do not come into conflict with each other after all. It's just that our judgments of justice and veracity turn out to be more accurate gauges of what all the principles truly converge on than our all-too-easily misinformed or distorted beliefs about what will promote the general good.

As we saw in our discussion of Clarke, belief in a multiplicity of non-conflicting ultimate moral ends can be combined with two different views about the nature of those ends: a non-conflict multiplist can hold that the ultimate moral ends are all simple, or that at least some of them include complex specifications and qualifications. I said that Clarke does not consider the matter in an expansive or coherent enough way to warrant our conclusively attributing to him any one of these views rather than the other, and I think the same is true of Butler. Because he held deep theological views that led him to assume moral conflict would never erupt, he did not expend his energy arguing for one version of non-conflict multiplism rather than the other.

Let me underscore the nature of the historical claim I have been trying to make about Clarke and Butler's non-conflict multiplism. I have not meant to claim that Clarke and Butler explicitly considered the idea of conflict between ultimate moral ends and then concluded, on the basis of consciously developed arguments grounded in rationalism and theology, that such conflict would never occur. My claim, rather, is that the possibility of such conflict wasn't on their philosophical radar, that it wasn't salient to their moral theorizing. And my contention is that they didn't address the possibility of such conflict because they had non-negotiable rationalist and theological commitments that restricted their philosophical vision to the prioritarian realm, where such conflict would not occur.

Hume, of course, would reject both the rationalism of Clarke and the theology of Butler. For Hume, morality is based on our sentiments, and there are no grounds for thinking that an omnibenevolent divine mind has given us those sentiments and designed the world in which they operate. But if morality rests on a non-theological sentimental base, the stage is set for conflict multiplism—for the view that not only is there a multiplicity of ultimate moral ends but also that those ultimate moral ends can sometimes come into conflict with each other. For as just about everyone eventually learns, we cannot rely on all of our sentiments always perfectly harmonizing. Our sentimental constitution and the world at large are not set up to ensure that we will never have to choose between different things we care about. Virtually everyone can count on having to face, at some point, a situation in which the only way to attain one thing she cares about is to forgo another thing she cares about. But if morals are based on what we care about, and if we don't have prior rationalist or theological reasons for thinking that all of our moral cares will always harmonize with each other, then it should come as no surprise to find ourselves sometimes facing situations in which one of our ultimate moral ends conflicts with another.

This, then, is the recipe for Humean conflict multiplism. Start with observations of what people take to be of ultimate moral importance. Find, like Clarke and Butler, that Hutcheson's monism was wrong, and that people take to be of ultimate moral importance a multiplicity of different things. Remove the rationalist and theological blinders that prevented Clarke and Butler from considering whether those ultimate moral ends can come into conflict. Find that those ends do come into conflict.

2

Hume's Moral Pluralism

Both Hutcheson and Butler aimed to describe everday commonsense moral judgments. Both took themselves to be charting persons' actual moral responses, to be presenting data gleaned from a cautious observation of human life. But Butler presented powerful reasons for holding that Hutcheson was wrong to claim that our moral judgments track only our thoughts about general benevolence. Commonsense everyday moral judgments of justice, veracity, friendship, gratitude, promise-keeping, and the like, Butler argued, are not all reducible to or derived from approval of motives to promote the welfare of all of humanity. Our assessments of such things reveal vectors of moral concern that are independent of approval of the motive to promote the "Good of the Whole."

Multiplism in Hume

Hume clearly agreed with Butler in this dispute. Humean morality is not based entirely on the tendency to promote the happiness of humanity in general. According to Hume, our moral character judgments are based on our approval of four different tendencies of personal traits: their tendencies to be useful to others, to be useful to the agent herself, to be immediately agreeable to others, and to be immediately agreeable to the agent herself (*T* 3.3.1.24–7; 3.3.5.1, 3.3.2.16; *E* 9.1; D 37). The first of these four principles—approval of qualities that are useful to others—might look to be similar to Hutchesonian approval of general benevolence.[1] But Hume's other three principles are clearly responsive to different things. We approve of qualities that are agreeable *not* because we think their agreeability is a small piece of usefulness. We approve of their agreeability for its own sake. The value we place on that which is agreeable cannot be reduced to, or placed on the same scale as, the value we place on what is useful. We may believe that the useful quality of, say, discretion produces more long-term benefit for humanity than the immediately agreeable quality of wit. But we don't value wit because we think it does the same job as discretion, only not as well. The value we place on wit is not merely an inferior version of the value we place on discretion. Indeed, what we value about wit (its agreeability) is something concerning which discretion is inferior. We value discretion because it is "naturally fitted" to do one job, and we value wit because it does well at a different job (*T* 3.3.1.30). And just as the value of agreeability to others and the value of usefulness to others can be distinguished in this way, so too can the values of usefulness to self and usefulness to others, as well as the values of agreeability to self and usefulness to self.[2] We approve of perseverance because we think it is very useful to its possessor, not merely because we think it is mildly useful to humanity as a whole. We approve of cheerfulness because it makes its possessor's life much more agreeable, not because it might be a little bit useful to people in general.[3]

A good illustration of the distinctness of usefulness and agreeability is the reaction most people have to Dr Martin Ellingham in the BBC series *Doc Martin*. Ellingham is an exceptionally effective physician. He cures many ailments, saves many lives. On the vector of usefulness to others, he scores extremely high. But Ellingham is also socially unpleasant, humorless, insensitive. On the vector of agreeability to others, he scores very low. If people took agreeability to be on the same scale as usefulness—if agreeability were valued because it is part of, or contributes to, usefulness—Ellingham would be more approved of than anyone else in town. The medical benefits he provides would massively outweigh the pleasantness of others people's company and the unpleasantness of his own. But that's not how the folk assess Ellingham. Ellingham isn't judged to be a moral paragon whose good works massively outweigh and thus make virtually morally irrelevant his personal disagreeableness. Ellingham is judged, rather, to be good in one respect, but bad in another respect. If someone like Ellingham were to say, "I've saved more lives than anyone else you know, and so you should think of me as the most virtuous of your acquaintances, regardless of the social unpleasantness I occasion," the typical villager would be unmoved. The problem with Ellingham is not that he would be even more useful if he were agreeable. The problem is that, while in one morally important aspect of life he's a success, in a different morally important aspect he's a failure.

A counterpart to Ellingham is the character of Harold Skimpole from Dickens's *Bleak House*. Skimpole is extraordinarily pleasant company, kind, witty, emotionally generous. He scores extremely high on the agreeability scale. He is, however, also incredibly impractical, and his undisciplined inattention to worldly matters places his friends and family in serious financial difficulties. On the usefulness scale, he scores extremely low. But even though the problems he creates turn out to be highly significant, Skimpole is not deemed a complete personal failure. The practical problems he creates do not outweigh the personal pleasantness he produces, nor does his personal pleasantness cancel out his practical culpability. Or put the other way: even though Skimpole is the most sparkling dinner companion in town, he is not deemed a complete personal success. He is taken to have real and important virtues of good company, even while he is also taken to have real and important vices of irresponsibility.

Earlier, I argued that while Clarke thinks there is one common feature that all moral duties possess (they are all fit), he should not be taken to hold that that feature is the single fundamental justificatory or normative ground of morality. Similarly, we can say of Hume's view that while having the property of eliciting approval (from the general point of view[4]) is the unifying explanation of all of the grounds of our moral judgments, that property is not itself a justifying ground of our moral judgments. That I approve of X will always be a Humean explanation of my judging S to be virtuous. But that is not to say that my approving of S is the justificatory reason for my judgment of her virtue. The justificatory reason will be that S is agreeable or useful to self or others.

Wanting to make clear his rejection of Hutcheson's monism, Hume takes great pains to highlight that on his view virtue consists of four independent vectors of moral thought—that the four different categories of natural virtue cannot be reduced to or derived from each other.[5] Here are just a few quotations that indicate that Hume had this multiplist purpose in mind.[6]

We Take Some Qualities to be Meritorious Because they are Useful to Others

We may observe, that, in displaying the praises of any humane, beneficent man, there is one circumstance which never fails to be amply insisted on, namely, the happiness and satisfaction, derived to society from his intercourse and good offices... As these topics of praise never fail to be employed, and with success, where we would inspire esteem for any one; may it not thence be concluded, that the Utility, resulting from the social virtues, forms, at least, a *part* of their merit, and is one source of that approbation and regard so universally paid to them. (*E* 2.6–8)

We Take Some Qualities to be Meritorious Because they are Useful to their Possessors

[Q]ualities, which tend only to the utility of their possessor, without any reference to us, or to the community, are yet esteemed and valued. (*E* 6.22)

There are many other qualities of the mind, whose merit is deriv'd from the same origin. *Industry, perseverance, patience, activity, vigilance, application, constancy,* with other virtues of that kind, which 'twill be easy to recollect, are esteem'd valuable upon no other account, than their advantage in the conduct of life... As on the other hand, *prodigality, luxury, irresolution, uncertainty*, are vicious, merely because they draw ruin upon us, and incapacitate us for business and action. (*T* 3.3.4.7–8)

We Take Some Qualities to be Meritorious Even Though they are Not Useful

All this seems to me a proof, that our approbation has, in those cases, an origin different from the prospect of utility and advantage, either to ourselves or others. (*T* 3.3.3.4)

We Take Some Qualities to be Meritorious Because they are Agreeable to Others

These attentions and regards are immediately *agreeable* to others, abstracted from any consideration of utility or beneficial tendencies: They conciliate affection, promote esteem, and extremely enhance the merit of the person, who regulates his behaviour by them. (*E* 8.2)

We Take Some Qualities to be Meritorious Because they are Agreeable to their Possessors

As some qualities acquire their merit from their being *immediately agreeable* to others, without any tendency to public interest; so some are denominated virtuous from their being *immediately agreeable* to the person himself, who possesses them. (*T* 3.3.1.28)

Hume's catalogue of the virtues is thus closer to Clarke and Butler's pictures of the content of morality than to Hutcheson's monistic picture. Hutcheson and Hume are alike in holding to a sentimentalist explanation of our moral judgments. But Hume's description of the content of those judgments is more like Clarke and Butler's in that he insists that they are based on a multiplicity of ultimate moral ends.

We've seen, though, that Butler and Clarke believed that different ultimate moral ends will never come into conflict with each other, and that this belief was based on deep theological and rationalist commitments. What does Hume, who rejects those theological and rationalist commitments, say about such matters?

Hume's Conflict Multiplism

In a number of places, Hume describes the convergence of our moral concerns, pointing out that we approve of one and the same thing for a number of different reasons. We approve of benevolence because it is useful to others, but usefulness is only "a *part* ... of its merit" (*E* 2.22; Hume's italics). We also approve of benevolence because it is immediately agreeable to others, where that immediate agreeability is not reducible to usefulness (*E* 7.19–22; *T* 3.3.3.2–4). There are two different reasons we approve of honesty and promise-keeping: both because such qualities are useful to others and because they are useful to their possessors (*E* 6.13). Courage, too, is useful to others and to its possessor; courage is also immediately agreeable, thus laying claim to approval from all four principles of virtue (*T* 3.3.2.14.1; *E* 7.11). A good body can lay similar claim, being useful and agreeable to its possessor and to others (*T* 3.3.5.2.2–4). All of these findings of moral convergence would fit comfortably within the non-conflict multiplism of Butler and Clarke.

Hume clearly differs from Butler and Clarke, however, by stating unabashedly that the different kinds of approval can and sometimes do diverge. Hume tells us that pride is immediately agreeable and useful to its possessor (*T* 3.3.2.1; 3.3.2.8) but also that it is disagreeable and disadvantageous to others (*T* 3.3.2.6–10). Anger is disagreeable to its possessor and to others, but it is useful to its possessor (*T* 3.3.3.7). "Heroism, or military glory" is disadvantageous to others and perhaps even to its possessor, but it is immediately agreeable to its possessor and perhaps to others (*T* 3.3.2.15).[7]

Hume is particularly forthcoming about the potential for such conflict in "A Dialogue."[8] There he writes, "It is needless to dissemble . . . We must sacrifice somewhat of the *useful*, if we be very anxious to obtain all of the *agreeable* qualities; and cannot pretend to reach alike every kind of advantage" (*D* 47). Hume points to "luxury" and "free commerce between the sexes" as examples of things that are agreeable and yet also disadvantageous: treating these things in accord with one principle of moral concern can be incompatible with treating them in accord with another. Conflict between agreeability and usefulness can also erupt in the forming of judgments of political leaders who possess qualities that are agreeable but disadvantageous (*E* 7.22–4).

Perhaps the most important cases of moral conflict Hume describes are between natural virtues and artificial virtues. Hume's leading example of artificial virtue is justice, and he makes a special effort to explain our approvals of just conduct.[9] But he is also perfectly clear that in some situations the just course of action will be incompatible with the course of action favored by our approval of natural virtue. Justice can demand that we give money to someone even if he is "a vicious man, and deserves the hatred of all mankind," or a miser who "can make no use of" it or "a profligate debauchee" who "wou'd rather receive harm than benefit" (*T* 3.2.1.13, 11, and 14; see also *T* 3.2.6.9 and App. 3.6). Meanwhile, there may be other people who are wonderful in every way and who have urgent needs that can only be met if they receive the money instead. It may even be the case that the matter has been conducted in "secret" so that the public will not be harmed by the "example" set by giving the money to those in great need rather than to the vicious, miserly, or debauched (*T* 3.2.1.11). In such situations, to do what is just will be incompatible with doing what is agreeable and useful. The demands of justice will conflict with natural virtue.

The other artificial virtues Hume examines are promise-keeping, allegiance to government, and chastity, and he acknowledges that each of these can conflict with natural virtue by obligating us to do what is disadvantageous or disagreeable. Hume highlights in particular the disadvantageousness of some acts of allegiance (*T* 3.3.9.3) and the disagreeability and uselessness of the demands of chastity (*T* 3.2.12.3–7).

Artificial virtues can also come into conflict with each other. Different artificial virtues have different jobs—they're fitted to different ends—and those different jobs or ends will not always harmonize. Hume makes this point when stressing the independence of promise-keeping and allegiance (which is crucial to his attack on contractarian accounts of the origins of government). He writes, "[S]ince there is a separate interest in the obedience to government, from that in the performance of promises, we must also allow of a separate obligation. To obey the civil magistrate is requisite to preserve order and concord in society. To perform promises is requisite to beget mutual trust and confidence in the common offices of life. The ends, as well as the means, are perfectly distinct; nor is the one subordinate to the other" (*T* 3.2.8.5). He goes on, "But 'tis not only the *natural* obligations of interest, which are distinct in promises and allegiance; but also the *moral* obligations of honour and conscience: Nor does the merit or demerit of the one depend in the least upon that of the other . . . As there are here two interests entirely distinct from each other, they must give rise to two moral obligations, equally separate and independent" (*T* 3.2.8.7). Given this independence of promise-keeping and allegiance, it is entirely possible that a course of action required by one of these moral ends will be incompatible with the course of action required by the other. The moral end of chastity is different again from those of allegiance and promise-keeping; Hume accounts for our approval of chastity with considerations that there is no reason to think could be derived from the ends of the other artificial virtues (*T* 3.2.12.3). And once again the independence of chastity makes it possible for its requirements to conflict with the requirements of justice, promise-keeping, and the like.[10]

So: Hume maintains that there is a multitude of ultimate moral ends. Some of those ends ground natural virtues and some ground artificial virtues. Different kinds of conflict can arise between all of these different moral ends—between one natural virtue and another natural virtue, between a natural virtue and an artificial virtue, between one artificial virtue and another artificial virtue. This is a conflict multiplism that is deep and broad.

Hume's Explanation of Conflict Multiplism

What is Hume's explanation for humans' having these various, potentially conflicting moral ends? Obviously, he will not rely on Clarke-style rationalism or Butler-style theology to explain them. Nor does he rely on an explanatorily basic moral sense, as Hutcheson does. Hume's account of our moral responses is based, rather, on two mental mechanisms quite different from his predecessors': (1) sympathy and (2) the addiction to general rules.

Humean sympathy is not an internal sense that has as its only role the issuing of approvals and disapprovals, which is what the Hutchesonian moral sense was. Its operations are more pervasive than that. Humean sympathy is what underlies our general tendency to identify with others and thus to feel the same kind of thing we believe they are feeling. It is the mental mechanism by which the feelings of others are transmitted to us. Because of sympathy, when I consider someone who I think is angry, I tend to feel angry. When I consider someone who I think is sad or excited or envious, I tend to feel sad or excited or envious.

Because of sympathy, when I consider someone who I think is experiencing a positive emotion, I tend to feel a positive emotion. If the person's positive emotion has been caused by the personal quality of someone, and if I am considering the situation from a general point of view, the positive emotion I experience will be a sentiment of approval directed to the bearer of that personal quality. And the point of importance for our purposes is that sympathy is exceedingly *ecumenical* about the kinds of positive emotions it will transmute into approval in this way (*T* 3.3.1.7–10 and 29; 3.3.6.1).[11] A quality of someone can cause a positive emotion by causing other people to have an immediately agreeable experience. A quality of someone can cause a positive emotion by causing the person herself to have an immediately agreeable experience. A quality of someone can cause a positive emotion by promoting the long-term welfare of others. A quality of someone can cause a positive emotion by promoting the long-term welfare of the person herself. In each of these cases, when we consider the person or persons who are experiencing positive emotions, sympathy transmits the positive emotion to us, and thus, if we are considering the situation from the general point of view, we will feel approval toward the quality that caused it.

The phenomenological feel of these approvals toward different kinds of qualities might differ from each other to some extent.[12] Approval of that which is agreeable to self might feel a bit different from approval of that which is useful to others, which might differ again from approval of that which is agreeable to others, and so on. But Hume thinks these responses are similar enough to rightly be taken to all be morally significant nonetheless.[13] The sentiment of approbation that agreeability elicits may be "somewhat *different* from that, which attends the other virtues. But this, in my opinion, is not a sufficient reason for excluding them from the catalogue of virtues. Each of the virtues, even benevolence, justice, gratitude, integrity, excites a different sentiment or feeling in the spectator. The character of *Cæsar* and *Cato*, as drawn by *Sallust*, are both of them virtuous, in the strictest sense of the word; but in a different way: Nor are the sentiments entirely the same, which arise from them" (*T* 3.3.4.2; see also *E* 7.29 and App 4.3–6 and 21–2). If we experience a positive feeling when considering a certain quality from a general point of view, then we will take it to be morally significant, even if it feels somewhat different from other positive feelings we have had when considering other qualities from a general point of view. Each of these feelings will have the kind of salience to our thinking about how we ought to interact with people that is characteristic of morality. And this explains the existence of the different vectors of our judgments of virtue: we feel fully fledged approval toward different kinds of positive emotion-producing qualities.

But as we saw in our earlier discussion of justice and the artificial virtues, we sometimes approve of particular instances of conduct (such as returning money to a miser or certain cases of chastity) that do not cause people to experience positive emotions—instances of conduct that are neither useful nor agreeable to self or others. Hume cannot rely solely on positive emotion-transmitting sympathy to explain such moral responses. In order to account for the full range of our approvals, Hume needs to deploy his second crucial mental mechanism: our addiction to general rules.[14]

Our addiction to general rules is our associative tendency to think or feel the same thing about two objects that resemble each other but differ in some crucial respect. Hume explains how this mechanism works in moral contexts when he writes,

As to [moral obligations], we may observe, that the maxim wou'd here be false, that *when the cause ceases, the effect must cease also*. For there is a principle of human nature, which we have frequently taken notice of, that men are mightily addicted to *general rules*, and that we often carry our maxims beyond those reasons, which first induc'd us to establish them. Where cases are similar in many circumstances, we are apt to put them on the same footing, without considering, that they differ in the most material circumstances, and that the resemblance is more apparent than real. (*T* 3.2.9.3)

Our addiction to general rules is our tendency to *overgeneralize*. It (along with sympathy) accounts for our approval of "virtue in rags," which is an instantiation of a quality that typically brings happiness to people but fails to do so in a particular case because of unusual, unfortunate circumstances (*T* 3.3.1.19). We originally approve of discretion, for instance, because it is useful and because sympathy leads us to approve of what is useful. And discretion is useful in so many cases that we eventually come to associate discretion with approval. We develop the powerful habit or disposition to feel approval whenever we consider discretion. Now there are some atypical situations in which a person's discretion will serve no purpose whatsoever, when it is not useful at all. But the association we have formed between discretion and approval is strong enough that it will lead us to feel approval when we consider discretion even in those cases in which it is not useful. Our reactions follow the general rule of approving of discretion, and they follow that rule even in those unusual cases in which discretion does not have the useful effects that originally caused us to approve of it.

Similarly, our addiction to general rules plays a crucial role in our approvals of artificial virtues in situations in which they are not useful (T 3.2.2.24). Most of the time, justice, promise-keeping, allegiance, and chastity are useful, and in each of those useful cases we will (as a result of the mechanism of sympathy) feel approval for the instantiations of those artificial virtues.[15] We will thus develop the associative habit of feeling approval when considering justice and the other artificial virtues. Once this associative habit becomes strongly ingrained enough, it will outrun the precise conditions that originally gave rise to it. We will thus be disposed to feel approval toward an instantiation of an artificial virtue even in those atypical cases in which it is not beneficial. And the point of great importance here is that the approval that results from this associative habit is fully fledged. This is why we take the positive feeling we experience when considering even disadvantageous cases of discretion and justice (so long as we are considering matters from the general point of view) to be morally significant. Hume thus has a principled sentimentalist explanation of our approvals of some things that are neither useful nor agreeable (even if he also thinks that our approval in those cases is due to an associative habit that developed only because in most other cases those objects have been useful or agreeable).[16]

It's worth noting that Hume's use of sympathy and the addiction to general rules to explain the multiplicity of our moral ends coheres tightly with his psychology as a whole. It's not as though he whipped up these two mental mechanisms, ad hoc, to account for the multiplicity of moral ends he claims to have observed in our moral thought. Both of these mechanisms also play powerful and pervasive roles in Hume's explanations of a plethora of other (non-moral) phenomena. Sympathy plays a central role in his explanation of (among other things) beauty, pride, ambition, avarice, curiosity, revenge, and lust (T 2.2.5.15). The addiction to general rules plays a central role in his explanation of (among other things) prejudice and racial stereotyping, our distinguishing between "poetical enthusiasm, and a serious conviction" (T 1.3.10.11) and the embarrassment we feel for people who act foolishly but are not themselves aware of their own foolishness (*T* 2.2.7.5). Hume's general theory of human nature predicts that we will have a multiplicity of moral ends, and his observations of commonsense morality constitute confirmatory evidence of that general theory (*T* 3.3.1.25–31; 3.3.2.16).[17]

Mixed Moral Feelings

W. D. Ross is rightly celebrated for his nuanced description of central aspects of commonsense morality—aspects that fit squarely into what I have been calling conflict multiplism (Ross 1930, 17–27, 34–9). But Ross accounts for those aspects with a non-naturalist meta-ethics that many (including all Humeans) have found untenable (Ross 1930, 14–15, 29–33).[18] In this section, I will try to explain how Humean sentimentalist foundations can provide a fitting explanation of the phenomena Ross does such an excellent job of describing. If you find Ross's descriptions of commonsense morality compelling, and if you find the Humean explanations of moral phenomena metaphysically and epistemologically superior to Rossian non-naturalism, you will then have strong reasons to adopt the Humean pluralist position I am trying to develop.

The phenomena that are central to conflict multiplism are cases of moral ambivalence—the experience of moral considerations both in favor of and opposed to one and the same thing. Ross focuses his attention in chapter 2 of *The Right and the Good* on these sorts of cases, and Hume is also sensitive to them.[19]

One way in which I can be morally ambivalent is by having a positive moral reaction to one quality of a person (say, her kindness) while having a negative moral reaction to another quality of hers (say, her immoderation).[20] In a letter, Hume pointed out that if, as Hutcheson claimed, all virtue were based on benevolence, "no Characters could be mixt" (*Letters*, 34). But we plainly do have mixed moral responses to people. In the *History* and the *Essays*, Hume gives numerous examples of this kind of ambivalence. Henry I was brave, moderate, and a good friend, but he was also ambitious in a way that pushed him "into measures which were both criminal in themselves, and were the cause of further crimes" (*History*, 1.370–1). The Gunpowder Conspirators exhibited "intrepid firmness" and "courage" but also "bigoted zeal" and prejudice (*History*, 5.30–1). Sir Robert Walpole was "constant, not magnanimous; moderate, not equitable" (*Essays*, 575). About Charles I Hume writes, "The character of this prince, as that of most men, if not of all men, was mixed" (*History*, 5.542). Earlier we used Martin Ellingham and Harold Skimpole as examples of similarly mixed characters.

Let us turn our attention, however, to a second kind of moral ambivalence, as it elucidates particularly well the distinctive strengths of the Humean account—namely, the moral ambivalence we can experience towards a single quality, how a single quality can be favored by one vector of virtue and disfavored by another. Consider military glory. Military glory is both agreeable and disadvantageous. Will we, then, approve or disapprove of it? One could hold that there must be a simple answer to that question—that the mental machinery that produces approval and disapproval in us can issue only one product per item of evaluation. Clarke's rational apprehension of necessary truth and Hutcheson's monistic moral sense have that implication. But while some people may have a single univocal moral response to military glory, that isn't true of everyone. Many people have both morally favorable and morally unfavorable reactions towards it. Some instances of military glory they approve of. Other instances they disapprove of. And about still others they are ambivalent. The conduct of heroes such as Alexander the Great, Julius Caesar, and Napoleon may occasion this third, synchronic type of ambivalence. One may find oneself both admiring and condemning the conduct of such men—and not because one admires one of their qualities and condemns another. Rather, one may find oneself feeling a kind of admiration toward their militaristic drive while at the same time feeling a certain condemnation toward it.

Annette Baier has suggested that Hume does not endorse approval of military glory—that he disagrees with the admiration of glory that "the generality of mankind" evince and agrees with the condemnation of glory that "men of cool reflexion" evince (Baier 1991, 210–12). But I don't think Hume says that men of cool reflection fail to see anything at all of worth in military glory; it's just that they see more clearly than others that there is something morally significant to be said against it as well. It's worth noting, moreover, that Baier doesn't think we should prefer utility to agreeability in all other cases in which they conflict. Indeed, she is particularly eloquent in her descriptions of how agreeability is something that matters to us independently of utility (Baier 1991, 198–219). And I think it's undeniable that many people do find the astounding military success of someone like Caesar to be, well, glorious. No doubt, Hume thinks admiration for military brilliance ought to be tempered by consideration of the devastation it can cause. But his pluralism implies—plausibly, I think—that we feel evaluative weight on both sides.

Next consider extensive public-spiritedness, the drive to benefit humanity as a whole even if it means sacrificing the good of specific individuals. I'm thinking here of persons who are so focused on doing something for the public good that they end up acting in ways that detract from the happiness of those near and dear to them. In some cases, we might approve of this kind of devotion to the public good: think of a committed scientist whose quest to cure a terrible disease leads her merely to botch some day-to-day matters, such as missing a dentist's appointment or forgetting a wedding anniversary. In other cases, we might disapprove of it: think of a scientist whose commitment to work makes her significantly neglectful of her children. Towards still others we might have positive and negative responses at the same time.

Or consider intensely driven artists and athletes. Their accomplishments might be very agreeable. But the single-mindedness that enables them to achieve their lofty goals can lead them to act in ways that detract from the long-term interests of not only themselves but also their parents, spouses, and children. Of some instances of such single-minded artistic and athletic pursuit we may approve, of some we may disapprove, and about still others we may be (synchronically) ambivalent.

The same kind of ambivalence can arise in cases involving injustice. Consider a husband who steals medicine for his wife, or a father who steals bread for his children. (See *T* 3.2.1.13; 3 2.6.9.) It doesn't take much imagination to fill in details in ways that will lead us to approve of some of these cases of injustice, to disapprove of other cases, and to have mixed moral responses in still others.

Hume's sentimentalist conflict multiplism explains all of this beautifully. It explains how one and the same quality can produce different feelings of approval or disapproval in us. These feelings (as we discussed in the previous section) might not have exactly the same phenomenological feel as each other, but they may be similar enough for us to take both of them to have moral significance (*T* 3.3.4.2; see also *E* 7.29, App 3–6 and 21–2). Hume thus has an explanation not only of how it is that we can come to have mixed moral feelings about a person's character as a whole (approving of one of her qualities and disapproving of another of her qualities) but also of how it is that we can come to have mixed moral feelings about a single quality—both in the sense of approving of some instantiations of it and disapproving of other instantiations of it, and in the sense of approving and disapproving at the same time of some individual instantiations of it. There is for a sentimentalist like Hume nothing at all mysterious about such mixed moral feelings. There are many other things in life about which we have mixed feelings, many other things towards which we have both positive and negative responses. So why shouldn't we have mixed feelings about morally significant features as well, given that our moral responses are sentiments that are sensitive to a number of different dimensions of human welfare and rule-following?

This Humean view can and needs to include a distinction between feelings of approval and disapproval, on the one hand, and final all-in moral judgments, on the other.[21] There has been much written about how on Hume's view our moral judgments need not track precisely our occurrent feelings—about how our moral judgments can align to our dispositions to feel approval and disapproval toward qualities from a general point of view, regardless of whether we are actually (occurrently) responding to those qualities from the general point of view at the moment we make the judgment.[22] This dispositional aspect of the Humean view of moral judgment is important, but it is not what I mean to focus on here. What I mean to focus on is that we can have a feeling of disapproval toward something (whether we take that in an occurrent or dispositional sense) and still refrain from making a final all-in judgment that it is vicious.[23] And that's because we may also have a feeling of approval toward it (in either the occurrent or dispositional sense). One and the same thing can elicit from us a feeling of disapproval and a feeling of approval, since one and the same thing can be favored by one vector of virtue and disfavored by another. We can thus see how the Humean can explain well what Ross is rightly celebrated for acutely describing: our experience of recognizing morally significant considerations both in favor of something and in opposition to it, and of our coming to make a single final all-in judgment about that thing. Ross explains these experiences as resulting from our recognition of mind-independent prima facie and actual duties (Ross 1930, 17–20, 23–4, 28–31). The Humean says that they are the result of our mixed moral feelings.

Once we have this distinction on board, moreover, we can see the error of criticisms of Hume such as that advanced by Rosalind Hursthouse. Hursthouse claims that Hume's view fails because it implies that many more things are virtues than are in fact virtues, and because it implies that one and the same thing can be both a virtue and a vice. As Hursthouse writes when discussing Hume's four-fold disjunctive view, "But, as we all know, it is all too easy for something to meet a disjunctive condition, let alone one with four disjuncts … [I]t is disastrously obvious that the four causes of pleasure are bound to yield many inconsistent or inconclusive results" (Hursthouse 1999b, 70–1).

Hume's programmatic statements about his account of virtue are indeed emphatically disjunctive (see, for instance, T 3.3.1.24; 3.3.5.1; E 9.1), and he makes it clear that certain traits are approved of "only" or "merely" because of the benefits they provide to the agent herself (T 3.3.1.26; 3.3.1.25; 3.3.1.28–9; 3.3.4.5; 3.3.4.8; E 9.1.12; 6.2.22). But when we are clear about what Hume's philosophical project is, we see that this disjunctive aspect is a strength of his view, not a weakness. Hursthouse believes that Hume fails to tell us what the correct moral judgments are, that he doesn't give us an account of virtue that we can use as guidance or a goal in our lives. But Hume is not presenting a proposal about how we ought to live. His project, rather, is to explain the things people actually happen to do.[24] Now the phenomena Hume seeks to explain in book 3 of the *Treatise* and in much of the *Second Enquiry* are people's praisings and blamings. It's a plainly observable fact that people praise and blame many different sorts of things, and Hume sets out to explain the psychological mechanisms that underlie that activity. Hume's claim is that people praise and blame based on what they think is useful or agreeable to self or others—that a person's praisings and blamings are responsive to her beliefs about usefulness and agreeability. Of course a person could have false beliefs about whether something is useful or agreeable, and to the extent that her beliefs are false her moral judgments that are responsive to those beliefs will seem misguided to those who have the relevant true beliefs. But Hume's main concern is to show that a person's moral judgments are responsive to her beliefs about such things. Most people, for instance, don't praise celibacy and self-mortification because most people think that such practices are disagreeable and fail to produce any benefit (*E* 9.3). That's consistent, however, with Hume's also holding that someone who thinks that those practices are useful will praise them. Hume's view will be falsified only if we find that people praise things that they think are neither useful nor agreeable (*contra* Hursthouse 1999b, 75–6). It will not be falsified by—indeed, it will gain confirmation from—people's praising things that they think are useful, even if Hume himself thinks those people are factually mistaken about the usefulness of such things.

Moreover, once we realize that something's being useful or agreeable to self or others can be for a person an *initial* but not necessarily a *conclusive* reason to praise it—once we distinguish between a feeling of approval and a final all-in judgment— we see that far from being disastrous, the expansiveness of Hume's disjunctive view is a great strength. A moral monist might think that on reflection all of our evaluative reasons will always line up on the same side of every question. But that's not the way things work out for most of us. Most of us at least occasionally face situations in which there are evaluative weights that pull in opposite directions. The military courage of a general in wartime is one such example that we've already examined. The frugality of a friend is another: we might approve of our friend's financial discipline while at the same time disapproving of his refusal to use his money in a way that will provide him with what we take to be legitimate pleasure. Another example might be someone's powerful commitment never to break the rules: we might respect the principledness of such a person's conduct while at the same time wishing that she would lighten up a bit. Hursthouse argues that Hume's view is a failure because it can't tell us whether these things—military courage, frugality, punctiliousness about the rules—are virtues or vice. But the fact is that we have mixed moral feelings about many of these things; we don't have a single positive or negative response to all of them all of the time; we can and do have both positive and negative responses to them. And Hume's four-fold account explains why we experience this kind of evaluative ambivalence, why we think some are virtuous to some extent without being entirely virtuous, and others are vicious to some extent without being entirely vicious. It's those views that cannot account for this sort of ambivalence—those views that affirm only a single ultimate end, or only a single set of completely harmonious ends—that fail to capture crucial evaluative phenomena. It's Hume's view, with its expansive account of the different bases of our evaluative responses, that captures the contours and borders of values as we actually experience them.

What do we do when we find ourselves in a situation in which we recognize both a consideration that morally favors something and a consideration that morally disfavors it? The Humean and the Rossian will both say that in some situations in which we see conflicting moral considerations we come to think that the considerations on one side of the question clearly and decisively override those on the other. In those situations, we will quickly arrive at a final all-in judgment that the object of evaluation is, say, vicious. But while the Rossian account will revert to our apprehension of mind-independent prima facie and actual duties to explain this situation, the Humean will take this situation to be akin to one in which we have both a desire for and aversion to one and the same thing, and in which the aversion massively outweighs the desire. The strawberry pie looks delicious, but because I know that I am severely allergic to strawberries I am not at all tempted to try it. Loyalty to one's fellows is something we generally approve of, but when it leads a gang member to commit crimes we have no hesitation at all in judging him to be vicious.

In other situations, however, the conflicting moral considerations may seem to us to be more evenly matched. And the Humean will hold that those kinds of cases are akin to ones in which (I'm not allergic to strawberries but) my desire for the strawberry pie is in conflict with my close-in-strength aversion to putting on weight or feeling overly full. In such a case, I might waver, hesitate, be at least uncertain about what to do. Similarly, in some morally significant cases the conflicting considerations might be evenly enough matched to make it initially unclear to me what final all-in judgment to make.

In some of these difficult cases we may refrain from fixing on a single moral verdict. Do we judge Alexander's military drive to be virtuous or vicious? How about the zeal to find a cure that leads a scientist to be careless about nontrivial matters pertaining to her loved ones? Or the competitive drive that leads an athlete to sacrifice her long-term welfare? The artistic commitment that led Gauguin to leave his family and go to Tahiti? Perhaps some might have single up-or-down moral responses to cases like these, but the Humean can also accommodate responses that are less simple and decisive. A person might approve and disapprove of Alexander and Gauguin (because she is responsive to different Humean vectors of virtue), which is to say that she might recognize considerations both for judging them to be virtuous and for judging them not to be virtuous. She might not find either of the conflicting considerations to be powerful enough to completely over-ride the other. And there might be no feature of her situation that compels her to come down decisively on one side or the other. She thus might remain ambivalent, finding it more fitting to recognize both the good and bad aspects of such persons' qualities rather than commit to univocal positive or negative verdicts.

Evaluations of Gauguin and the cancer-scientist may very well be influenced by moral luck (see Williams 1981). Assessments of Gauguin would then be higher because his paintings are masterpieces than they would be if his paintings were dross. If the scientist fails to discover anything at all of medical value our assess-ment of her may be lower than if she discovers a miracle cure. But a nice feature of Humean pluralism is that it explains why those luck-sensitive assessments need not constitute the entirety of our moral evaluations of such people. Learning that Gauguin and a familially neglectful scientist have succeeded in their endeavors may positively affect our assessment of them without making our mixed moral feelings about them go completely away; we may still recognize a moral reason to criticize their conduct even while appreciating the value of what they have done. Humean pluralism tells us that that is because, while their successes give them a higher score on one dimension of moral importance, on a different dimension of moral importance they continue to score low.

These mixed moral responses are closely analogous to a type of aesthetic response that (I think) is far from uncommon. Consider our reactions to authors whose writing style is appealing in one sense and unappealing in another. I find the florid expansiveness of Thomas Wolfe's prose to be both poetic and indulgent. I think there are reasons to praise Wolfe's writing style and also reasons to criticize it. But what is my final aesthetic judgment of Wolfe? Well, there is no compelling need to commit to a single up-or-down verdict, and so I don't. About the qual-ity of Wolfe's writing—as about the moral status of Caesar and Gauguin's lead-ing characteristics—I can remain poised between two judgments, recognizing considerations on both sides of the question without taking either to be decisive. I feel the same ambivalence about the painter Rene Magritte and the writer Jorge Borges: I find the idea-centeredness of their works both intellectually thrilling and emotionally somewhat disengaged. Evaluative ambivalence can, in these cases, be a point of equilibrium.

Hume is one of the few philosophers I can think of who has paid close atten-tion to this kind of evaluative ambivalence. He points out that the "amours and attachments of Harry the IVth of France" and the "excessive bravery and reso-lute inflexibility of Charles the XIIth" were disadvantageous (E 7.22–4). But these very qualities of Harry and Charles were also agreeable. So what is our final moral verdict of Harry and Charles? Hume does not seem to think that there must be a simple up-or-down answer. What he seeks to do, rather, is explain the mixed moral feelings Harry and Charles evoke, without giving any indication that a single definitive verdict is called for. In the *Treatise*, Hume describes the similarly mixed moral feelings we may have toward those who are friendly but indolent (*T* 3.3.1.24) and those who are extravagantly proud and ambitious (*T* 3.3.2.14).[25] As Dees has done a wonderful job of showing, Hume's *History* contains a number of character sketches that reveal the same kind of moral ambivalence.[26] And "A Character of Sir Robert Walpole" is virtually a case study in it, with Hume concluding, "As I am a man, I love him; as I am a scholar, I hate him" (*Essays*, 576).

This kind of evaluative ambivalence will not always result from epistemic uncertainty.[27] For the Humean, it need not be the case that there is some determinate fact of the matter as to whether Harry, Charles, Caesar, or Gauguin was virtuous or vicious—any more than there must be some determinate fact as to whether Thomas Wolfe was a great writer.[28] We may have mixed evaluative feelings about all such things even after we are fully informed, and there may be no single up-or-down verdict out there (or in us) to discern.

There are, however, some situations in which we recognize conflicting moral considerations but are compelled to come to some kind of univocal judgment—when remaining indefinitely poised between two verdicts is simply not an option. The most obvious examples of such situations are those in which we have to make a decision about what to do—when we recognize moral considerations in favor of two incompatible courses of action and yet must make a choice about which course to take. Hume directs his attention more toward third-personal evaluations of character than toward first-personal deliberations about what to do, but his conflict multiplism also applies well to the latter. For one thing, as Hume points out, our moral judgments of others affect how we decide to treat them (*T* 3.3.1.25). If a person's company is pleasantly agreeable, that will give us reason to treat him in one way; if a person's behavior is deleterious, that will give us a reason to treat him in another way. And if one and the same person's conduct is both agreeable and deleterious, we may be faced with a situation in which we recognize competing considerations for treating him in incompatible ways. A good example of someone who is agreeable but disutile is Mr Skimpole from Dickens's *Bleak House*. And indeed Skimpole does evoke in Esther and John Jarndyce an evaluative ambivalence that leads them in various circumstances to be uncertain about what they ought to do. Should he be allowed to visit the house? Should they pay off his debts?

More generally, the different principles of Humean morality explain conflicting views we may develop about how to live with each other—about the construction of social arrangements. In "A Dialogue," Hume points out that "luxury" and "free commerce between the sexes" are agreeable and disadvantageous, while more Spartan and less licentious arrangements are disagreeable but advantageous (D 46–7). We might be forced to make a decision to follow either a restrictive or permissive policy about such practices. There may arise external and internal disagreements about the best policy to follow with regard to such competing social arrangements, and Hume's four-part view of virtue constitutes an explanatory framework for such disagreements—a plausible framework for explaining why people might have conflicting views about these arrangements, and why people offer certain kinds of considerations as reasons for their views.

Perhaps the most important kinds of cases Hume discusses in which we are compelled to opt for one side or another are those involving conflicts between justice and the other virtues. Hume makes it clear that we can end up in situations in which we must choose to do either the just thing or the thing that is agreeable or beneficial, but not both. Hume can explain how the same kind of conflict can occur in cases in which one can keep a promise or do what is useful, but not both. It is just these sorts of phenomena—moral conflicts between, for instance, keeping promises and making others happy—that Ross uses his concepts of prima facie and actual duties to account for (Ross 1930, 34–9). We see now that Humean pluralism can account for them equally well by pointing to the mental mechanisms of sympathy and our addiction to general rules, and by explaining how those mechanisms produce in us a response of approval toward justice and promise-keeping *and* a response of approval toward unjust promise-breaking that produces more happiness.

What do we do when faced with conflict between our moral ends? What should we do? This is a question we might want anyone who affirms conflict multiplism to face. And it is just this question that separates prioritarianism from pluralism. Conflict multiplists can hold that there is a strict priority ordering for resolving all conflict between moral ends—which is ordered conflict multiplism, the far right side of prioritarianism. Or they can hold that there is no such strict priority ordering—which is non-ordered conflict multiplism, or pluralism. In the next section, I will illustrate the difference between these two views by describing the ordered conflict multiplism of Reid and Rawls, on the one hand, and the non-ordered conflict multiplism (or pluralism) of Price and Ross, on the other. In the section after that, I will ask where Hume falls in this dispute.

Ordered Multiplism (Reid and Rawls) vs. Pluralism (Price and Ross)

Ordered conflict multiplists hold that whenever different ultimate moral ends come into conflict there is a strict, invariable normative hierarchy that gives determinate guidance about which moral end ought to be obeyed. Ordered multiplists could hold, for instance, that truth-telling, promise-keeping, and promoting human happiness are all ultimate moral ends and that these three ends can require incompatible actions. But they can still be prioritarian by also holding that whenever two of the ends conflict, one of them will have strict priority or normative trumping power over the other. So an ordered conflict multiplist might hold, for instance, that truth-telling always trumps promise-keeping and the promoting of human happiness, and that promise-keeping always trumps the promoting of human happiness.

The other kind of conflict multiplist—the non-ordered conflict multiplist, or (as we will call it) pluralist—agrees that there is a multiplicity of potentially conflicting ultimate moral ends but denies that there is any invariable normative hierarchy for resolving such conflict. Pluralists will not deny that in specific cases one ultimate moral end will override another. But they will deny that there is a normative order or über-principle that tells us that every instantiation of one ultimate moral end will always override every instantiation of another ultimate moral end. So pluralists will hold that in some cases in which truth-telling, promise-keeping, and human happiness come into conflict, truth-telling will override the other two. But they will also hold that in other cases, promise-keeping may be the overriding end. In still other cases, human happiness may override the other two.[29]

Thomas Reid is a fine example of an ordered conflict multiplist. As we've seen, Reid rejects benevolence-monism, contending that there are multiple "first or self-evident principles, on which all moral reasoning is grounded" (Reid 1983, 321, 351). Reid's list of these "first principles of morals" contains eleven items divided into three categories (Reid 1983, 352 ff.). Reid also thinks that the first moral principles considered as general propositions fit together harmoniously (in effect denying modally strong conflict pluralism, which holds that moral ends inherently conflict with each other[30]). But Reid does affirm (modally weak) conflict multiplism, in that he allows that one of the first moral principles can require an action that is incompatible with what another of the first moral principles requires. He writes, "Between the several virtues, as they are dispositions of mind, or determinations of will, to act according to a certain general rule, there can be no opposition. They dwell together most amicably, and give mutual aid and ornament, without the possibility of hostility or opposition, and, taken altogether, make one uniform and consistent rule of conduct. But, between particular external actions, which different virtues would lead to, there may be an opposition ... [I]t may happen, that an external action which generosity or gratitude solicits, justice may forbid" (Reid 1983, 357–8). Reid also maintains, however, that it is self-evident that certain moral principles have invariable priority over others—that there is a strict ordering for resolving conflict between ultimate moral ends. As he puts it, "that *unmerited generosity should yield to gratitude, and both to justice*, is self-evident. Nor is it less so, that *unmerited beneficence to those who are at ease should yield to compassion to the miserable*, and *external acts of piety to works of mercy*, because God loves mercy more than sacrifice" (Reid 1983, 358). While Reid does not provide a complete ordering of all moral ends, it seems pretty clear that he thinks such an ordering does exist and that it is self-evident, a priori. Reid is a conflict multiplist, but he is also a prioritarian.

The most well-known twentieth-century example of an ordered multiplism is Rawls's two principles of justice (although Rawls's view concerns political institutions rather than the individual moral judgments, which are our focus). Rawls's view has as ends both political liberty and economic benefit. But Rawls realizes that promoting one of these ends can sometimes be incompatible with promoting the other. Rawls maintains, however, that whenever such a conflict occurs, the end of political liberty always overrides the end of economic benefit. He proposes a ranking or lexical ordering "which requires us to satisfy the first principle in the ordering before we can move on to the second" (Rawls 1971, 43). Rawls is very clear, moreover, that this ordering eliminates the need for the pluralist, non-rule-based judgment about what to do when different duties conflict. As he puts it, "A serial ordering avoids, then, having to balance principles at all; those earlier in the ordering have an absolute weight, so to speak, with respect to later ones, and hold without exception" (Rawls 1971, 43; see also 61).

In contrast, Richard Price is a clear example of a non-ordered conflict multiplist—or pluralist. Price aligns with Butler, Hume, Reid, and Smith in his explicit rejection of the benevolence-monism of Hutcheson (Price 1787, 217–19, 226–30, 268). Price goes out of his way to stress the multiplist character of morality, writing, "Why must all moral good be reduced to one particular species of it, and kind affections, with the actions flowing from them, be represented, as alone capable of appearing to our moral faculty *virtuous*? Why may we not as well have an immediate relish also for truth, for candour, sincerity, piety, gratitude, and many other modes and principles of conduct?" (Price 1787, 228). Price then develops a multiplist view of morality with at least seven independent ultimate moral ends. It includes the Hutchesonian end of producing good for the whole of society (253), but also the distinct ends of promise-keeping (260), of veracity (256), of gratitude (254), of duty to God (231), of duty to self (248), and of justice (263). Price makes it clear that the non-benevolence-based ends are intrinsically right "*in themselves*, and *exclusive of their consequences*" (222), "independently of all considerations of utility" (231). Their violations are immediately wrong "independently of their effects," even when they are "productive of no harm, and even when in some degree beneficial" (223–4). Attention to our actual approvals and disapprovals, Price contends, proves "incontestably that actions evidencing kind affections are not the only ones we approve" (250), that "[p]ublick happiness cannot be the sole standard and measure of justice and injustice" (270: see also 249–50, 255).

So much is completely in line with Butler's criticism of Hutcheson in his *Dissertation*. But while Butler does not directly address the issue of moral conflict, Price is completely explicit about the possibility of different ends' requiring incompatible actions. While the various "heads of virtue" often agree "in requiring the same actions" (279), Price tells us, they also sometimes "interfere" with each other. He then goes on to say, "[I]n examining *single acts* and *particular cases*, we find that they lead us contrary ways. This perhaps has not been enough attended to, and therefore I shall particularly insist upon it" (279). Price gives as an example the conflict that can erupt between duties to self and to others. "[T]he pursuit of the happiness of others is a duty," he writes, "and so is the pursuit of private happiness; and though, on the whole, these are inseparably connected, in many particular instances, one of them cannot be pursued without giving up the other" (280).[31] "In like manner," he continues, "the nearer attachments of nature or friendship, the obligations to veracity, fidelity, gratitude, or justice, may interfere with private and publick good" (281).

So Price agrees with Butler that there are multiple independent ultimate moral ends. And Price agrees with Reid that those different ultimate moral ends can come into conflict with each other, requiring incompatible actions. Unlike Reid, however, Price crosses the crucial line from ordered conflict multiplism to non-ordered conflict multiplism—from prioritarianism into pluralism—by maintaining that there are no ordering principles that tell us how to act when different duties conflict. As Price sees it, in some situations of moral conflict one duty will override another, but in other situations the other duty will override the one. And there are no rules that tell us which kind of situation we are in. When the public and private good come into conflict, for instance, it is sometimes right to act on the former and sometimes right to act on the latter, and we lack any general principle for telling us when to we are in one situation or the other. As Price puts it in the continuation of a quotation we have already seen:

Thus, the pursuit of the happiness of others is a duty, and so is the pursuit of private happiness; and . . . in many particular instances, one of them cannot be pursued without giving up the other. When the public happiness is very great, and the private very inconsiderable, no difficulties appear. We pronounce as confidently, that the one ought to give way to the other, as we do, that either alone ought to be pursued. But when the former is diminished, and the latter increased to a certain degree, doubt arises; and we may thus be rendered entirely incapable of determining what we ought to chuse. We have the most satisfactory perception, that we ought to study our own good, and, within certain limits, prefer it to that of another; but who can say how far, mark precisely these limits, and inform us in all cases of opposition between them, where right and wrong and indifference take place? (231)

Conflict also occurs between other moral ends, Price tells us, and the same lack of a priority ordering characterizes those cases as well. "In like manner, the nearer attachments of nature or friendship, the obligations to veracity, fidelity, gratitude, or justice, may interfere with private and publick good, and it is not possible for us to judge always and accurately, what degrees or circumstances of any one of these compared with the others, will or will not cancel its obligation, and justify the violation of it" (281). Far from affirming an indubitable a priori priority ordering of the different moral ends, as Reid did, Price maintains that there is no such ordering at all.

The most famous twentieth-century non-ordered conflict multiplist—or pluralist—is Ross, who denies that there are any invariable general rules that tell us what to do in every case in which one prima facie duty conflicts with another. Ross writes:

> Every act ... viewed in some aspects, will be *prima facie* right, and viewed in others, *prima facie* wrong, and right acts can be distinguished from wrong acts only as being those which, of all those possible for the agent in the circumstances, have the greatest balance of *prima facie* rightness ... For the estimation of the comparative stringency of these *prima facie* obligations no general rules can, so far as I can see, be laid down. We can only say that a great deal of stringency belongs to the duties of "perfect obligation"—the duties of keeping our promises, or repairing wrongs we have done, and of returning the equivalent of services we have received. For the rest, "the decision rests with perception." This sense of our particular duty in particular circumstances, preceded and informed by the fullest reflection we can bestow on the act in all its bearings, is highly fallible, but it is the only guide we have to our duty. (Ross 1930, 42–3; see also 23)[32]

Ross does say here that there is a general sense in which obligations to keep promises and repay debts have greater "stringency" than duties to promote the good. But that "stringency" is not so strong as to amount to an invariable lexical priority, as Ross also thinks that there are cases in which the utility produced by breaking a promise will justify doing so (Ross 1930, 28 and 38–9).[33]

Hume: Prioritarian or Pluralist?

Which kind of conflict multiplist is Hume? Does he think there is a strict hierarchical ordering of potentially conflicting ultimate moral ends? Hume does make a few comments that seem to suggest at least a partial ordering of moral ends. But at the same time, trenchant aspects of his view fit better with a denial of any invariable ordering. Let us explore these issues now.

Here is a passage that suggests that Hume thought, as a descriptive matter, that commonsense morality takes usefulness to others to have priority over the other kinds of natural virtue:

> In all determinations of morality, this circumstance of public utility is ever principally in view; and wherever disputes arise, either in philosophy or common life, concerning the bounds of duty, the question cannot, by any means, be decided with greater certainty, than by ascertaining, on any side, the true interests of mankind. If any false opinion, embraced from appearances, has been found to prevail; as soon as farther experience and sounder reasoning have given us juster notions of human affairs; we retract our first sentiment and adjust anew the boundaries of moral good and evil. (*E* 81; see also 78, 82)

It seems that Hume is saying here that "public utility" is morally dominant in commonsense moral judgments—that whenever any vexing moral questions arise, people generally think the answer boils down to what will best promote "the true interests of mankind."

Here is a second passage that suggests that Hume thought that usefulness to others has priority over the other three vectors of natural virtue:

> Moral good and evil are certainly distinguish'd by our *sentiments*, not by *reason*: But these sentiments may arise either from the mere species or appearance of characters and passions, or from reflexions on their tendency to the happiness of mankind, and of particular persons. My opinion is, that both these causes are intermix'd in our judgments of morals; after the same manner as they are in our decisions concerning most kinds of external beauty: Tho' I am also of opinion, that reflexions on the tendencies of actions have by far the greatest influence, and determine all the great lines of our duty. (*T* 3.3.1.27)

Hume points out here that usefulness to others ("their tendency to the happiness of mankind, and of particular persons") and agreeability ("the mere species or appearance of characters and passions") both influence our moral judgments, but it is usefulness to others that has the "greatest influence" and determines "all the great lines of our duty." It doesn't seem unreasonable to take Hume here to be making some kind of claim about the priority of usefulness to others.

Here is a third passage that might seem to support an ordered multiplist reading of Hume.

> Heroism, or military glory, is much admir'd by the generality of mankind. They consider it as the most sublime kind of merit. Men of cool reflexion are not so sanguine in their praises of it. The infinite confusions and disorder, which it has caus'd in the world, diminish much of its merit in their eyes. When they wou'd oppose the popular notions on this head, they always paint out the evils, which this suppos'd virtue has produc'd in human society; the subversion of empires, the devastation of provinces, the sack of cities. As long as these are present to us, we are more inclin'd to hate than admire the ambition of heroes. But when we fix our view on the person himself, who is the author of

all this mischief, there is something so dazling in his character, the mere contemplation of it so elevates the mind, that we cannot refuse it our admiration. The pain, which we receive from its tendency to the prejudice of society, is over-power'd by a stronger and more immediate sympathy. (*T* 3.3.2.15)

Hume says here that heroism scores well on agreeability but scores badly on usefulness to others. And one possible reading of this passage has Hume going on to say the following: many people form moral judgments of heroism that are more influenced by approval of agreeability, but we ought to give normative priority to approval of usefulness, as the "men of cool reflexion" do.

None of these passages constitutes conclusive evidence that Hume thinks that in each and every case in which usefulness to others conflicts with any other moral ends we do or should take the former to have exceptionless normative trumping power. But they do suggest that Hume was sometimes drawn to the idea that usefulness to others has some kind of overridingness *vis-à-vis* usefulness to self and agreeability to self and others. These passages are also historically important in the development of monistic moral theorizing, as they look backward to Hutcheson's early utilitarianism and forward to the full flowering of utilitarianism in Bentham.

A different picture emerges, however, when we turn to one of Hume's most explicit statements about conflict between usefulness and agreeability. As we've seen, Hume says in "A Dialogue": "It is needless to dissemble... We must sacrifice somewhat of the *useful*, if we be very anxious to obtain all of the *agreeable* qualities; and cannot pretend to reach alike every kind of advantage" (D 47). But he certainly doesn't imply that, as a descriptive matter, commonsense morality always sides with the useful in such cases. Indeed, the entire point of "A Dialogue" is that different cultures take to be correct different resolutions of this type of conflict. Now that point is on its own compatible with the prescriptive claim that we ought to resolve conflicts between agreeability and usefulness in favor of usefulness. But the structure of "A Dialogue" resists that prescriptive claim. Hume argues that the moral differences between cultures can be explained by showing that virtually everyone's moral judgments are based on the same principles of morality; almost everyone has the same ends at his or her justificatory base. Hume also believes, however, that the differences between the relative priorities different cultures give to the same set of moral principles do not always admit of principled adjudication. In the last few paragraphs of "A Dialogue," Hume does maintain that certain kinds of "artificial lives," such as Diogenes' and Pascal's, are morally condemnable. But his discussion of such moral mistakes comes *after* and *in contrast to* his discussion of the different ways different cultures have resolved conflicts between usefulness and agreeability. Hume's point is that while there is *no* invariable trans-cultural justificatory ground for preferring the English way (which tends to resolve conflicts between usefulness and agreeability in favor of the former) to the French way (which tends to resolve those conflicts in favor of the latter), there *is* a trans-cultural justificatory ground (i.e. one constituted by the set of all four principles of virtue) for condemning the artificial lives of Diogenes and Pascal.[34]

A non-ordered—pluralist—reading is also consonant with the view of aesthetic merit Hume advances in "Of the Standard of Taste." Hume argues that there are universal aesthetic standards, principles for judging works of art that are rightly acknowledged by all. But he also thinks that there is no way of adjudicating between different emphases on these various principles. "Mirth or passion, sentiment or reflection; whichever of these most predominate in our temper, it gives us a peculiar sympathy with the writer who resembles us...The ear of this man is entirely turned towards conciseness and energy; that man is delighted with a copious, rich, and harmonious expression. Simplicity is affected by one; ornament by another...Such preferences are innocent and unavoidable, and can never reasonably be the object of dispute, because there is no standard, by which they can be decided" (*Essays*, 244). If a literary work fails miserably to live up to certain aesthetic principles, it is rightly disdained. But there is no über-standard that implies that one legitimate aesthetic principle has invariable trumping power over another.

Moreover, Hume never suggests a strict ordering that will resolve all types of moral conflict. One type of potential conflict Hume doesn't give any indication there is a strict order to resolve is between promising and obedience to the law. As he explains, "[S]ince there is a separate interest in the obedience to government, from that in the performance of promises, we must allow of a separate obligation...The ends, as well as the means, are perfectly distinct; nor is the one subordinate to the other" (*T* 3.2.8.5). Another kind of potential conflict Hume does not seem to think there is any strict priority for resolving is between general benevolence and particular benevolence (*E* 2.6–7; App 2.5 footnote). General benevolence is the motive to benefit very large swaths of humanity—communities, countries, perhaps people as a whole. Particular benevolence is the motive to benefit much smaller groups—those few with whom one has direct contact, the near and dear (such as the kinds of acts Butler thinks are required by gratitude and friendship). There are passages in the *Treatise* that suggest that the principle of usefulness to others is sensitive only to cases of particular benevolence, that the principle of usefulness to others leads us to judge a person based only on how her conduct affects the welfare of those in her immediate sphere of influence (*T* 3.3.1.18; 3.3.3.2). But there are passages in the *Enquiry* that suggest that the principle of usefulness to others is also sensitive to general benevolence, that this principle leads us to judge a person based on how her conduct affects the welfare of much larger groups of people (*E* 5.39; 9.5). Now it seems to me that commonsense takes into moral account both particular and general benevolence—both a person's concern for those near and dear to her *and* her concern for humanity more generally. And Hume himself notes our sensitivity to these two different dimensions of benevolence when he says that our moral sentiments "arise...from reflexions on [passions'] tendency to the happiness of mankind, *and* of particular persons" (*T* 3.3.1.27; italics added). But these two tendencies—(1) to approve of what benefits humanity generally, and (2) to approve of what benefits those few who are near and dear—can come into conflict. The conduct that benefits one's friends or family (gratitude, friendship) can be incompatible with the conduct that benefits one's community, country, or humanity as a whole. What is the right thing to do in such cases? Mill manages to avoid this question by maintaining, implausibly, that whatever most benefits my friends and family will almost always end up most benefiting humanity as a whole (Mill 1861/2001, 18–20). Some recent consequentialists do squarely address the question, and then go on to maintain that the right thing to do is promote the happiness of humanity as a whole, even if it means sacrificing the happiness of those near and dear (Singer 1972; Kagan 1989; Unger 1996). But such a strict maximizing consequentialism conflicts with a great deal of commonsense, as those contemporary consequentialists themselves readily acknowledge. So it's no surprise that Hume does not say, as a descriptive matter, that commonsense morality gives strict priority to general benevolence over particular benevolence. Nor does he say, as a prescriptive matter, that general benevolence ought always to override particular benevolence. At the same time, he never says (what Butler seems to) that people always take, or ought always to take, particular benevolence to override general benevolence. What he says, rather, is this: "[W]e may observe in our common judgments concerning actions [that] we blame a person who either centers all his affections in his family, or is so regardless of them, as in any opposition of interest, to give the preference to a stranger or mere chance acquaintance" (*T* 3.2.2.8). It seems to me that what fits best both with what Hume says and doesn't say is a view that resists a strict ordering of general and particular benevolence, a view that grants neither invariable trumping power. In some situations one will override the other and in other situations the other will override the one.

Hume's discussions of the relationship between justice and usefulness also resist a strict priority reading. As we've seen, Humean justice can demand that money or property go to someone even if it would be more useful for it go to someone else. Hume makes it clear that in some of these circumstances justice ought to be followed even though it is disadvantageous—even though the just act is "productive of pernicious consequences" (App 3.3; see also *T* 3.2.1.11–14). But he also makes it clear that there are some circumstances in which the usefulness of injustice makes it right to do the unjust thing. It is acceptable, for instance, to violate property law "after a shipwreck" or when a besieged city is "perishing with hunger" (E 3.8). We thus find Hume telling us that when justice and usefulness conflict, justice will sometimes override usefulness and usefulness will sometimes override justice. This is pluralism, not prioritarianism.

The point that Hume makes about shipwrecks and besieged cities connects with a long tradition of theorizing about justice, and it's important to see the ways in which Hume agrees and disagrees with past theorists. In the natural law tradition, as Fleischacker has shown, it was common to hold that it is morally acceptable for a person to take something that the everyday laws of property imply do not belong to her, so long as she urgently and absolutely needs that thing for her survival (Fleischacker 2004, 215–19). Thus, Aquinas says that "if the need be so manifest and urgent, that it is evident that the present need must be remedied by whatever means be at hand (for instance when a person is in some imminent danger, and there is no other possible remedy), then it is lawful for a man to succor his own need by means of another's property, by taking it either openly or secretly: nor is this properly speaking theft or robbery" (Aquinas, *Summa Theologiae*, II-II, q 66, a 7 (New York: McGraw Hill, 1964–73)). Similarly, Grotius says that "in case of necessity men have the right to use things which have become the property of another" (Grotius, *Law of War and Peace*, 2.6.1; translated by F. W. Kelsey (Indianapolis: Bobbs Merrill, 1925)). Grotius gives as an example a voyage on which the provisions have failed; in such a case, everything, regardless of prior ownership claims, "ought to be contributed to the common stock" (Grotius, 2.6.3). But Aquinas and Grotius do not maintain that in cases of urgent and absolute need a person is justified in violating the laws of justice. Their view, rather, is that the laws of justice themselves include specifications or qualifications that imply the lawfulness of a needful person's use of another's property. Aquinas writes, "In cases of need all things are common property, so that there would seem to be no sin in taking another's property, for need has made it common" (Aquinas II-II, q 66, a 7); as we've just seen, he goes on to say that "it is lawful for a man to succor his own need by means of another's property, by taking it either openly or secretly: nor is this properly speaking theft or robbery." And Grotius maintains that under conditions of great need things revert to common ownership, so that "if a man under stress of such necessity takes from the property of another what is necessary to preserve his own life, he does not commit a theft" (Grotius, 2.6. 4). So in the natural law tradition as represented by Aquinas and Grotius, there is no conflict between justice and need. The duties implied by each of these fit together perfectly. When great need justifies using some resource, it is not unjust to use it; when justice forbids using some resource, there cannot be a great need to use it.[35] It is, moreover, easy to see why Aquinas and Grotius held such a prioritarian position. The natural law tradition attributes all moral principles to the designing mind of a perfect lawgiver and characterizes our obedience as rational. But neither rationality nor a perfect designing mind would issue laws that imply incompatible results. Now a thought that seems irresistible to virtually everyone—Aquinas, Grotius, and Hume included—is that a person whose literal survival requires using a certain material resource does not do something wrong by using it, even if the normal laws of property would imply that it belongs to someone else. The adherents of the natural law tradition are thus driven to the conclusion—driven by their belief in the legitimacy of taking what is urgently needed, and in the divine, rational origins of morality—that in such cases the laws of property do not apply in the normal way, that the person using the resource does not violate the demands of justice.

Humean sentimentalism, of course, offers a very different view of the origin of morality. On the Humean account, morality originates in our psychological tendencies and how they are shaped by contingent interactions with the empirical world. Those tendencies are more coarse-grained than the precise moral specifications that Aquinas and Grotius assume when denying moral conflict. Those tendencies produce chunky moral principles that occasionally come into competition with each other. They are more like trees growing out of the same soil than pieces of a jigsaw puzzle.[36] In their discussions of justice and necessity, Aquinas and Grotius emphasize the purpose of justice, which is to promote human welfare. Aquinas and Grotius think that from the fact that justice in general serves that purpose it follows that obeying a rule when doing so will promote vital human welfare cannot be unjust. Hume also thinks that justice in general promotes human welfare, and he thinks we approve of justice in general because it promotes human welfare; if justice in general did not promote human welfare, it would, on Hume's account, not be a moral virtue. But the mental mechanisms that cause us to approve of justice as a moral virtue are not so finely tuned as to perfectly discriminate between the great many cases in which obedience to certain rules promotes human welfare and the few cases in which obedience to those rules does not. We are "addicted to general rules," which results in our approving of things that generally serve a purpose even in those unusual cases in which they do not serve that purpose. We have come to think that kindness and honesty are moral virtues because they benefit others; if they did not benefit others, we would not think of them as moral virtues. But our attitudes towards those traits are not so finely tuned that we fail to approve of them in those cases in which they fail to benefit others. We are built to generalize from the great many cases to the very few. Virtue in rags is still really virtue: we approve of kindness and honesty even in someone whose kindness and honesty fail to produce any benefit for others (*T* 3.2.1.19). Similarly, according to Hume, people came to think that chastity and modesty are virtues because they prevent genealogical confusion; if chastity and modesty had not prevented genealogical confusion, people would not have come to think of them as virtues. But that does not mean that people have thought that there is nothing at all morally wrong with any particular instance of sexual behavior just so long as there is no chance that it will lead to reproduction. Particular instances of chastity and modesty have been taken to be moral virtues even in situations in which there has been no possibility of genealogical confusion (*T* 3.2.12.7). And, Hume is perfectly clear, the same kind of moral generalizing characterizes our attitudes towards justice. We think of justice in general as a moral virtue because of the good it does for humanity, but that general tendency encompasses in its net those unusual cases in which justice does not produce good. Giving money to a seditious bigot, if that's the course of action the laws of property imply, is truly just even if more good would come by giving it to a family man. Using someone else's stores without her permission really does violate property, even if you have great need of them.[37] And the mental mechanisms that have caused us to approve of justice have enough psychological momentum to produce in us approval of giving the money to the bigot even while the psychological momentum of other tendencies leads us to approve of helping the family man. The Humean moral mind is not a mathematical problem-solver, not a precisely engineered machine. It's more like a meeting of generally harmonious siblings, whose common genetics and upbringing doesn't ensure invariable agreement.

Hume, of course, did not offer evolutionary explanations. But the chunky, sometimes conflicting, moral ends that his theory implies cohere better with a broadly evolutionary approach than the perfectly fitted, jigsaw-like moral principles of Aquinas and Grotius. Evolutionary pressures produce traits that serve certain purposes. But evolutionary pressures don't produce traits that are so finely tuned or precisely drawn that in each and every case they always do only what will serve those purposes, nor do they always lead us in exactly the same direction as every other trait that evolutionary pressures have produced. The traits that result from evolutionary pressures are more coarse-grained than that, less precise. They may generally serve the purpose that explains their existence, and they may generally pull in the same direction as other traits; but once they have come into existence, they can in particular circumstances frustrate their original purpose, as well as pull in different directions from each other.[38] I don't mean to push this analogy too far: we should not completely assimilate the Humean account of morality to Darwinian explanations of physical features. My point is simply that once we are in the realm of naturalistic explanations of human phenomena—in the realm of explanations based on human biology and psychology, and how they are shaped by contingent interactions with the empirical world—we should not be surprised to find tendencies that sometimes fail to promote the goal that initially gave rise to them and sometimes come into conflict with each other.

MacIntyre takes Hume's discussion of the money owed to the seditious bigot to be evidence that Hume, in contrast to the natural law tradition represented by Aquinas and Grotius, thought that it is always wrong for a person to take what the rules of property forbid, even if the person needs that thing for her literal survival (MacIntyre 1988, 307). Fleischacker correctly points out that this is a misinterpretation of Hume. Hume agrees with Aquinas and Grotius that in cases of great need, such as a shipwreck or siege, it is morally acceptable for a person to take what the rules of property forbid. But Fleischacker goes on to say that Hume agrees with Aquinas and Grotius in holding that in cases of great need it is not unjust for a person to take what the rules of property would otherwise forbid—that Hume "maintains the natural law tradition intact on these matters" in that he thinks "that justice falls away altogether in the face of necessity" (Fleischacker 2004, 216–17). Here I think Fleischacker is mistaken. Hume is trying to explain the same particular moral judgments as Aquinas and Grotius: that we think *both* that a rich person can have a morally decisive claim to certain resources that would do more good if they went to a poor person *and* that it is morally acceptable for a person in great need to take what does not belong to her. But Hume explains those phenomena pluralistically: with multiple moral ends that come into conflict with each other in ways that we sometimes think ought to be resolved in one way and other times think ought to be resolved in the opposite. We reach the same moral verdict about particular cases as Aquinas and Grotius. When we reach Hume, however, it's new wine in old bottles.

Confirmation of this pluralist interpretation of Hume comes from the section of the *Treatise* titled "Of the Laws of Nation." There, Hume contends that the rules of justice ("the three fundamental rules of justice, the stability of possession, its transference by consent, and the performance of promises") apply to princes (*T* 3.2.11.2). But he also maintains that it is sometimes legitimate for princes to violate the rules of justice—indeed, that it is legitimate for princes to violate justice more often than it is for a private person to do so. We are, Hume writes, "more easily reconciled" to "any transgression of justice among princes and republics, than in the private commerce of one subject with another" (*T* 3.2.11.5). We "give a greater indulgence to a prince or minister, who deceives another, than to a private gentleman, who breaks his word" (*T* 3.2.11.4). The rules of justice do have force on princes. There truly is a "*moral* obligation" for a prince to be just (*T* 3.2.9.4). But when considerations of state are strong enough, it can be legitimate for a prince to breach justice. In the prince's case, the obligations of justice "may lawfully be transgress'd from a more trivial motive" (*T* 3.2.11.2). This, then, is another clear instance in which Hume says that justice may sometimes be overridden. He is not saying here that the rules of justice do not apply in these cases; he is saying that they apply but that it is legitimate for the prince to transgress them. And while his point is that such legitimate transgressions of justice are more common in the case of a prince than private people, he puts the point in a way that implies that there are also cases in which a private person may legitimately transgress justice, although it requires a less "trivial motive" for her to do so.[39]

In the final paragraph of "Of the Laws of Nations," moreover, Hume makes comments that fit very well with the pluralist idea that conflicts between different moral ends must be decided on a case-by-case basis and not by an invariable priority ordering. He writes, "Shou'd it be ask'd, *what proportion these two species of morality bear to each other?* I wou'd answer, that this is a question, to which we can never give any precise answer; nor is it possible to reduce to numbers the proportion, which we ought to fix betwixt them" (*T* 3.2.11.5). It should be noted that Hume is not here discussing the relationship between two different ultimate moral ends, such as justice and benevolence, which has been our topic. He is, rather, comparing the morality of a prince to the morality of a private person. Nonetheless, this passage does reveal his non-prioritarian view of our moral thinking, his view that our moral thinking does not include any strict prioritizing of different moral ends.

Hume does certainly believe that justice and the other artificial virtues would never have developed if they hadn't been useful to society (*T* 3.3.1.9; *E* 3). The virtue of justice as a whole can only be explained by referring to its societal usefulness. But the fact that societal usefulness plays an essential role in the genetic development of the virtue of justice does not mean that we approve of each and every just act because we think it is socially useful. Indeed, as we've seen, Hume is perfectly clear that we approve of some instances of justice even while thinking they are not socially useful. But that does not mean that we will necessarily *not* approve of all socially useful acts that are unjust. We may feel approval toward an act that is socially useful while at the same time feeling disapproval toward it because it is unjust. And Hume does not think there is any invariable lexical ordering that will tell us that one of those sorts of approvals always overrides the other.

There are, as well, elements deep within Hume's sentimentalism that militate against joining his view to a lexical ordering of ultimate moral ends. The Humean view will not be able to fund a priority ordering by reason alone. Reason provides information that enables us to see in particular situations what an end requires and what failing to fulfill the end will lead to (*T* 2.3.3 and 3.1.1; *E* 1.9; App 1.2). Reason may show us how we can bring ends that initially seemed in conflict into harmony. But conflict between Humean moral ends will sometimes be unavoidable even after reason has done everything it can do. In such cases of sentimental conflict—conflict between sentimentally grounded ultimate ends—reason alone cannot gain traction. Hume explains, "[U]ltimate ends of human actions can never... be accounted for by *reason*, but recommend themselves entirely to the sentiments and affections of mankind, without any dependence on the intellectual faculties" (App 1.18). We have a plurality of ultimate ends. And if reason cannot justify one ultimate end, neither will it be able to justify giving one ultimate end invariable normative priority over another. If reason can't tell me to prefer the scratching of my finger to the destruction of the whole world, it certainly won't be able to tell me to prefer, say, agreeability to others to usefulness to self, or usefulness to others to justice.

Hume points out that we typically engage in more reasoning when trying to determine what serves the ends of utility than when trying to determine what serves the ends of agreeability (App 1.2–3). But our needing to engage in more reasoning to serve the ends of utility than to serve the ends of agreeability does *not* imply that the ends of utility are normatively superior to the ends of agreeability. The greater cognitive activity involved in promoting utility is morally important only because of the end it serves; that that end has ultimate moral significance is due to our sentimental make-up; and the ends of agreeability have the same kind of sentimental origin as the ends of utility (i.e. both are based on approvals experienced from general points of view). This point is one that Joshua Greene fails to appreciate, for Greene acknowledges that all of our moral ends are based in Humean sentiment, but he then goes on to try to justify privileging the end of utility over other moral ends on the grounds that judgments based on the former typically require more cognitive activity than judgments based on the latter (Greene 2008).

So if the Humean view were to include a comprehensive invariable moral priority ordering, it would have to be funded by sentiment. But what sentiment could fill this bill? Humean moral considerations are based on approvals and disapprovals we feel when we consider matters from general points of view. There are situations in which we can feel for one and the same thing both Humean approval and Humean disapproval. So there can be Humean moral considerations both for and against the same thing. If there were an invariable comprehensive ordering of such considerations, that ordering itself would be a kind of über-moral consideration—a moral consideration that tells us how to rank other moral considerations, a second-order moral consideration. Such a consideration would have to be based on a special sentiment, a sentiment that is moral and yet differs from all the other moral sentiments in that it possesses a ranking authority the others lack. But Hume himself doesn't include such an ordering meta-moral sentiment in his account, and it's very difficult to see how he could.

If all of our ultimate moral ends aimed at the very same goal, then we could rank them based on how effective they are at achieving it. But to say that they are distinct ultimate ends is just to say that they do not aim at the same goal. We care about agreeability to self not because we think agreeability to self is a little bit of usefulness to humanity in general. We care about agreeability to self for its own sake. We disapprove of individual instantiations of promise-breaking not because we think each of them on its own detracts from the public good. We disapprove of individual instantiations of promise-breaking in and of themselves. Our senti-mental make-up leads us to experience the production of immediately agreeable experiences as intrinsically worthy and to experience promise-breaking as intrin-sically unworthy—just as it leads us to experience the promotion of the public good as intrinsically worthy and the detraction from the public good as intrinsi-cally unworthy.[40] Each of these things serves its own end.

Our approval of what is beneficial, of what is agreeable, of promise-keeping, of justice: each of these is a fully fledged moral sentiment. Each is itself the basis of an ultimate moral consideration. Each is the sort of thing that gives rise to moral status itself. And it is hard to see how, on a Humean view, there can be any moral ground beneath them from which they can all be (morally) ranked. If you hold that a plurality of sentiments is at the very bottom level of moral justification, how can you also hold that there is some moral justificatory principle that funds a com-prehensive invariable ordering of morally justificatory considerations?[41]

That is not to say that Humean pluralism implies that it is impossible for us to make justified decisions in cases in which moral principles come into conflict. In non-moral cases in which my desires come into conflict, I can make decisions about how to act and can give sensible reasons for doing so even though there is no priority ordering of types of desires for me to rely on. There are times, for instance, when I want to go to a musical performance, when I want to exercise at the gym, and when it is impossible for me to do both. Sometimes I decide to exercise and can sensibly justify my decision by saying that in this case exercising is more important to me than going to the show (let us say that I have not done any exercise for a while and that the performer is relatively undistinguished). Other times I decide to go to the show and can sensibly justify my decision by saying that in that case going to hear the music is more important to me than exercising (let us say that it is a really fantastic performer whom I will not get the chance to see again). This kind of justification for acting on one desire over another makes good sense to us. And Humeans can make the same kind of sense out of our justifica-tions for giving priority to one moral end over another in particular cases. In some cases I can decide to neglect to do something useful in order to keep a promise, and it can be legitimate for me to justify my action by saying that (in this case) the promise overrides the usefulness. But in other cases I can decide to break a promise in order to do something useful, and it can be legitimate for me to justify my action by saying that (in that case) the usefulness overrides the promise.

Price, Ross, and the Humean pluralist are all alive to the fact that we sometimes have to decide between two incompatible options that both have something morally in their favor. Price, Ross, and the Humean pluralist all deny, for instance, that promising invariably overrides usefulness, or vice versa (or that benefit to society as a whole invariably overrides benefit to specific individuals, or vice versa). But Price and Ross are mind-independent moral realists, not sentimentalists, and thus their diagnosis of these cases will be profoundly different from the Humean's. Price and Ross must contend that our experience of moral conflict is our apprehension that the implication of one mind-independent, a priori moral truth is incompatible with the implication of another mind-independent, a priori moral truth. And, according to Price and Ross, when we find ourselves in a situation of moral conflict, we must try to determine which of the two incompatible implications has the mind-dependent property of being an actual duty.[42] The Humean pluralist, in contrast, holds that our experience of moral conflict is at bottom the same as our experience of having two conflicting desires, and that when we find ourselves in a situation of moral conflict we end up doing something similar to what we do when we have to decide between incompatible desires of ours. And it seems to me that within the category of pluralists, the Humean sentimentalist explanation is clearly superior to the Price-Ross mind-independent, a priori explanation. We understand and have plenty of experience of conflicting desires and of having to decide between them: this fits perfectly well with our general view of human psychology and its interactions with the world. The idea of incompatible implications of mind-independent, a priori truths is altogether stranger. Pluralism and sentimentalism make the best couple.

On the Humean view, all moral reasons will give out at a point well short of necessity. Given that Humeanism is sentimentalist, it holds that our ultimate moral ends depend on our contingent sentimental make-up. Our ultimate moral ends are things that have moral importance for us, but we will not be able to give a justificatory reason for why they have that moral importance. They are the spots at which our moral justifications end.[43] And given that Humeanism is a pluralism, it holds that our sentimental make-up is such that it leads us to morally care about a multiplicity of potentially conflicting things for their own sakes.

It didn't have to be that way. We could have been built to morally care about only one thing (as Hutcheson thought). We could have been built to morally care about a multiplicity of things that never conflict with each other (as

Clarke and Butler thought). But if Hume is right, the psychological origins of our moral concerns have caused us to care about a multiplicity of potentially conflicting things for their own sakes. And if that's the way it is, we might very well face situations in which we can give no moral reason for taking one moral reason to override another moral reason—which is not the same as having no moral reasons at all.

3

Humean Non-Consequentialist Ends

I have argued that Hume develops a robustly pluralist view of morality, one that includes several different kinds of ultimate ends. But many have argued that sentimentalism in general and Humeanism in particular cannot accommodate one of the most important—if not *the* most important—kind of moral end: namely, non-consequentialist moral ends. According to this criticism, sentimentalists in general and Humeans in particular may be able to explain our having a plurality of consequentialist goals; they may be able to explain the practical reasons that arise from the desirability of certain states of affairs. But they cannot explain the practical reasons we have that are independent of the desirability of states of affairs. And yet, those non-consequentialist practical reasons are at least as central to our moral thinking as the consequentialist ones. So for all the variety of the Humean-sentimentalist picture of morality, it is still fatally incomplete.

In this chapter, I will try to show that this criticism is unfounded. Humean sentimentalism coheres with a pluralism that includes not only consequentialist moral ends but non-consequentialist ones as well. And it's to Humeanism's credit that it does so, as our moral thinking does indeed include both of those kinds of ends.[1]

The Non-Consequentialist Objection

John Balguy raised an early version of the objection that moral sentimentalism cannot accommodate the non-consequentialist aspects of our moral thinking, just two years after Francis Hutcheson published the first systematic development of it. As Balguy understood it, Hutcheson's sentimentalism implied that what makes an action virtuous is its effects, such as the advantages or pleasures it produces. According to Balguy, however, what actually makes an action virtuous is an intrinsic quality it possesses, which is independent of any effects the action may have. As Balguy rhetorically asks, "Is virtue no otherwise good or amiable, than as it conduces to public or private advantage? Is there no absolute goodness in it? Are all its perfections *relative* and instrumental?" (Balguy 1728/1991, 402). Actions produce consequences, and some of those consequences may be "natural goods." But the morality of an action is independent of the natural goodness it brings into existence. As Balguy puts it, "[M]oral good is an *end*, an *ultimate end* of one kind, as *natural good* is of another...However pleasure may be the consequence or appendage of virtue, yet, strictly speaking, it is not the end of a moral agent, nor the object of a moral affection, but virtue alone, antecedent to all considerations, and abstracted from every natural good" (Balguy 1728/1991, 403; see also 407–8).

Kant objected to sentimentalism on similar grounds. According to Kant, sentimentalism can explain only the motives we have to promote "a certain interest [whether it be] one's own or another's" (Kant 1785/2002, 233). Sentimentalism can account only for the ends that a person has that consist of "*what he intends to accomplish* through his action" (Kant 1785/2002, 228). The ends of morality, however, are "abstract[ed] completely from every end that has to be *brought about*" or "produced" (Kant 1785/2002, 238). The goal of producing desirable states of affairs, which is the only kind of goal sentimentalism can accommodate, gives rise only to hypothetical imperatives, but morality "can be expressed only in categorical imperatives" (Kant 1785/2002, 226).

Like Balguy and Kant, Rawls thought that sentimentalism—or at least *Hume's* sentimentalism—was unable to explain the moral concerns we have that are not based on the desirability of outcomes. In explaining this idea, Rawls distinguished between "object-dependent desires" and "principle-dependent desires" (Rawls 2000, 46–7). An object-dependent desire is a desire to produce certain states of affairs. A principle-dependent desire is a desire to act on a principle, distinct from the states of affairs that acting in that way will produce. Hume's sentimentalist psychology, Rawls claims, can explain only object-dependent desires—only desires to produce certain results (Rawls 2000, 48–50). But in fact we also have principle-dependent desires. We sometimes prefer a course of action even though its outcomes are less desirable. We sometimes perform actions because we think they are required by a principle that is not results-oriented. And Hume's sentimentalism cannot accommodate this.

The most important recent version of this non-consequentialist objection is Stephen Darwall's. It's Darwall's version that I will focus on in the rest of this chapter.

According to Darwall, Hume's approval-based account of morality[2] can accommodate only judgments based on desires for states of affairs.[3] As a result,

Humeanism cannot account for commonsensical opposition to certain kinds of moral trade-offs. As Darwall puts it:

In accepting a norm of justice requiring me to restore a seditious bigot's property, I take there to be a reason for doing so that cannot be reduced to a reason for (desiring) the existence of any state, even the state of the money's being returned. Perhaps the world would be a better place if the money went to Oxfam; that might be a more desirable state of affairs. And even if I think that a property-restoring act's being done is a better state, the reason I will credit in accepting a norm of justice requiring me to restore the property will differ from any deriving from (or consisting in) the value of that state. Imagine...that I can bring about more such valuable states by the shocking spectacle of violating the norm myself thereby causing, say, two other would-be violators not to go through with their previously intended violations. The (agent-relative, second-person) reasons for acting that derive from a norm of property would not recommend that I do so. Reasons for action cannot, in general, be reduced to reasons to desire states, and, in particular, a reason of justice to return a seditious bigot's property cannot be. Or so someone who has the motive of justice must think if she is to regulate her conduct in the way she must for a whole plan or scheme to be collectively beneficial. But...this conflicts with Hume's general theory of motivation. (Darwall 2006, 191)[4]

In returning the money to the seditious bigot, the just person is not trying to produce a certain outcome. She is not trying to bring the world into accord with her desire for a certain state of affairs. She is, rather, acting on principle, heeding the normative call for an action "pure and simple" (Darwall 2006, 157). This normative call is impervious to the lure of trading one unjust action (of one's own) for two just actions (of others). That's because the attraction of such a lure would be based on the desirability of certain outcomes, but the normative call is not based on the desirability of certain outcomes. It's a call to follow a norm, not a desire that has a state of affairs as its object. According to Darwall, however, the official Humean view takes all reasons to be based on desires that do have outcomes or states of affairs as their objects. More specifically, the Humean view takes all of an agent's reasons to be based on the agent's desire to experience more rather than less pleasure. As Darwall puts it in an earlier work, "Hume's theory of action thus not only employs the traditional idea that the will invariably aims at the good: it also interprets that idea hedonistically and egoistically" (Darwall 1995, 294). If the only reason a person has to perform an action is that it will produce an outcome whose observation will give her a pleasurable feeling (of, say, approval), then she will have an even more powerful reason to perform an action that produces an outcome whose observation will give her two pleasurable feelings (of approval). Because the Humean agent will have every reason to trade off something that will cause her to feel one pleasure (of approval) for something that will cause her to feel two pleasures (of approval), Hume cannot accommodate a reason not to trade off one of one's own just acts for two just acts of other people. But we *do* think there is a reason not to trade off one of one's own just acts for two just acts of other people. The Humean view thus fails as an account of our moral thinking.[5]

In response, I will try to show that the Humean theory can in fact accommodate our non-trade-off judgments and is thus not open to the non-consequentialist objection. The approach I will take to defending Hume is not the only possible one. We could also highlight Hume's acknowledgement that some of our motives (such as to punish our enemies, benefit our friends, and be kind to children) are unconnected to any thought of producing pain or pleasure; as he writes, "Beside good and evil, or in other words, pain and pleasure, the direct passions frequently arise from a natural impulse or instinct, which is perfectly unaccountable" (*T* 2.3.9.8). Or we could follow Garrett, who has defended Hume by explaining his capacity to accommodate the motive to follow a "policy" that has long-term benefits rather than simply to act on a "case-by-case evaluation of interest," which would explain why a person may in a particular situation perform an action that she does not expect to produce an outcome that will give her pleasure (Garrett 2007). But what I will try to show is that Humean moral psychology includes pleasurable moral sentiments that accord perfectly well with the non-trade-off moral judgments at the heart of the objection, and that Darwall and others who have advanced the objection have failed to notice this because they have attributed to Hume a view of pleasure that is more simplistic than the one he actually develops.

Beauty and Trade-Offs

The non-consequentialist objection moves from the claim that Humean sentimentalism can account only for desires for states of affairs whose observation one finds pleasurable to the claim that Humean sentimentalism cannot account for our opposition to certain kinds of moral trade-offs (such as our opposition to performing one unjust action in order to cause other people to perform a multitude of other, just actions). But there is a desire for a type of state of affairs that would block that move: namely, an agent's desire for the state of affairs in which *she herself* does not perform an unjust act. I may desire that the world contain as many just acts as possible, regardless of who performs them. But I may also have a distinct desire that the world contain just acts *performed by me*. That second desire may not be merely another instance of the first. And the pain I receive from performing an unjust act myself might be so much weightier than the pain I receive from observing two others' unjust acts that we do not need to refer to anything else to explain my resistance to trading off one of my just acts for two of two others.

The distinction between agent-relativity and agent-neutrality is helpful in explaining this point. An agent-neutral desire has as its object a state of affairs that can be described without any reference to the agent who has the desire. An agent-relative desire has as its object a state of affairs that cannot be described without reference to the agent who has the desire. The agent-neutral desire for a world in which just actions are performed may not be able to fund the non-trade-off judgments at the core of the non-consequentialist objection. But the agent-relative desire for a world in which I myself perform just actions can fund such judgments. So if Humeanism can accommodate agent-relative desires of this kind, the crucial final move of the objection will be blocked.[6]

To make this general sentimentalist approach plausible, let's first consider artistic motivation. An artist, call her Jane, has a desire to produce a beautiful object herself, say a painting. Jane also has a desire that the world contain as many beautiful objects as possible, regardless of who produces them. From her possessing those two desires, can you infer that Jane will prefer not to create a painting she wants to create if she believes that by doing so she can spur two other people to produce two beautiful paintings? No. The satisfaction Jane receives from producing a beautiful painting herself is quite different from, and quite possibly much weightier than, the pleasure she receives from observing a beautiful painting produced by someone else. The satisfaction of creating a beautiful work of art isn't simply one unit of something that the pleasure of observing two other works of art is two units of. That both feelings are pleasurable reactions to states of affairs does not give you any reason to hold that Jane will think it better to trade her own artistic creation for the observation of two others' creations. Or consider the desire to write a novel or run a marathon and the desire to read others' novels or watch others finish marathons. You may want to write a novel or run a marathon because you think you will get great satisfaction out of it. You may also want two other people to finish novels or marathons because you think you will enjoy reading or watching them. I cannot infer on this basis alone, however, that you will prefer to abandon your own novel or marathon in order to spur two other people to finish theirs.

It's not even the case that the pleasurable emotional response Jane has to observing an already-existent beautiful object will necessarily have more deliberative weight with her than the pleasurable emotional response she would have to two new beautiful objects' coming into existence. Let us say that Jane observes an object and that her observation is pleasurable in a way that leads her to judge it beautiful. Does this give you reason to think that she will, all other things being equal, choose to destroy the original object so that two other objects that give her the same kind of pleasure will be brought into existence? I think it's pretty clear that it does not. Imagine that the original object is a painting. Jane realizes that by destroying the painting she will inspire multiple other people, spurred to artistic creation by fury at her destructive act, to create paintings that she will find just as beautiful as the original. And let us say that she chooses not to destroy the painting. Do we need to postulate that she has some desire that *conflicts* with the aesthetic pleasure she receives from the original painting in order to explain her not destroying that painting? No. Jane's aesthetic response to the original painting itself seems perfectly compatible with her choosing that the painting continue to exist even if destroying it would lead to the production of two other beautiful paintings. (This is a case I will come back to later.)

But if you know that Jane finds an object beautiful, can't you legitimately infer that, all other things being equal, she will prefer that more objects like it exist rather than fewer? Perhaps. That inference, however, does not imply any consequentialist-vs.-non-consequentialist distinction between the pleasure Jane receives from a beautiful object and her reasons for moral action. From the fact that Jane thinks she morally ought to perform a particular action it may be legitimate to infer that, all other things being equal, she will prefer more actions like it to be performed rather than fewer. But what the non-consequentialist objection requires is that her having a pleasurable emotional response to an object warrants the inference that, all other things being equal, she will choose a state of affairs in which that original object is destroyed so that more objects like it will exist, over a state of affairs in which the original object persists but fewer objects like it exist overall—and this inference is not warranted. Concluding that Jane will prefer the trade-off of one actual desirable object for the bringing into existence of multiple possible desirable objects is just as unwarranted with regard to her responses to beautiful objects as it is with regard to her responses to acts of justice. Her aesthetic appreciation of a beautiful object gives you no more reason to think that she would destroy that object in order to spur other people each to create multiple beautiful objects than her appreciation of just action gives you reason to think that she would act unjustly in order to spur multiple other people to act justly.

How does this discussion of Jane's aesthetic reactions help the Humean respond to the non-consequentialist objection? The aesthetic case helps because it's an example of a set of evaluations and motivations that are plausibly taken to be based on sentiment and yet do not lead to the intrapersonal trade-offs at the heart of the objection. If we find nothing amiss in combining a sentimentalist account of aesthetics with non-consequentialist features of our aesthetic reasons, then why think there is anything amiss in combining a sentimentalist account of morality with non-consequentialist features of our moral reasons?[7] The satisfaction Jane receives from creating a beautiful work of art is not merely one unit of a kind of pleasure that she receives two units of when she observes two other artists' works of art. There is thus no conceptual bar to the sentimentalist's denying that the pleasurable response to her own just acts is merely one unit of the pleasure Jane could receive two units of by observing two other people perform just acts. In the next four sections, I will try to show that the details of Hume's account of pleasurable sentiments, motivation, and evaluation cohere perfectly with such a denial.

The Non-Fungibility of Humean Pleasures

Bentham thought that all pleasures were fungible and that as a result decisions about what to do can be entirely quantitative matters.[8] This Benthamite position is based on the idea that all pleasures can be reduced to the selfsame impression, to a single, distinct psychological state.

Hume rejects this view of pleasures as fungible. Humean pleasures do not all reduce to quantifiable, commensurable units, for Hume denies that there is a simple impression of pleasure *per se*. He writes:

['T]is evident, that under the term *pleasure*, we comprehend sensations, which are very different from each other, and which have only such a distinct resemblance, as is requisite to make them be express'd by the same abstract term. A good composition of music and a bottle of good wine equally produce pleasure; and what is more, their goodness is determin'd merely by the pleasure. But shall we say upon that account, that the wine is harmonious, or the music of a good flavour? In like manner an inanimate object, and the character or sentiments of any person may, both of them, give satisfaction; but as the satisfaction is different, this keeps our sentiments concerning them from being confounded, and makes us ascribe virtue to the one, and not to the other. Nor is every sentiment of pleasure or pain, which arises from characters and actions, of that *peculiar* kind, which makes us praise or condemn. (*T* 3.1.2.4)

While there are multiple impressions that are pleasurable, pleasure simpliciter is merely an abstract idea. We can form a mental grouping, or associated set, of all impressions that are pleasurable, but there is no one impression that is simply pleasure itself.

This feature of Hume's account should immediately make us question whether he is committed to holding that a person will always prefer two things that give pleasure to one thing that gives pleasure. For Humean pleasure is not a single, discrete mental experience that can be chopped up into fungible units that can be compared in the way that consequentialist trade-offs require. My appreciation of a musical composition and my appreciation of a fine bottle of wine are both determined by the pleasure they give me. But that does not imply that I would trade the single pleasure of listening to one musical composition for the two pleasures of drinking two bottles of wine. The pleasures involved aren't sensibly chopped up, quantified, and measured in the way that such trade-offs presuppose.[9]

Someone might try to reassert the objection by claiming that it requires only trade-offs between experiences of approval. The charge is that Hume is committed to holding that we will always prefer two experiences of approval (of the moral acts of others) to one experience of approval (of my own moral act). And even if trade-off implications don't follow in any clear way in cases in which there are different kinds of pleasures, they do follow in cases in which it is approval that is on both sides. Comparing the pleasure of a bottle of wine to the pleasure of a musical composition might be akin to comparing apples to oranges. But comparing approvals to approvals is apples to apples.

This reassertion of the objection fails, however, because even comparing two pleasures that go by the same name can be a case of comparing apples and oranges. The aesthetic case is once again instructive. The desire an artist has to create a beautiful painting and the desires an artist has for multiple other people to create beautiful paintings might both be said to be based on aesthetic pleasure. But that does not give us grounds for claiming that the artist will prefer to forgo the single pleasure of creating a beautiful painting so that she can experience the two pleasures of observing two other persons' beautiful creations. (Indeed, there's something deeply suspect about this quantitative way of speaking about aesthetic pleasure in the first place.) Similarly, your receiving pleasure from a painting you find beautiful does not warrant my believing that you will prefer that painting be destroyed so that two equally beautiful paintings will be created. And as we have already seen in Chapter 2, Hume points out that sentiments that are classified as approval differ from each other in a similar ways. The sentiment of approval that one virtue elicits can be "somewhat *different* from that, which attends the other virtues...Each of the virtues, even benevolence, justice, gratitude, integrity, excites a different sentiment or feeling in the spectator" (*T* 3.3.4.2; see also *E* 7.29 and App 4.3–6 and 21–2).[10] The virtues that make us love our friends lead us to feel a sentiment toward them that differs from the sentiment that the virtues of heroes we admire make us feel. Approval of a trait agreeable to its possessor is not a smaller amount of the same thing that approval of a trait useful to others is a larger amount of. Approval of a trait that is useful to its possessor is not a smaller amount of the same thing that approval of a trait that is useful to others is a larger amount of. We've seen Hume make all of these points in his pluralist account of the bases of our moral judgments. All of these points fit with his view of the pleasures as non-fungible, the idea that pleasurable sentiments do not all reduce to some quantity of one selfsame impression or mental state. (Pleasure *per se* is, for Hume, merely an abstract idea.) And these points about the variability of moral pleasure enable Hume to resist the implication of the simplistic trade-offs at the heart of the non-consequentialist objection—just as he can resist the idea that we would always trade one beautiful musical composition for two good bottles of wine.

Most importantly, at the heart of the non-consequentialist objection are *interpersonal* trade-offs—trade-offs of one approval-of-myself for two approvals-of-others. But Hume's account of the motivational influences of the indirect and moral passions implies that self-approval has a deliberative weight of a different kind from the deliberative weight of approval of others. The non-consequentialist objection will work only if Hume is committed to holding that the interpersonal comparison of self-approval to approval-of-others is an apples-to-apples comparison, but on Hume's own account it's apples-to-oranges. The kind of asymmetry of the motivational profiles of these pleasures is something we have already seen in our discussion of artistic creation. We will now see how Hume builds that motivational asymmetry into his account of the indirect and moral passions.

Pride and Love

Let's return to Jane. She now faces two courses of action. If she takes the first course of action, she'll be proud of herself, or at least will avoid the painful feeling of humiliation. If she takes the second course of action, she'll feel humiliated, but she'll also cause herself to feel love for three people toward whom she is currently indifferent. So: the first course of action promises a net result of one pleasurable impression (namely, a feeling of pride or the avoidance of a feeling of humiliation). The second course of action promises one painful impression (humiliation) and three pleasurable impressions (love for three other people), for a net result of plus two. Can we therefore infer that Jane will prefer the second course to the first— that she'll bring onto herself one feeling of humiliation so that she can also experience three feelings of love? Of course not. Pride and humiliation and love don't operate in the quantifiable, interpersonally fungible way such trade-offs require. And Hume's account of the passions fits perfectly well with these non-trade-off phenomena.

On Hume's account, pride and love are pleasurable indirect passions. Neither of them is on its own an immediate motive to action (T 2.2.6.3–6).[11] But both influence the will in indirect ways. What I want to highlight is the difference between how the two of them influence the will.

According to Hume, my thinking that I will feel pride as a result of performing an action can never be the sole explanation of my being motivated to perform it. There must be some other consideration that initially leads me to be motivated to perform it. But my thinking that action will make me feel pride will add to that initial motive. Hume writes:

Supposing that there is an immediate impression of pain or pleasure, and that arising from an object related to ourselves or others, this…, by concurring with certain dormant principles of the human mind, excites the new impressions of pride or humility, love or hatred. That propensity, which unites us to the object, or separates us from it, still continues to operate, but in conjunction with the indirect passions, which arise from a double relation of impressions and ideas. These indirect passions, being always agreeable or uneasy, give in their turn additional force to the direct passions, and encrease our desire and aversion to the object. Thus a suit of fine cloaths produces pleasure from their beauty; and this pleasure produces the direct passions, or the impressions of volition and desire. Again, when these cloaths are consider'd as belonging to ourself, the double relation conveys to us the sentiment of pride, which is an indirect passion; and the pleasure, which attends that passion, returns back to the direct affections, and gives new force to our desire or volition, joy or hope. (*T* 2.3.9.4)

My feeling pride in a thing cannot on its own explain my desire for it, since my feeling pride in it must itself be explained by some feature of it that I find desirable. However, the prospect of feeling pride will "encrease" or give "new force" or "additional force" to my desire or volition. When I have an antecedent desire to produce some result, my thinking that this result will cause me to feel the pleasure of pride will strengthen the antecedent desire. Perhaps in addition to wanting to buy a suit, I am also averse to spending the money that it will cost. If it were simply a contest between my desire for the suit based on its beauty and my resistance to the suit based on its cost, the latter would win out. But then I realize how proud I will feel walking into the office in my new suit, and my desire to buy it grows in strength. With the additional force that the prospect of feeling pride adds, my desire to buy the suit now wins out.

Humean pride is a pleasurable feeling (toward oneself). Humean love is a pleasurable feeling (toward another). Like pride, love is not itself an immediate motive to action. Like pride, love nonetheless influences the will in indirect ways. But the way love influences the will differs from the way pride does—and this difference accounts for Jane's resistance to trading off one feeling of humiliation for three feelings of love.

Pride influences an agent by strengthening her motive to do something that she thinks will lead her to feel the pleasurable sentiment of pride. The main influence of love, in contrast, is not to motivate an agent to bring about states of affairs in which she will have pleasurable experiences of love. Indeed, love does not influence an agent's will chiefly by adding to, or giving rise to, motives to create for herself experiences of feelings of pleasure at all. Love, rather, influences an agent chiefly by giving rise in her to a motive to make the person she loves happy. Hume writes:

The passions of love and hatred are always followed by, or rather conjoin'd with benevolence and anger. 'Tis this conjunction, which chiefly distinguishes these affections from pride and humility... [L]ove and hatred are not compleated within themselves, nor rest in that emotion, which they produce, but carry the mind to something farther. Love is always follow'd by a desire of the happiness of the person belov'd, and an aversion to his misery: As hatred produces a desire of the misery and an aversion to the happiness of the person hated.... [B]enevolence and anger are passions different from love and hatred... [but] ... conjoin'd with them, by the original constitution of the mind. As nature has given to the body certain appetites and inclinations, which she encreases, diminishes, or changes according to the situation of the fluids or solids; she has proceeded in the same manner with the mind. According as we are possess'd with love or hatred, the correspondent desire of the happiness or misery of the person, who is the object of these passions, arises in the mind, and varies with each variation of these opposite passions. (*T* 2.2.6)

Love influences an agent's will by causing her to have a motive to benefit the person for whom she feels love. Love is a pleasurable sentiment and it has motivational influence, but that influence does not mainly concern an agent's desires for states of affairs in which she herself experiences more pleasure.

Hume thinks, for instance, that we tend to feel esteem for people who have "power and riches" and "contempt" for people who exhibit "poverty and meanness." He also thinks that this "esteem and contempt are to be consider'd as species of love and hatred" (*T* 2.1.5.1). But he does not equate our esteem for the rich with desire for certain kinds of outcomes that produce pleasure in us. The esteem we feel for a rich person is pleasurable, but Hume nowhere suggests that such esteem is the same as a desire to observe as many rich people as possible. The state of mind of esteeming a rich person is that of having a positive feeling about her, not that of having a motive to change the world in any particular way. Just as my aesthetic appreciation of an object is distinct from my wanting to own the object or maximize the number of moments of my observation of it, so too my esteem for a rich person is distinct from my wanting anything in particular at all. Indeed, Hume takes great pains to argue that our esteem for the rich is neither equivalent to, nor based on, our desire for any advantages we might expect to gain from their wealth. He maintains "not only that we respect the rich and powerful, whether they shew no inclination to serve us, but also when we lie so much out of the sphere of their activity, that they cannot even be suppos'd to be endow'd with that power" (*T* 2.2.5.10). The esteem we feel for the rich is "disinterested," distinct from states of mind with a world-to-mind direction of fit (*T* 2.2.5.11).

Because Hume takes esteem to be a species of love, and because he claims that the passion of love "is always followed by, or rather conjoin'd with benevolence," he must hold that when we feel esteem for a rich person we also tend to feel a certain amount of good will toward her, even if that good will's motivational force is relatively weak. As he explains it, "love and esteem are at the bottom the same passion" (*T* 2.2.2.10), and "benevolence attends both" even if benevolence "is connected with love in a more eminent degree" (*T* 3.3.4.15). And it is, in fact, plausible to hold that if I esteem another person I will, all other things being equal, prefer that her welfare be promoted rather than obstructed. That preference, however, is not necessarily a desire for as many outcomes as possible that produce in me feelings of pleasure, which is what the non-consequentialist objection requires. Hume's view may entail that the esteem I feel for a wealthy person is always conjoined with a desire for that particular person's happiness, but it does not entail that this esteem is equivalent to, or is even always conjoined with, a preference for the state of affairs in which the original wealthy person is made poor while a few more people overall are made wealthy over the state of affairs in which the original person remains wealthy while no one else is made wealthy. The Humean position can consistently deny, as Hume himself surely would want to, that my good will toward a wealthy person whom I esteem implies my having the preference to destroy this person's wealth so that multiple different people could be made wealthy. My esteem—like my feelings of love in general—has an agent-relative character that spreads to the desires associated with them, and not the agent-neutral character that implies interpersonal trade-offs.

One way to underscore the difference between pride and love's influence on the will is to note the temporal asymmetry between them. It's the *prospect* of feeling pride that influences the will: the thought that doing something will cause me to feel pride in the future will "encrease [my] desire" to do it. But we aren't typically motivated to perform an action because we think that it will cause us to feel love in the future for someone whom we do not currently feel love for. Rather, *occurrent* feelings of love give rise to motives to benefit the beloved in the future: we feel love actually for a person and that feeling causes us to "desire...the happiness of the person belov'd." Because I will feel pride toward myself by doing something, I have a stronger motive to do it. In contrast, it's not typically the case that because I will feel love for S by doing something, I develop a motive to do it. Rather, because I occurrently feel love for S, I am motivated to do things that will make her happy.[12]

The difference between the motivational profiles of the *occurrent* pleasurable sentiment of love and the *prospect* of feeling the pleasurable sentiment of pride in the future helps explain what might otherwise have seemed puzzling about one of the aesthetic cases we have discussed. Jane observes a painting that gives her aesthetic pleasure. She realizes that if she destroys the painting she will spur two other people to create two equally beautiful paintings that she will then be able to observe, resulting in two aesthetic pleasures. Even if we eliminate all non-aesthetic considerations of potential punishment and property violation and the like, it's still natural to think that Jane will choose not to destroy the original painting, even if doing so will spur the creation of two equally beautiful paintings. How can Humean sentimentalists explain this? They can do so by holding, plausibly, that aesthetic pleasure is like love. Like love, aesthetic pleasure is not in and of itself a motive to action. Like love, aesthetic pleasure gives rise in Jane to a desire to promote the well-being of the thing she feels it about. In the case of love, this would be a desire for the beloved's happiness; in the case of aesthetic pleasure, this would be a desire for the preservation of the object. Crucially, however, her desire to promote the well-being of the object of her love or aesthetic pleasure is not the same as a desire to feel more sentiments of love or aesthetic pleasure.[13] It would be very odd for Jane to destroy a person she loves in order to create a situation in which she would feel love for two other people whom she currently does not love; it would be odd in the same way for her to destroy one object she gets aesthetic pleasure from in order to spur others to create two such objects. The explanation for this is that the pleasurable sentiments of both love and aesthetic pleasure do not chiefly motivate "in prospect"—i.e. it's not the future prospect of feeling love and aesthetic pleasure that is their main motivational influence. These feelings are, rather, directed toward the object of the affection (see Cohon 2008, 171). That is not to say that the expectation of feeling a pleasurable sentiment can never be a motive to action, nor even to say that the thought that a course of action will cause one to feel love or aesthetic pleasure will never strengthen one's motive to take that course. The point here is merely that there is a difference between a prospective pleasurable sentiment that motivates chiefly by *pulling* the agent toward her own future pleasure, and an occurrent pleasurable sentiment that motivates chiefly by *pushing* the agent to act for the benefit of the object of the sentiment—and Hume's discussions of the motivational profiles of pride and love show that he was well aware of that difference.

The mere fact that pride and love are both pleasurable does not imply that they are a single kind of pleasure that each person invariably seeks to experience the maximum amount of and which will thus lead to trade-off judgments. Indeed, it is just the variability of these different experiences that Hume was intimately aware of and attempted to capture by developing his complex and nuanced account of the indirect passions. This variability is what makes Hume's account pluralist. There is a sense in which we can say that for Hume value is based on pleasure, or pleasurable emotional responses to certain things. But there are different kinds of pleasure—different kinds of pleasurable emotional responses—that do not all reduce to one thing. Pleasurable emotional responses are multifarious; it is not the case that pleasure is a single, common coin. But given that, on Hume's pluralist account of pleasurable emotional responses, the indirect passions of pride, humility, love, and hatred do not imply agent-neutral maximizing trade-offs, it would hardly be surprising if his account of the moral sentiments resists that implication as well. And when we turn to Hume's texts, we do in fact find that his moral sentiments are akin to the indirect passions and aesthetic appreciation in that they are emotional responses that are not equivalent to, nor necessarily give rise to, the agent-neutral maximizing desires that lead to the implausible trade-off judgments that the non-consequentialist objection foists on the Humean position. He has a pluralist account of moral pleasures that explains his pluralist account of moral judgment.

Approval of Self and Approval of Others

The differences between the motivational influences of Humean pride and love also characterize the differences between the motivational influences of Humean self-approval and approval of others. Hume foregrounds this connection when he says that "virtue and the power of producing love or pride" are "equivalent," as are "vice and the power of producing humility or hatred" (*T* 3.3.1.3; see also 3.3.1.31).[14]

On Hume's account, approval is like pride and love in that it is not itself an immediate motive to action but rather influences the will indirectly. There are, however, different ways approval exerts its influence. Approval of oneself influences the will the way pride does. Approval of others influences the will the way love does.

Hume explains how approval of oneself can influence the will in the following passage, in which he is summing up three different ways in which the virtues of benevolence benefit their possessor (I've added the numbers).

[1] [T]he immediate feeling of benevolence and friendship, humanity and kindness, is sweet, smooth, tender, and agreeable, independent of all fortune and accidents. [2] These virtues are besides attended with a pleasing consciousness or remembrance, and keep us in humour with ourselves as well as others; while we retain the agreeable reflection of having done our part towards mankind and society. [3] And though all men show a jealousy of our success in the pursuit of avarice and ambition; yet are we almost sure of their good-will and good-wishes, so long as we persevere in the paths of virtue, and employ ourselves in the execution of generous plans and purposes. What other passion is there where we shall find so many advantages united; [1] an agreeable sentiment, [2] a pleasing consciousness, [3] a good reputation? (*E* 9.2.21)

Hume tells us here that there are three different but converging reasons that a person with the benevolent virtues is better off: (1) the affections that are virtuous (e.g.
"humanity and kindness") are themselves pleasant; (2) one will feel the pleasure of
approval toward oneself (i.e. one will have "a pleasing consciousness" and a good
"humour with [oneself]") when one acts on the affections that are virtuous; and
(3) one will have a "good reputation" and receive the "good-will and good-wishes"
of others if one acts on the affections that are approved of as virtuous. (1) and
(3) are not constituted by a person's having feelings of approval or disapproval.
It's (2) that concerns the way approval and disapproval of one's own character can
give one a reason to be virtuous. (2) is what Hume has in mind when he says that
"in all ingenuous natures, the antipathy to treachery and roguery is too strong to
be counterbalanced by any views of profit or pecuniary advantage. Inward peace
of mind, consciousness of integrity, a satisfactory review of our own conduct;
these are circumstances very requisite to happiness" (E 9.2.23). In addition, Hume
relies on this view of self-approval's motivational influence in the conclusion to the
Treatise, when he says that acting virtuously gives us the pleasure of "inward satisfaction" and acting viciously makes us feel the pain of not being able to "bear [our
own] survey" (T 3.3.6). A person will be happier if she feels self-approval rather
than self-disapproval. That is not to say that self-approval is the only reason a person has for virtuous conduct. Indeed, the primary reason a virtuous person will act
virtuously is that she has a direct or immediate motive to do what benefits others.
Self-approval can nonetheless strengthen that primary motive.

The motivating influence of self-approval is thus like the motivating influence
of pride in that it is prospective and depends on the existence of an independent, desirable feature. Suppose I am considering a future course of conduct, and
I think, prospectively, that if I acted in that way I would feel approval toward
myself. Hume holds that I would only feel approval because the course of conduct
has some desirable feature, for example, its agreeability or usefulness to others.[15]
So if I think that my performance of an action would cause me to feel approval of
myself, I must have a motive to perform the action that is prior to and independent
of the prospect of my feeling approval toward myself. I could, for instance, want to
perform an action just because it will benefit others without having any thought
whatsoever about its causing me to feel approval.[16] Nonetheless, it is also the case
that the prospect of feeling approval can increase or give additional force to that
prior desire, just as a feeling of pride can increase or give additional force to the
desire to do something that will make me feel proud. Just as I will have an independent desire to possess a suit of clothes that will cause me pride (since my feeling
pride is based on the clothes' having some antecedently desirable quality), so too
I will have an independent desire to perform actions that I will approve of (since

my approval is based on some prior desirable feature of the action). And just as the prospect of feeling pride at possessing the clothes can strengthen my motivation to possess it, so too can the prospect of approving of an action strengthen my motivation to perform it.[17]

Here is how the influence of self-approval can work in practice. I am considering whether to do something that will be useful to other people. I have a motive to do it because I have a desire to make other people happy. But I also have motives that pull in the opposite direction, maybe motives based on narrowly selfish desires for material gain. Failing to perform the action will, however, lead me to feel self-disapproval, and knowing this strengthens my motivation to perform the action, and thus helps to override my narrowly selfish motives to do otherwise. It is just this kind of strengthening of the motive to virtue that Hume points to when explaining why most of us will be better off eschewing sensible knavery. People with "ingenuous natures" care about the welfare of others. Their concern for others is a motive for them to benefit others. And their motive to benefit others will be strengthened because benefitting others will lead them to avoid self-disapproval, enabling them to experience "a satisfactory review of [their] own conduct" and a "consciousness of [their own] integrity" (E 9.2.23).

Now consider the influence on the will of the moral sentiments of approval and disapproval about the conduct of other people.

Hume contends that my approval of a person will cause me to feel love for that person.[18] We have seen that Hume claims that my love for a person will also cause me to feel benevolence toward that person, or to desire her happiness. Humean psychology thus implies that when I approve of a person I will also have a desire for that person's happiness. Hume makes just this point at T 3.3.1.3. and 3.3.1.31. When you come to approve (or disapprove) of someone, it will influence your will by giving rise in you to a motive to make that person happy (or miserable).

Hume refers to this motivational influence of other-approval in his discussion of "dexterity in business." He writes:

Here is a man, who is not remarkably defective in his social qualities; but what principally recommends him is his dexterity in business, by which he has extricated himself from the greatest difficulties, and conducted the most delicate affairs with a singular address and prudence. I find an esteem for him immediately to arise in me; His company is a satisfaction to me; and before I have any farther acquaintance with him, I wou'd rather do him a service than another, whose character is in every other respect equal, but is deficient in that particular. (T 3.3.1.25)

The crucial bit here is the claim that I would rather do a service to a person with this character trait than do a service to a person without it. According to Hume, this is evidence that the trait is a virtue, which is to say that judging someone virtuous influences the will by causing a desire to benefit her. Similarly, when explaining the similarities between the natural abilities and qualities that are more traditionally thought of as virtues, Hume says that even if we choose to "refuse to natural abilities the title of virtues, we must allow, that they procure the love and esteem of mankind; that they give a new luster to the other virtues; and that a man possess'd of them is much more intitled to our good-will and services, than one entirely void of them" (T 3.3.4.2). If I approve of someone, Hume tells us here, I will have more "good-will" toward him than I will toward someone I don't approve of and be more inclined to do him a "service." The motivational influence my approval of other people has on me is to give rise in me to a desire for their happiness.

We can now see that the asymmetry we've already noted between the influence of pride and love also exists between approval toward self and approval toward others. Pride and self-approval influence the will *prospectively*: we do things that will cause pride and self-approval in the future. But love and other-approval mainly influence the will *occurrently*: we do things for other people because we currently feel love or approval toward them. And while pride and self-approval strengthen one's motivation to do something that will make oneself happy, love and other-approval give rise to a new motive to benefit someone else.

With the pieces we have in place—the examples from aesthetics, the non-fungibility of Humean pleasures, and the motivational asymmetry between pride and self-approval, on the one hand, and love and approval of others, on the other—we can now describe clearly the failure of the non-consequentialist objection.

The Humean Answer to the Non-Consequentialist Objection

On Hume's view, the prospect of feeling self-approval can strengthen one's desire to act morally. And there is nothing in Hume's view that speaks against that desire's playing a non-consequentialist role in one's moral thinking. One's wish to feel self-approval is what Hume calls an "ultimate end." It gives "immediate satisfaction" (E App 1. 20). It's not something one desires because it produces anything else, such as fungible units of pleasure *per se*. One desires it for its own sake.

Consider again Jane. She has promised her dying father that she will donate his money to a certain cause. Jane thinks that if she breaks her promise, she will feel bad about herself—will feel shame and self-disapproval. This feature of a possible course of action—that it will make her feel shame or self-disapproval—gives her a basic or ultimate reason not to do it. This reason is not reducible to the desire for any quantifiable measure of fungible units of pleasure. It functions in just the way we would expect from a non-consequentialist consideration. Jane's wish to avoid shame and self-disapproval issues a normative call that is as "pure and simple" as anything a non-consequentialist could hope for. The fact that that wish is based on sentiment does not preclude its having that kind of normative call.

Jane will also experience a painful sentiment—of disapproval—if she learns that someone else has broken a deathbed promise to his parent, or if she learns that two people have each broken deathbed promises to their parents. Hume does not think, however, that the unpleasantness of disapproval of others influences the will chiefly by motivating the person who feels disapproval to act in ways that will make her feel approval instead. The main motivating influence of one's disapproval toward others is to give rise in one to the desire for their misery (or punishment), just as the main motivating influence of love or approval is to give rise in one to the desire for their happiness. So the main motivational effect on Jane of others' committing injustice will be Jane's desire to see the wrong-doers punished. On Hume's view, the *prospect* of feeling love or approval towards others is not motivationally salient—which is in stark contrast to the intense motivational salience of the prospect of self-directed feelings of pride or approval, shame or disapproval, about oneself. Therefore, it is simply not true that Hume is committed to holding that Jane will prefer to trade off one of her own unjust acts for two just acts of two other people. Explicit and central features of Hume's account of moral motivation block that implication.

It would be weird if Jane preferred to do something that made her feel humiliation so that she could cause herself to feel love for three people toward whom she is currently indifferent. It would be weird if Jane was an artist and yet always preferred to spur other people to create rather than ever create anything herself. It would be weird in the same way if Jane preferred to do something that made her feel disapproval of herself so that she could cause herself to feel approval toward three other people. The desires to avoid humiliation, to create art, and to avoid self-disapproval have an agent-relative character to which Hume's account of the indirect passions and the moral sentiments is acutely sensitive. These desires are not simply thrown into some Benthamite hopper of uniform impressions of pleasure to be maximized. Hume's moral pluralism is built on a pluralism of emotional responses.

Even if we allow that Jane does have some motivating desire to prevent a state of affairs in which she would feel hatred or disapproval toward two other people—even if we bracket the separate point (discussed in the previous paragraph) of the different motivational influences of self-approval and other-approval—there would still be no grounds for attributing to Hume the view that the strength of that desire must be greater than the strength of her desire to avoid feeling shame and disapproval of herself. The pleasure of feeling pride or self-approval is not interchangeable with the pleasure of feeling love or approval of others. Feeling the former is not, on Hume's view, feeling a certain sum of pleasures of which feeling the latter is feeling twice as much. Feeling good about oneself is pleasurable and feeling good about other people is also pleasurable, but they are different sentiments, not greater and lesser amounts of the same sentiment. They're apples and oranges. Comparing them is no more a purely quantitative matter (where two approvals of others necessarily have twice as much deliberative weight as one approval of self) than is comparing the enjoyment of one beautiful musical composition to the enjoyment of two good bottles of wine.

Even if we were to allow that Humean self-approval and other-approval *are* fungible—which is just what I have been arguing against—it still would not be plausible to claim that Hume is committed to a trade-off of one act of one's own immorality for two acts of others' immorality. This is because the pain of shame and disapproval of one's own act is not a single, isolated sentiment. Feeling shame or self-disapproval is not a discrete experience temporally clipped to a one-and-done episode that caused it, not a single emotional moment that pops like a firework and then disappears. It persists and spreads throughout one's mental life, as Hume was well aware. Feeling pride or self-approval gives us a "pleasing consciousness or remembrance, and keep[s] us in humour with ourselves." The "inward peace of mind" of realizing you've acted well, as well as the self-recrimination of knowledge of your own knavery, is a chronic condition.

There are thus no grounds for foisting on Hume the view that a person such as Jane will invariably prefer to perform an action that makes her feel shame and self-disapproval in order to prevent two others from performing actions that will make her feel hatred and other-disapproval. We may suppose that Jane prefers that the world contain fewer immoral acts rather than more. But Jane also (agent-relatively) prefers that she herself perform fewer immoral acts rather than more. And Hume is no more committed to holding that the latter preference collapses into the former than he is to holding that the satisfaction of completing a novel is one unit of pleasure of which the pleasure of reading two novels by two other people is two units, or that feeling humiliation is one negative unit of which feeling love for two people is two positive units. Indeed, Hume's description of the long-lasting and pervasive mental effects of the results of reviews of our own conduct explains very well how the ultimate end of feeling pride and self-approval in what we ourselves have done can override the prospect of many other more momentary pleasures.

Some may worry that Hume is now susceptible to another objection, namely, that his view gives us the wrong kind of reason to treat others morally.[19] Don't we think we should treat people as morality demands because that's what's owed them and not because it produces in us the pleasure of self-approval? If Hume can explain only the latter sort of reason and not the former, doesn't his theory fail on that account?

Hume's view of moral motivation is not susceptible to this wrong-kind-of-reason charge because his view does not imply that the pleasures of self-approval and pains of self-disapproval are the only or primary reasons we have for virtuous conduct. The primary reason Jane has for doing what is moral is that it will be agreeable or beneficial or just. On Hume's account, if Jane is virtuous, she will typically be motivated immediately by her concern for others' welfare, social order, and the like. Indeed, Jane will approve of her own conduct just because it is typically motivated by those other concerns. What the prospect of self-approval or self-disapproval does is strengthen her motivation to act on those other concerns, which is of course very important in cases in which different considerations exert motivational force in the opposite direction.

This also explains how the Humean view can respond to the following, related objection (which Julia Annas put to me): if a person acts morally because she thinks doing so will enable her to avoid the painful experience of self-disapproval, then her motive for acting in that way will be selfish; but if her motive for an action is selfish, then she won't be able to approve of herself for performing that action. There are several reasons this objection does not discomfit the Humean. First, the agent who acts so as to avoid self-disapproval does not thereby *fail* to act on any other, approval-inducing motive. Suppose the agent is motivated to keep her promise or assist another because she cares about keeping her promises or about others' welfare. Suppose also that she realizes that if she fails to keep her promise or doesn't lend assistance she will feel disapproval of herself, and this thought strengthens her motivation to perform the action. That doesn't imply that she is no longer acting on the motive to keep her promise or assist another. The first motive is still there and worthy of approval. The aversion to self-disapproval doesn't make those other motives disappear or cease functioning. Secondly, Hume does not think that actions motivated by the desire to make oneself happy are never worthy of approval. Indeed, traits that are useful or beneficial to the agent herself constitute half of the catalogue of Hume's virtues, and the motive to perform actions that will prevent one from feeling disapproval of oneself fits comfortably into that half of his catalogue. Thirdly, an agent's being more strongly motivated to do something because she'll feel self-disapproval if she doesn't do it need not be taken to be a conscious mental event. Her concern to keep her promises or for others' welfare may be all that she's consciously aware of. But she may still be the sort of person who will disapprove of herself if she does not act in those ways, and her being that sort of person (rather than being a knave who does not feel self-disapproval) can account for some of the strength of her motivation to act in those ways, even if she doesn't consciously represent to herself the prospect of feeling painful self-disapproval if she acts differently. Hume himself discusses the case of someone who lacks a first-order motive to do what is virtuous but who does what is virtuous anyway because he does not want to feel the painful feeling of self-disapproval (*T* 3.2.1). Hume does not suggest, however, what would surely be implausible, that if such a person realized that he was acting morally in order to avoid self-disapproval he would thereby feel self-disapproval for his own selfishness.

Jane is considering whether to perform one action or another. She is motivated to do the first because it will make someone happy or it will prevent harm or it is just. But the second will make her a great deal of money, and that creates a countervailing motive. If Jane does the first she will approve of herself and if she does the second she will disapprove. And this strengthens her motivation to do the first.

So what is Jane's reason for doing the first instead of the second? Well, the answer might have different parts. Jane may think that the first will make someone happy or prevent harm or be just. But she may also think, "I'd feel terrible about myself if I did the second." The thought that she'd feel terrible about herself if she did the second is distinct from the thought of making others happy or preventing harm or being just (even if the former depends on the latter). The thought that she'd feel terrible about herself is sentiment-based and self-oriented—it's a thought about what will cause her to have painful or pleasurable experiences. Those features do not, however, make it the wrong kind of reason, at least not if our task is to account for the full array of considerations that play a role in our moral thinking.[20] People like Jane can be motivated in part by how they think they'll feel about themselves if they act one way rather than another. The prospects of experiencing sentiments of self-approval or self-disapproval can and do function as ultimate ends in our moral thinking. To its credit, Hume's account explains why this is so.

4

Prioritarianism and Pluralism in Adam Smith*

We have seen that Clarke, Butler, and Reid rejected monism, explicitly affirming a multiplicity of ultimate moral ends. Clarke, Butler, and Reid were also gripped by the prioritarian idea that full moral understanding would provide principled and determinate verdicts to all our moral questions—that morality does not harbor justificatory gaps between ends and judgments. Consequently, Clarke, Butler, and Reid advanced views according to which either the multiplicity of moral ends never come into conflict with each other, or, if such conflicts do occur, there is a strict hierarchical ordering for resolving them.

Hume too rejected monism. And Hume had his prioritarian moments, at times suggesting that moral conflict should always be resolved in favor of public utility. But Hume was also drawn to the opposing, pluralist idea—that moral ends can come into conflict in ways that do *not* admit of principled resolution.[1] Indeed, Hume's sentimentalist account of morality, combined with his attention to certain phenomena of commonsense moral thinking, made this anti-prioritarian view almost irresistible.

Adam Smith struggled at times to find his footing along the border between prioritarianism and pluralism. In the end, however, Smith, like Hume, was more deeply drawn to the pluralist position. Or so in this chapter I'll try to show.

Smith's Multiplism

In part VII of *The Theory of Moral Sentiments*, Smith examines two "systems" of virtue: that which holds that virtue consists entirely of self-interest, and that which

---

* I wish to express special thanks to Ryan Hanley, who commented on numerous drafts of this chapter and helped me improve it immeasurably.

holds that virtue consists entirely of benevolence (*TMS* 294–306). Smith thinks both of these systems get something importantly right—each identifies a crucial aspect of morality. The problem with both systems is that they identify as essential to morality only one thing while ignoring all others. Their problem is that they're monistic rather than multiplist.

The self-interested system, of which Epicurus was the leading proponent, held that "pleasure and pain were the sole ultimate objects of natural desire and aversion" (*TMS* 295), and that "to obtain this great end of natural desire was the sole object of all the virtues" (*TMS* 296). This system reduced every virtue—prudence, temperance, magnanimity, justice, beneficence, etc.—to the capacity to improve its possessor's ratio of pleasure to pain. Smith does not quarrel with the idea that responsible self-management is virtuous. Where Epicurus went wrong was in not acknowledging that moral judgments can also be based on ends entirely distinct from self-interest (*TMS* 298). "By running up all the different virtues too to this one species of propriety," Smith writes, "Epicurus indulged a propensity, which is natural to all men, but which philosophers in particular are apt to cultivate with a peculiar fondness, as the great means of displaying their ingenuity, the propensity to account for all appearances from as few principles as possible. And he, no doubt, indulged this propensity still further, when he referred all the primary objects of natural desire and aversion to the pleasures and pains of the body" (*TMS* 299). Like Hume, Smith believes that those who try to reduce everything to self-interest allow their "love of *simplicity*" to lead them into "much false reasoning in philosophy" (*E* App. 2.6).

In the chapter following his discussion of Epicurus' self-interest monism, Smith argues against the competing benevolence-monism of Hutcheson. Toward that end, Smith cites traits that are virtuous not because they benefit others but because they reflect responsible self-management, such as prudence, temperance, and constancy. Smith reiterates here Hume's anti-Hutchesonian idea that a significant subset of what we take to be virtues are traits that are beneficial to the agent herself, and that we do not think those traits earn their virtue entirely from their effects on society as a whole. Smith also argues against Hutcheson's benevolence-monism view by pointing out that it implies that virtue concerns only the "effects" of character traits on human happiness, when in fact we also morally judge traits based on non-consequentialist notions of propriety or suitableness. He writes:

As some of the other systems which I have already given an account of, do not sufficiently explain from whence arises the peculiar excellency of the supreme virtue of beneficence, so this system [i.e. Hutcheson's benevolence-monism] seems to have the contrary defect, of not sufficiently explaining from whence arises our approbation of the inferior virtues of prudence, *vigilance*, circumspection, temperance, constancy, firmness. The view and aim of our affections, the beneficent and hurtful effects which they tend to produce, are the only qualities at all attended to in this system. Their propriety and impropriety, their suitableness and unsuitableness, to the cause which excites them, are disregarded altogether. (*TMS* 304)

Both monistic "systems of moral philosophy" go wrong by narrowing virtue to a single point. And by failing to recognize the importance of a multiplicity of moral ends, "they tend, in some measure, to break the balance of the affections, and to give the mind a particular bias to some principles of action, beyond the proportion that is due to them" (*TMS* 306).

Smith's multiplism about virtue is also evident in his distinguishing between "the amiable and respectable virtues" (*TMS* 23).[2] Both of these sets of virtues are grounded in a person's desire to be in sentimental accord with others. But the "amiable" virtues come from a person's ramping up her emotional reaction to the plight of others so that her feelings are more akin to their first-hand experiences, while the respectable virtues come from a person's dampening down her emotional reaction to her own circumstances so that her feelings are more akin to the experiences of the people who are observing her. We approve of the person who shows more-than-usual compassion for the misfortunes of others *and* of the person who shows less-than-usual distress at her own misfortunes. These two sets of virtues, based though they are on the single sympathetic mental mechanism of bringing one's emotions into accord with others, are distinct objects of moral judgment. Our approval of the person "whose sympathetic heart seems to re-echo all the sentiments of those with whom he converses, who grieves for their calamities, who resents their injuries, and who rejoices at their good fortune [exclamation point]!" is different from our approval of the "reserved" person whose own misfortune occasions a "silent and majestic sorrow, which discovers itself only in the swelling of the eyes, in the quivering of the lips and cheeks, and in the distant, but affecting, coldness of the whole behaviour" (*TMS* 24).

In his account of justice, Smith makes clear his belief that, in addition to our concern for benevolence toward humanity, we also have non-consequentialist moral concerns. He does this by calling attention to our retributivist reactions to egregious crimes. Yes, such crimes do tend to harm humanity and for that reason should be discouraged. But our desire to see them punished is fueled by our disapproval of the acts in themselves, distinct from any thoughts of future consequences. Our first response to egregious crimes is simply that they deserve to be punished, not that such punishment will benefit society.

But though it commonly requires no great discernment to see the destructive tendency of all licentious practices to the welfare of society, it is seldom this consideration which first animates us against them. All men, even the most stupid and unthinking, abhor fraud, perfidy, and injustice, and delight to see them punished. But few men have reflected upon the necessity of justice to the existence of society, how obvious soever that necessity may appear to be. That it is not a regard to the preservation of society, which originally interests us in the punishment of crimes committed against individuals, may be demonstrated by many obvious considerations. (*TMS* 89)

Smith goes on to present evidence that we approve of some punishments on grounds distinct from their tendency to promote the general happiness. We may approve of the execution of a sentinel who falls asleep on his watch only because we think such punishment has beneficial future consequences. But we approve of the punishment of "detestable crimes" (such as murder and parricide) on different grounds, independently of their tendency to promote "the safety of numbers" or "the interest of the many" (*TMS* 91). As Smith says, "The very different sentiments with which the spectator views those different punishments [the difference, that is, between one's reluctant acceptance of the death penalty for a sleeping sentinel, and one's unambiguous ardor to see a vicious murderer executed], is a proof that his approbation of the one is far from being founded upon the same principles with that of the other" (*TMS* 90).

Elsewhere, Smith reiterates that different moral judgments are based on different approvals of different features. He writes, "If we attend to what we really feel when upon different occasions we either approve or disapprove, we shall find that our emotion in one case is often totally different from that in another, and that no common features can possibly be discovered between them. Thus the approbation with which we view a tender, delicate, and humane sentiment, is quite different from that with which we are struck by one that appears great, daring, and magnanimous" (*TMS* 324–5). This is the same point we saw Hume make when he discussed the different kinds of approval that lie at the base of positive judgments of the great and good (*T* 3.3.4). Both Smith and Hume take pains to make clear the distinct bases of virtue.

On the basis of these claims, it seems perfectly safe to attribute to Smith some form of multiplism, not monism. He's explicitly, consciously arguing against monistic views. When we try to place Smith on one side of the prioritarian/pluralist divide, however, things become less clear.

Smith's Prioritarian Leanings

There are strands in Smith's *Theory of Moral Sentiments* that fit with the theological prioritarianism of Butler. According to the Butlerian theological view, as we've seen, the promotion of the good of humanity is God's only ultimate moral end. But we humans are too cognitively and emotionally limited to conform our conduct to such an expansive goal. So we have been implanted with several more restricted principles, principles that have been designed so that, when we act on them, we will promote the general good of humanity even though that is not our conscious goal. Such is what Butler maintained in a passage we've already looked at from "Of the Love of Neighbor" (Butler's 1729/1983a, 66). Butler says the same thing in his "Dissertation," where he writes:

The happiness of the world is the concern of him, who is the Lord and the Proprietor of it: nor do we know what we are about, when we endeavour to promote the good of mankind in any ways, but those which he has directed; that is indeed in all ways, not contrary to veracity and justice...And though it is our business and our duty to endeavour, within the bounds of veracity and justice, to contribute to the ease, convenience, and even cheerfulness and diversion of our fellow-creatures: yet from our short views, it is greatly uncertain, whether this endeavour will, in particular instances, produce an overbalance of happiness upon the whole; since so many and distant things must come into the account. (Butler 1736/1983, 385)

Smith says something very similar in the section in which he argues (just as Butler did in the "Dissertation") against Hutchesonian benevolence-monism. Smith writes: "Benevolence may, perhaps, be the sole principle of action in the Deity, and there are several, not improbable, arguments which tend to persuade us that it is so. It is not easy to conceive what other motive an independent and all-perfect Being, who stands in need of nothing external, and whose happiness is complete in himself, can act from. But whatever may be the case with the Deity, so imperfect a creature as man, the support of whose existence requires so many things external to him, must often act from many other motives" (TMS 305). A perfect being, Smith tells us here, would have the single moral end of benevolence. But we're imperfect, so we've been implanted with other principles to act on, and that's because acting on those principles best serves the end of benevolence as the perfect being understands it. Butler's idea that from a God's eye point of view, benevolence is the one fundamental moral end on which all other ("inferior") moral principles are based is something Smith seems to be endorsing when presenting his critique of Hutchesonian monism.

Smith also manifests the same prioritarian tendencies as Butler when elucidating our judgment that it is just to punish wrong-doers. Such judgments, according to Smith, can be independent of our beliefs about what will best promote the happiness of humanity. Our judgments concerning punishment of "detestable crimes" (TMS 91) look backward to what the wrong-doer did, not forward to the consequences of punishing. But Smith then goes on to maintain that our instinct to punish has been implanted in us by God (or Nature) because it serves the ultimate purpose of promoting the good. He writes:

We are not at present examining upon what principles a perfect being would approve of the punishment of bad actions; but upon what principles so weak and imperfect a creature as man actually and in fact approves of it. The principles which I have just now mentioned, it is evident, have a very great effect upon his sentiments; and it seems wisely ordered that it should be so. The very existence of society requires that unmerited and unprovoked malice should be restrained by proper punishments; and consequently, that to inflict those punishments should be regarded as a proper and laudable action. Though man, therefore, be naturally endowed with a desire of the welfare and preservation of society, yet the Author of nature has not entrusted it to his reason to find out that certain application of punishments is the proper means of attaining this end; but has endowed him with an immediate and instinctive approbation of that very application which is most proper to attain it. (*TMS* 77)

According to Smith, what explains our desire to punish in a way that does not involve thoughts about promoting the good of humanity is that such a desire in fact best serves the purpose of promoting the good of humanity. This explanation once again echoes Butler's account of morality and Butler's criticism of Hutcheson (in his "Dissertation" and "Love of Neighbors").

The same echo can be heard in Smith's discussion of our sense of duty or conscience. Our sense of duty or conscience, according to Smith, leads us to have moral concern for things other than merely benevolence or the promotion of the good of humanity. But it is God's concern for the good of humanity that is the ultimate explanation of our moral concerns.

The happiness of mankind, as well as of all other rational creatures, seems to have been the original purpose intended by the Author of nature, when he brought them into existence. No other end seems worthy of that supreme wisdom and divine benignity which we necessarily ascribe to him; and this opinion, which we are led to by the abstract consideration of his infinite perfections, is still more confirmed by the examination of the works of nature, which seem all intended to promote happiness, and to guard against misery. But by acting according to the dictates of our moral faculties, we necessarily pursue the most effectual means for promoting the happiness of mankind, and may therefore be said, in some sense to co-operate with the Deity, and to advance as far as in our power the plan of Providence. By acting otherways, on the contrary, we seem to obstruct, in some measure, the scheme which the Author of nature has established for the happiness and perfection of the world, to declare ourselves, if I may say so, in some measure the enemies of God. (*TMS* 166; cf. 168)

Our conscience does not always represent the right action to us as that which promotes happiness. But promoting happiness is nevertheless what conscience has been designed to do.

While developing this view of conscience, Smith affirms the existence of "general rules of morality" that, it seems, a virtuous agent takes to be inviolable. He extols, for instance, the "sacred regard to general rules" that constitutes the "essential difference between a man of principle and honour and a worthless fellow. The one adheres, on all occasions, steadily and resolutely to his maxims, and preserves through the whole of his life one even tenour of conduct. The other, acts variously and accidentally..." (*TMS* 163). He maintains, as well, that these rules of morality are "justly regarded as the Laws of the Deity" (*TMS* 161)—that the belief that a strict obedience to those rules will be rewarded by God and transgressions will be punished is "confirmed by reasoning and philosophy" (*TMS* 167). The moral rules are "to be regarded as the commands and laws of the Deity, promulgated by those vicegerents which he has thus set up within us... Those vicegerents of God within us, never fail to punish the violation of them, by the torments of inward shame, and self-condemnation; and on the contrary, always reward obedience with tranquility of mind, with contentment, and self-satisfaction" (*TMS* 165–6). Smith seems to be endorsing here a view that takes the moral rules to be akin to commands that ought always, without exception, to be obeyed. This sounds like a prioritarian view, a view that does not allow that we ever ought to act in a way that conflicts with an ultimate end.

It's notable, as well, that during this discussion of general moral rules, Smith makes some of his most Butlerian claims. He says, for instance, that our moral perceptions "carry along with them the most evident badges of... authority" and goes on to sketch a phenomenological argument for the authority of conscience that would work well as a précis of the position Butler argues for in his sermon, "Upon Human Nature" (*TMS* 165; see Butler 1729/1983b, 25–33). As we've seen, Butler is prioritarian: he does not think virtuous agents will ever have to act contrary to any (properly understood) moral principle. Because Smith seems in this part of *TMS* to be endorsing the general Butlerian view, it's not unreasonable to attribute to him some kind of prioritarian view as well.

It's true that Smith compares justice and beneficence, and maintains that the former is more important to the preservation of human society than the latter. "Beneficence," he writes, "is less essential to the existence of society than justice. Society may subsist, though not in the most comfortable state, without beneficence; but the prevalence of injustice must utterly destroy it" (*TMS* 86). But that does not show in and of itself that he thought that justice and beneficence would ever come into conflict with each other. Indeed, Smith's main point in this passage is that, because violations of justice are greater threats to society than non-beneficence, Nature or God has implanted in humans a stronger sense of punishment for the former (*TMS* 82–91). "In every part of the universe we observe means adjusted with the nicest artifice to the ends which they are intended to produce; and in the mechanism of a plant, or animal body, admire how every thing is contrived for advancing the two great purposes of nature, the support of the individual, and the propagation of the species" (*TMS* 87). The general tenor of these teleological remarks seems to fit with the Butlerian view, according to which a true understanding of our moral ends will reveal their complete compatibility with each other.

In other passages, however, Smith presents a different view, one that has all the hallmarks of anti-prioritarian pluralism. Let's turn to those now.

Smith's Pluralist Leanings

We have seen that Smith distinguishes between the "the soft, the gentle, the amiable virtues" of "indulgently" feeling for others and the "the great, the awful and respectable" virtues "of self-denial" (*TMS* 23). Smith says "the man of the most perfect virtue" will exhibit to the fullest both sets of virtue (*TMS* 152). Smith also acknowledges, however, that there are circumstances in which one set of virtues pulls apart from the other.

Under the boisterous and stormy sky of war and faction, of public tumult and confusion, the sturdy severity of self-command prospers the most, and can be the most successfully cultivated. But, in such situations, the strongest suggestions of humanity must frequently be stifled or neglected…As it may frequently be the duty of a soldier not to take, so it may sometimes be his duty not to give quarter; and the humanity of the man who has been several times under the necessity of submitting to this disagreeable duty, can scarce fail to suffer a considerable diminution…It is upon this account, that we so frequently find in the world men of great humanity who have little self-command but who are indolent and irresolute, and easily disheartened, either by difficulty or danger, from the most honourable pursuits; and, on the contrary, men of the most perfect self-command, who no difficulty can discourage, no danger appal, and who are at all times ready for the most daring and desperate enterprises, but who, at the same time, seem to be hardened against all sense either of justice or humanity. (*TMS* 153)

In certain situations, in order to fully exhibit one set of virtues, a person may have to develop a character that will almost inevitably lead him to fail to fully exhibit the other set of virtues. To be a good soldier, one may have to develop a character that leads one to fail to manifest the forgiveness or leniency that is appropriate in some non-military contexts. To be a compassionate caregiver or educator one may have to develop a kind of flexibility that leads one to fail to manifest the uncompromising fixity that is appropriate in some military or judicial contexts. And while Smith does not explicitly deny that there is a prioritarian ordering of these two sets of virtue, it's notable that no such ordering is on offer in this passage. Smith seems to be making the same point here that Hume made in "A Dialogue": all virtue is based on the same basic principles, but different circumstances can cause those principles to exert conflicting passions, and the principles themselves will not unequivocally tell us that one type of resolution of those conflicts is correct and all others incorrect.

Smith also rejects a strict priority ordering of the multiplicity of virtues concerning the good of others. There is virtue in promoting the welfare of your family. There is virtue in promoting the welfare of your friends. There is virtue in promoting the welfare of those who have benefitted you in the past. There is virtue in promoting the welfare of your countrymen. There are times, however, when acting to promote the welfare of one of these is incompatible with acting to promote the interests of another. And there exist no rules for adjudicating such conflict. Smith writes,

> When those different beneficent affections happen to draw different ways, to determine by any precise rules in what cases we ought to comply with the one, and in what with the other, is, perhaps, altogether impossible. In what cases friendship ought to yield to gratitude, or gratitude to friendship; in what cases the strongest of all natural affections ought to yield to a regard for the safety of those superiors upon whose safety often depends that of the whole society; and in what cases natural affection may, without impropriety, prevail over that regard; must be left altogether to the decision of the man within the breast, the supposed impartial spectator, the great judge and arbiter of our conduct... We shall stand in need of no casuistic rules to direct our conduct. These it is often impossible to accommodate to all the different shades and gradations of circumstance, character, and situation, to differences and distinctions which, though not imperceptible, are, by their nicety and delicacy, often altogether undefinable. (*TMS* 227)

The need for pluralist judgment—for non-codifiable balancing of competing moral considerations—is as conspicuous here in Smith as it is in Hume and Ross.

In his later, fuller discussion of casuistry, Smith's rejection of a prioritarian ordering of conflicting duties is equally pronounced. Casuists, Smith tells us, hold that there are "exact and precise rules for the direction of every circumstance of our behavior" (*TMS* 329). In fact, however, there are multiple basic ethical principles, and there is no strict method for adjudicating between them.

Smith presents as a counterexample to the casuists' "exact and precise rules" the case of a traveler who, on fear of death, promises a highwayman a certain sum of money. Some philosophers have maintained that travelers who make such promises are never obligated to pay the money. Others have maintained that such travelers are always obligated to pay.[3] (In my own utterly unscientific experience of asking friends and colleagues, I've encountered a similar diversity of opinions.) But the truth, according to Smith, is that in some cases a traveler who has made such a promise ought to pay and in other cases a traveler ought not to pay—and there is no strict principle that can tell us whether we are in the first type of situation or the second. "If we consider the matter according to the common sentiments of mankind, we shall find that some regard would be thought due even to a promise of this kind; but that it is impossible to determine how much, by any general rule that will apply to all cases without exception" (*TMS* 331).

As Smith sees it, there is truly a standing moral duty to keep your word, and that includes the word you've given to a highwayman threatening your life. Promises even of this kind have moral weight, which is derived from "that most sacred rule of justice, which commands the observance of all serious promises" (*TMS* 330), from that "inviolable sacredness of that part of [our] character which makes [us] reverence the law of truth and abhor everything that approaches to treachery and falsehood" (*TMS* 331). As a result, a person who was "quite frank and easy in making promises" to threatening highwayman and who then "violated them with as little ceremony" would deserve our censure. A "gentleman who should promise a highwayman five pounds [i.e. a relatively paltry sum] and not perform, would incur some blame" (*TMS* 331).

But as real as the moral weight to keep a highway promise is, there may also be a countervailing moral weight not to keep it, based on the good that could be brought about, or the bad that could be prevented, by using the money for some other purpose. If the sum promised "was very great," for instance, it might be "proper" not to pay.

If it was such, for example, that the payment of it would entirely ruin the family of the promiser, if it was so great as to be sufficient for promoting the most useful purposes, it would appear in some measure criminal, at least extremely improper, to throw it, for the sake of a punctilio, into such worthless hands. The man who should beggar himself, or who should throw away an hundred thousand pounds, though he could afford that vast sum, for the sake of observing such a parole with a thief, would appear to the common sense of mankind, absurd and extravagant in the highest degree. Such profusion would seem inconsistent with his duty, with what he owed both to himself and others, and what, therefore, regard to a promise extorted in this manner, could by no means authorise. (*TMS* 331–2)

We recognize a moral duty to keep our promises. But we also recognize that that duty can be overridden by our duty "to the public interest [or] to those whom the laws of proper beneficence should prompt us to provide for" (*TMS* 332). And what reveals perfectly clearly Smith's anti-prioritarianism in this matter is his insistence that there are "no precise rules" for determining when to keep the promise and when to use the money for some good purpose—when to favor justice and when to favor beneficence—when these two reasons for acting "are inconsistent" (*TMS* 332). Smith writes:

To fix, however, by any precise rule, what degree of regard ought to be paid to it [i.e. to a promise extorted by a highwayman], or what might be the greatest sum which could be due from it, is evidently impossible. This would vary according to the characters of the persons, according to their circumstances, according to the solemnity of the promise, and even according to the incidents of the reencounter: and if the promiser had been treated with a great deal of that sort of gallantry, which is sometimes to be met with in persons of the most abandoned characters, more would seem due than upon other occasions. (*TMS* 332)

Sometimes a promise should be kept. Sometimes a promise should be broken. And there is no prioritarian method for determining when to keep or break it. Anti-prioritarian, pluralist judgment—judgment that outstrips the general rules of morality—is required.

Of course it's unlikely that any of us will find ourselves wrestling with the question of whether to keep our promise to pay ransom to a highwayman. But Smith's point about such cases easily generalizes. We have a duty to keep our word (whether given to a friend, coworker, highwayman, or whomever). We have duties to promote good results (such as helping the poor) and to prevent bad ones (such as bankrupting our families). Sometimes these two kinds of duties really do come into conflict with each other (*contra* Butler). And (*contra* Reid) there are no precise and exact meta-rules that always determine for us which duty overrides and which is overridden.

Smith's anti-prioritarian pluralism is also evident in his ensuing discussion of the attitude one should have toward breaking a promise in those circumstances in which it is proper for one to do so. What Smith says there is that even though breaking a promise may, all things considered, be the right thing to do, the promise-breaker should nonetheless feel some shame for what he has done. He writes:

> Fidelity is so necessary a virtue, that we apprehend it in general to be due even to those to whom nothing else is due, and whom we think it lawful to kill and destroy. It is to no purpose that the person who has been guilty of the breach of it, urges that he promised in order to save his life, and that he broke his promise because it was inconsistent with some other respectable duty to keep it. These circumstances may alleviate, but cannot entirely wipe out his dishonour. He appears to have been guilty of an action with which, in the imaginations of men, some degree of shame is inseparably connected. He has broken a promise which he had solemnly averred he would maintain; and his character, if not irretrievably stained and polluted, has at least a ridicule affixed to it, which it will be very difficult entirely to efface; and no man, I imagine, who had gone through an adventure of this kind would be fond of telling the story. (*TMS* 332–3)[4]

"Some degree of shame" or "dishonor" can attach even to an action that is, all things considered, correct to perform. As we will discuss in Chapter 10, this idea fits best with the view that there is more than one fundamental duty and that these different fundamental duties can imply incompatible courses of action. Indeed, that a moral stain can accrue even to the performance of the best available action is the most common evidence that has, over the last forty years, been offered in favor of moral pluralism. Smith's affirmation of this phenomenon, coupled with his explicit rejection of "exact and precise rules" for adjudicating moral conflict, amounts to a powerful case for taking him to be a pluralist.

Smith's discussion of highway promises is not the only place where he endorses the idea that creating benefit or preventing harm can sometimes override the rules of justice. Just as it might be correct to break a promise to a highwayman if doing so is necessary to create great benefit or prevent great harm, so too may it be acceptable to force someone to sell his goods, even at a price or time he would want to resist, if doing so is necessary for the survival of others. As Smith writes in his *Lectures on Jurisprudence*, "It is a rule generally observed that no one can be obliged to sell his goods when he is not willing. But in time of necessity the people will break thro all laws. In a famine it often happens that they will break open granaries and force the owners to sell as what they think is a reasonable price" (Smith 1978, 197). Smith is making the same point we saw Hume make when, in the *Second Enquiry*, he affirmed the acceptability of violating justice in cases of shipwreck and siege: property rights can sometimes be overridden by competing goods. In the *Wealth of Nations*, Smith says something similar when he acknowledges that rules of justice may be overridden by the prospect of great harm. Smith writes, "To hinder, besides, the farmer from sending his goods at all times to the best market, is evidently to sacrifice the ordinary laws of justice to an idea of publick utility, to a sort of reasons of state: an act of legislative authority which ought to be exercised only, which can be pardoned only in cases of the most urgent necessity" (Smith 1776/1976, 539). To hinder the farmer from selling his goods on the open market is a violation of the laws of justice. Such violations are almost always unacceptable. In cases of "urgent necessity," however, when the public good will be greatly served, such violations "ought" to occur and "can be pardoned."[5]

It's true that Smith maintains that the rules of justice are more precise and accurate than the rules of the other virtues (*TMS* 174–6). He writes: "The rules of justice may be compared to the rules of *grammar*; the rules of the other virtues, to the rules which critics lay down for the attainment of what is sublime and elegant in composition. The one, are precise, accurate, and indispensable. The other, are loose, vague, and indeterminate, and present us rather with a general idea of the perfection we ought to aim at, than afford us any certain and infallible directions for acquiring it" (*TMS* 175–6). But the greater precision and accuracy of justice does not imply its invariable normative priority over all the other virtues. It implies only that we can determine what justice demands by deploying exact and precise rules while we cannot do the same thing to determine what is demanded by gratitude, friendship, or prudence. But that's consistent with the demands of one of those other virtues sometimes overriding the demands of justice. (Indeed, the point of the passages at *TMS* 194–6 is not that justice has normative trumping power over the other virtues but rather that justice differs from the other virtues in that it involves more conscious and explicit deployment of rules than they do)

Justice might demand that you pay a highwayman exactly £1,000, but that doesn't on its own imply that your harder-to-precisify duty to your children could not make it correct not to pay him. A grain-owner may have the right to demand exactly £100 per ton of corn, but that does not imply that the urgent needs of peasants cannot make it justifiable to pay him only £80—even if we cannot state precisely what standards of urgency would need to be met in order to make that justified.

It's also true that Smith maintains that justice is essential to human society in a way that beneficence is not. He writes, "Society may subsist, though not in the most comfortable state, without beneficence; but the prevalence of injustice must utterly destroy it" (*TMS* 2.2.3.3). He says, as well, that justice "is the main pillar that upholds the whole edifice" of society, while beneficence "is the orna-ment which embellishes, not the foundation which supports the building" (*TMS* 2.2.3.4). These quotations have led Otteson to conclude that Smith is committed to a "lexical priority—justice first, beneficence only thereafter" (Otteson forthcom-ing). But this conclusion does not follow. Let us grant that society cannot exist without justice but can exist without beneficence. Let us also grant that society is necessary for worthwhile human lives. There may therefore be a sense in which justice in general is more important than beneficence in general. But it does not follow from that general importance that justice must override beneficence in every particular case in which they conflict. That's because it's not the case that every particular violation of justice destroys society. If the choice is between having *only* justice or having *only* beneficence, then the former may be prefer-able. It may be more preferable still, however, to forgo in some particular cases justice for beneficence—namely, in those cases in which the violation of justice will produce benefits and not bring society crashing down. A set of actions that includes justice and beneficence—including some few cases of justice-violating beneficence—might be preferable to a set of actions that includes no violations of justice at all. The case is analogous to the relative values of water and oil. If we had to choose between having water with no oil or oil with no water, we'd obvi-ously take the first. Water is essential to human life in a way that oil is not. Water is in a general sense more important than oil. But that doesn't imply that in every situation in which we have to choose between obtaining more water or more oil, we should choose water. In some situations, the loss of some water will cause lit-tle harm while the gain of some oil will create great benefit. And just as it would be unreasonable to claim that we should never, under any circumstances, give up any amount of water for any amount of oil, so too it might be unreasonable to maintain that justice must hold no matter how much harm could be prevented by an isolated case of injustice.

Why Smith Might Lean More towards Pluralism

What Smith says about God's benevolence and conscience seems to imply a prioritarian reading. What he says about the tensions between amiability and self-command, about casuistry and highway promises, and about property and utility seems to imply a pluralist reading. So what is the best overall interpretation? Is Smith a prioritarian or a pluralist? Are his texts coherent?[6] Perhaps the best thing to say here is that Smith didn't consciously consider where to stand on the prioritarian-pluralist question, that he was pulled in both directions, and that there is no determinate answer as to which side or the other he belongs on. But I will hesitantly offer something more: a tentative reason for taking him to be more fundamentally committed to pluralism.

In the section entitled "Of the nature of self-deceit, and the origin and use of general rules," Smith argues against the Hutchesonian view that our moral judgments are based on a "peculiar faculty, such as the moral sense is supposed to be" (*TMS* 158). He also argues against the Clarkean-rationalist view that human moral judgment is originally based on general moral rules that are applied—in a top–down manner—to particular cases. It is a mistake, Smith says, to think "that the original judgments of mankind with regard to right and wrong, were formed like the decisions of a court of judicatory, by considering first the general rule, and then, secondly, whether the particular action under consideration fell properly within its comprehension" (*TMS* 160).[7] The truth, rather, is that we originally make moral judgments about particular cases, with the general rules developing only as inductive generalizations from those cases. He writes, "[T]he general rules of morality are…ultimately founded upon experience of what, in particular instances, our moral faculties, our natural sense of merit and propriety, approve, or disapprove of. We do not originally approve or condemn particular actions; because, upon examination, they appear to be agreeable or inconsistent with a certain general rule. The general rule, on the contrary, is formed, by finding from experience, that all actions of a certain kind, or circumstanced in a certain manner, are approved or disapproved of" (*TMS* 159; see also 319–20). As he puts it later,

When we read in history or romance, the account of actions either of generosity or of baseness, the admiration which we conceive of the one, and the contempt which we feel for the other, neither of them arise from reflecting that there are certain general rules which declare all actions of the one kind admirable, and all actions of the other contemptible. Those general rules, on the contrary, are all formed from the experience we have had of the effects which actions of all different kinds naturally produce upon us…The general rules which determine what actions are, and what are not, the objects of [approval and disapproval] can be formed no other way than by observing what actions actually and in fact excite them. (*TMS* 160)

Moral judgment, according to Smith, is a bottom–up, experience-driven affair. We have no a priori knowledge of general principles. The rationalist moral epistemology of "several very eminent authors"—i.e. the self-evident, a priori of rationalism of Clarke—is mistaken.

But from this position on the origin of moral judgment, it follows that we cannot say with certainty that certain kinds of considerations will invariably morally override other kinds of considerations. We have seen that Reid makes claims about the a priori self-evidence of just that sort of invariable overriding-ness. Reid says, for instance, that it's a priori self-evident that duties of grati-tude override duties of generosity, and that duties of justice override both of the other two. But Smith's moral epistemology—his position on the origins of moral judgment—will not countenance such moral claims. On Smith's empir-icist view of the origin of moral judgment, the correct judgment in cases of conflicting duties is not something we can determine in advance of actually considering and responding to the particular facts from an impartial perspec-tive.[8] Indeed, Smith's insistence on the primacy of moral particulars makes him look like a proto-particularist—and particularism is the most adamantly anti-prioritarian position there is.[9]

Moreover, Smith has a psychological story of how we come to rely on general moral rules that can explain why people may come to believe that there are a priori general moral principles, an explanation of why rationalists such as Clarke and Reid mistakenly thought that there are top–down a priori princi-ples.[10] It turns out that in a large majority of the particular cases we encounter, duties of justice override duties of gratitude and generosity. And "our continual observations" of cases "insensibly lead us to form to ourselves certain general rules concerning what is fit and proper" (*TMS* 159). We generalize from par-ticular cases, and eventually the generalizations acquire a psychological status that leads us to think of them as inviolable, and perhaps a priori (*TMS* 160; this view is a clear descendent of Hume's "addiction to general rules," which we have discussed). Smith may even think it salutary if people's generalizations become so firmly fixed that they come to believe that they are God-given rules that provide fully determinate and exceptionless guidance for every situation. It may perhaps be a good thing for our fellows to believe in prioritarianism. But as his discussions of casuistry make clear, Smith doesn't think that an invariable moral ordering of justice, gratitude, generosity, and the like really exists. Belief in prioritarianism may be psychologically understandable and even beneficial. But morality is in fact pluralist.

I am not entirely happy with this interpretative strategy for bringing into coherence Smith's prioritarian and pluralist-sounding passages. For one thing, despite what I've just said, I'm not sure that Smith's moral epistemology isn't compatible with a strict moral ordering after all, insofar as it seems possible that rules can be empirically derived and yet also have a prioritarian structure. For another, I worry that this interpretation rides roughshod over "Of the influence and authority of the general rules of morality, and that they are justly regarded as the laws of the deity." For it seems to me that in that chapter (which comes directly after the chapter I've relied on in the preceding three paragraphs) Smith endorses the view that the general rules of morality are sacred, inviolable, and God-given. That is to say, the reading I've just offered implies that Smith thinks that regarding the rules as sacred, inviolable, and God-given is a salutary mistake, but reading "Of the influence and authority of the general rules" in that way seems to me a strain.[11]

However that may be, the important point here—what I want to stress—is that we find within Smith's text the tension between, on the one hand, an a priori view that the multiplicity of our moral ends never come into conflict with each other, and, on the other hand, an empirical, observation-based view that such moral conflict does occur. Smith is not ambivalent about whether there is one ultimate moral end or more than one: he clearly affirms more than one. But he is ambivalent about whether those ultimate moral ends can come into conflict. This ambivalence is indicative of the transitional place Smith occupies in the history of morality. Behind lay the moral thinking of Butler, Clarke, and others who had a priori grounds for thinking that the multiplicity of human moral principles all partake of a rational or divinely ensured prioritarian coherence.[12] Ahead lay the monistic theorizing of Bentham and Kant, which ensured prioritarian justificatory determinacy through the affirmation of a single ultimate principle. Smith, along with Hume, was in the middle: intimately aware of our varied moral concerns, attracted by the lure of full prioritarian justification, but unwilling to accept as an article of faith that such justification will always be possible.

5

Contemporary Humean Moral Pluralisms

Humean moral pluralism includes three claims:

1. Sentiment plays an essential role in the development of our ultimate moral ends.
2. Our moral judgments are based on a multiplicity of independent ultimate moral ends.
3. The independent ultimate ends on which our moral judgments are based sometimes imply incompatible actions.

Each of these claims can be construed in a number of different ways. My main concern up to this point has been to explain how Hume and some of his eighteenth-century contemporaries understood them. But the work of Hume and his contemporaries is hardly the last word on these issues. In recent years updated versions of Humean moral pluralism have been advanced. These updated versions rely on arguments and methods unheard of in the eighteenth century (which is, of course, to be expected, and a good thing; it would not be to a view's credit if it could be supported only by eighteenth-century science). None of them endorses all the details of Hume's position, but they are nonetheless clear descendents of Hume in their affirmation of those three claims.

In this chapter, I will first sketch three of these contemporary Humean pluralist positions: those of Jonathan Haidt, Jesse Prinz, and Shaun Nichols. I will then describe an alternative position, the Universal Moral Grammar of John Mikhail, and use it as a springboard to discuss more directly the relationship between Humeanism and contemporary moral psychology.

Haidt's Sentimentalist Pluralism

In publications with several different collaborators, Haidt has developed an account of morality explicit about both its sentimentalism and its pluralism. Haidt initially built his account on the anthropological work of Shweder et al. and Rozin et al., who claimed to show that human moral judgment is based on three distinct emotions. The three emotions Shweder et al. and Rozin et al. focused on were contempt, anger, and disgust (although Rozin et al. note that in addition to those three, the "self-directed" emotions of shame, embarrassment, and guilt, and the "other-suffering emotions" of pity and sympathy, are also morally crucial: Rozin et al. 1999, 574–5). According to Shweder and Rozin's cross-cultural findings, these three emotions are the psychological ground of moral judgments all humans make. Each of these emotions gives rise to its own set of values—to "different types of 'goods,'" or ultimate ends (Shweder et al. 1999, 128, 141). Contempt lies at the base of norms concerning community, grounding our negative moral judgments of violations of social hierarchy and ties of interdependent personal relationships. Anger lies at the base of norms concerning autonomy or the protection of individuals, grounding our moral judgments about harms, rights, and justice. Disgust lies at the base of norms concerning sanctity, sin, and pollution, grounding our moral judgments about violations of what is sacred, the natural order, and tradition. Each of these three emotions has its own evolutionary history (Rozin et al. 1999, 575). And, crucially for pluralism, the norms based on these emotions can come into conflict with each other. As Shweder et al. put it, "The rub, of course, is that the three goods are often in conflict. In the material world…there may never have been a place or time when all three goods have been or could have been simultaneously maximized… [T]hey often come into conflict with one another and create 'moral dilemmas'" (Shweder et al. 1999, 141). Rozin et al. also note that, in addition to conflicts within the "other-critical hostility triad" of contempt, anger, and disgust, there will also be conflicts between that contempt–anger–disgust cluster and the distinct cluster of the "self-conscious" emotions of shame, embarrassment, and guilt, as well as conflict between those emotions and the "other-suffering" emotions of pity and sympathy (Rozin et al. 1999, 574–5).

Haidt's account has the same general structure as Shweder and Rozin's, but he identifies "five psychological foundations of morality." These five foundations or "psychological systems": are "harm/care, fairness/reciprocity, ingroup/loyalty, authority/respect, and purity/sanctity" (Haidt and Graham 2007, 99). Each of these is a non-rational feature of our psychology that produces "affective reactions of liking or disliking when certain patterns are perceived in the social world" (Haidt and Graham 2007, 104). According to Haidt, studies of our cognitive processes and evaluative intuitions show that it is these affect-based features, and not reason alone, that ground our moral judgments. While reasoning sometimes plays a role in our forming moral judgments, it is these five non-rational systems that are morally causally predominant (Haidt 2001; Haidt and Bjorkland 2008, 181,

185). The most influential of Haidt's studies purporting to show the non-rational basis of moral judgment are those concerning the phenomena of "moral dumbfounding" (Haidt 2001). In these studies, subjects were presented with scenarios that elicited from them negative moral judgments, such as a case of brother-sister incest. Included in the scenarios were details that undermined all the considerations that would typically be cited as reasons for the negative moral judgment. In the brother-sister incest scenario, for instance, it was stipulated that there was no chance of a pregnancy or of anyone's ever suffering any harmful repercussions; the brother and sister did it only once, their relationship was not harmed by it in any respect, and no one else ever found out. These details confounded the reasons many of the subjects offered for their negative moral judgment, but the subjects continued to make the same moral judgment nonetheless, even after the confounding. They were "morally dumbfounded," unable to provide any reason for their moral judgment but still refusing to withdraw or alter that judgment. The conclusion Haidt drew is that the subjects' moral judgment must be based (at least initially) on a non-rational, intuitive mental feature—on an aspect of their psychology that is independent of reasoning.

Haidt maintains that each of the non-rational systems on which our moral judgments are based has "its own evolutionary history" (Haidt and Graham 2007, 104). Each is distinct from the others, "modularized 'to some interesting degree'" (Haidt and Bjorkland 2008, 205). The five psychological systems are discrete "'taste buds' of the moral domain," each designed to respond to a different set of concerns (Haidt and Bjorkland 2008, 203). It should thus come as no surprise that the likings and dislikings of some of the systems may sometimes conflict with the likings and dislikings of others, given that they lack a common etiology and do not have the kind of rational basis that might ensure coherence. Haidt and Graham found, for instance, that when "values related to ingroup, authority, and purity were rejected, they were often rejected because they conflicted with virtues related to the harm and fairness foundations" (Haidt and Graham 2007, 110). And one of the central points of the article titled "When Morality Opposes Justice" is that there are many cases in which the ethical values based in "purity/sanctity," "authority/respect," or "ingroup/loyalty" are in conflict with the values based in "harm/care" or "fairness/reciprocity" (Haidt and Graham 2007). Haidt and Graham conclude that one of the most important implications for moral philosophy of their research is that "*monistic theories are likely to be wrong.*" They explain:

If there are many independent sources of moral value (i.e., the five foundations), then moral theories that value only one source and set to zero all others are likely to produce psychologically unrealistic systems that most people will reject. Traditional utilitarianism, for example, does an admirable job of maximizing moral goods derived from the harm/care foundation. But it often runs afoul of moral goods derived from the fairness/reciprocity foundation (e.g., rights), to say nothing of its violations of the ingroup/loyalty foundation (why treat outsiders equal to insiders?) the authority/respect foundation (it respects no tradition or authority that demands anti-utilitarian practices), and the purity/sanctity foundation (spiritual pollution is discounted as superstition). A Kantian or Rawlsian approach might do an admirable job of developing intuitions about fairness and justice, but each would violate many other virtues and ignore many other moral goods. An adequate normative ethical theory should be pluralistic, even if that introduces endless difficulties in reconciling conflicting sources of value. (Haidt and Graham 2007, 215)

Hume didn't use the same kind of studies and experimental techniques as Haidt to argue against moral rationalism, and the affective base of Hume's moral judgments (grounded in sympathy-induced approvals of the useful or agreeable to self or others) is narrower than Haidt's. But Haidt's view does share the three central tenets of Humean moral pluralism.

Prinz's Sentimentalist Pluralism

Like Haidt, Prinz affirms Hume's attack on the rationalist view that morality originates in reason alone. According to Prinz, there is a plethora of evidence that emotion is essential to moral judgment. Neuroimaging studies of moral cognition show that emotions accompany moral judgment (Prinz 2006, 30; he cites Moll et al. 2003, Sanfey et al. 2003, and Berthoz et al. 2002). Studies in which subjects' emotions are manipulated establish emotions' influence on moral judgment. In one such study, subjects seated at a disgusting desk (greasy pizza box, used tissue, crusty drink cup, etc.) were more likely to make negative moral judgments about the same situation than subjects seated at a clean desk (Prinz 2006, 31; he cites Schnall et al. 2005). "The same effect was obtained using disgusting films and 'fart spray'" (Prinz and Nichols 2010, 114). Prinz also argues that Haidt's moral dumbfounding studies, as well as studies involving hypnotism, show that emotions are sufficient for moral judgment. In the hypnotism studies, subjects who were hypnotized to feel the emotion of disgust formed negative moral judgments about cases that non-hypnotized subjects formed no moral judgment about at all (Prinz 2006, 31; he cites Wheatley and Haidt 2005). Given that there was nothing in the dumbfounded and hypnotized subjects' factual understanding of the cases that could account for their negative moral judgments, the best explanation of those judgments, according to Prinz, is that they were sparked entirely by negative emotions. Prinz also points to two branches of evidence for the claim that emotion is necessary for moral judgment. First, there is developmental evidence based on the way children learn about morality. As he explains, "Unlike language, children need a lot of training to conform to moral rules, and parents spend a lot of time giving their children moral instruction. Interestingly, the three main techniques that parents use to convey moral rules all recruit emotions (Prinz 2006, 31–3; he cites Hoffman 1983). And second, there is the evidence of psychopaths, whose fail-ure to understand morality is best explained by their emotional defects and not by any rational deficiency (Prinz 2006, 32; he cites Blair 1995, Blair et al. 1997).

Prinz is also like Haidt in holding that the emotional base of moral judgment is made up of not just one emotion but a multiplicity of distinct emotions. These different emotions produce different kinds of approval, which in turn cause us to have a multiplicity of different moral ends. Prinz distinguishes, in particular, between the "reactive" emotions that underlie the moral judgments we make of others and the "reflective" emotions that underlie the moral judgments we make of ourselves (Prinz 2007a, 69). The set of basic other-regarding moral emotions Prinz describes is similar to the contempt–anger–disgust triad advanced by Shweder et al. and Rozin et al., although Prinz suggests that contempt might not be basic but a blend of anger and disgust (Prinz 2007a, 69–79). Prinz also exam-ines other other-regarding emotions, such as admiration and gratitude, which he thinks underlie positive moral judgments we make of others (Prinz 2007a, 79–82). Distinct from all of those other-regarding emotions are the set of discrete basic self-regarding moral emotions, with guilt and shame being two of the negative self-regarding moral emotions, and gratification and dignity being two of the posi-tive ones. It's this variety of distinct emotional bases of moral judgment, according to Prinz, that accounts for the fact that "there are a plurality of basic moral values, rather than one single moral principle" (Prinz 2007a, 87–8). Prinz goes on to say, "There is a plurality of basic values because we can develop each of our emotional attitudes individually: we can acquire a distaste for killing in one way and a distaste for incest in another" (Prinz 2007a, 88; see also Prinz and Nichols 2010, 122).

In addition, Prinz argues that independent attention to the range of contents of human moral judgments makes it extremely implausible to hold the monistic view that there is a single underlying characteristic to all moral ends. "The class of mor-alized behavior *seems* to be disunified," Prinz writes (Prinz 2007a, 47). "On the face of it, we moralize a heterogeneous class of things" (Prinz 2007a, 49). Prinz uses as an example the great difficulty we would have in identifying one feature shared by all things classified as evil. "Do immoral acts have anything in common?," he asks. "Ostensibly, the answer is no. Immoral acts comprise a hodgepodge" (Prinz 2007a, 48). The conclusion Prinz draws from the evidence of "the disunity of morality" is strikingly Humean (Prinz 2007a, 47). The only feature that all immoral things have in common is that they give rise in us to negative moral sentiments, just as the only feature all moral things have in common is that they give rise in us to positive moral sentiments. Prinz: "I don't think we can single out any unique property as the reliable cause of our moral sentiments. The range of things that trigger disapprobation is radically disunified...There is no single response-independent property of actions or events that reliably triggers disapprobation in any of us. The only thing that unifies iniquities is the responses that they cause. It is for that reason that I think WRONG designates the power to cause disapprobation, and not some other property that can be characterized without reference to our responses" (Prinz 2006, 41). This is the very same point Hume makes when, after he has rejected the notion that all moral things are natural and all immoral things unnatural, he writes, "Thus we are still brought back to our first position, that virtue is distinguish'd by the pleasure, and vice by the pain, that any action, sentiment or character gives us by the mere view and contemplation. This decision is very commodious; because it reduces us to this simple question, *Why any action or sentiment upon the general view or survey, gives a certain satisfaction or uneasiness?* in order to show the origin of its moral rectitude or depravity, without looking for any incomprehensible relations and qualities, which never did exist in nature, nor even in our imagination, by any clear and distinct conception" (*T* 3.1.2.11). For both Hume and Prinz, morality originates in our emotional responses, and those emotional responses are varied enough to defy attempts to identify a single, monistic moral property.

Nichols' Sentimentalist Pluralism

Nichols' account differs from Hume's, Prinz's, and Haidt's in that Nichols holds that essential to the causal origin of morality are not only emotions but also a set of internally represented rules (Nichols 2004, 2008). Included in this set are rules to care for children, to punish the guilty, and not to harm innocents—as well, perhaps, as some of the other rules enshrined in lists such as Ross's prima facie duties and the Ten Commandments. Nichols' crucial sentimentalist claim is that we come to think of these rules in a distinctively important, non-conventional way only because they resonate with our basic emotions (Nichols 2004, 2008). We take rules concerning the care of children to be non-conventional and especially important because they resonate with our basic emotions of familial concern. We take rules concerning punishment and reparations to be especially significant because they resonate with our basic emotion of anger. Rules prohibiting harm to innocents are affectively backed by the distress we feel at the suffering of others. Rules concerning sexual deviance are affectively backed by disgust emotions (Gill and Nichols 2008, 146–8). If we had not possessed one of these basic emotions, we would not have taken the corresponding rule to be non-conventional and especially important. If we had not possessed any of these emotions, we would not have taken any of those rules to have this distinctive status.

A real-world instance of this latter possibility is the psychopath (see Nichols 2002; 2004, 65–82). Psychopaths, Nichols maintains, recognize many of the same rules of conduct as the rest of us. They can show that they are aware of rules prohibiting harming others, murdering, stealing, and the like. They can also show that they are aware of rules prohibiting jay-walking, driving without a driver's license, and parking without feeding a meter. But while normal people think the rules prohibiting harm, murder, and theft have a different character from the rules concerning jay-walking, driver's licenses, and parking meters, psychopaths see no difference (Blair 1995; Blair et al. 1997). Normal people think that violations of rules in the first group are less permissible than violations of rules in the second group, that violations of the first group (but not the second) are wrong because of the damage they do to other people, and that the rules of the first group (but not the second) are independent of authority. Normal people think that the rules in the first group have a special non-conventional status that distinguishes them from the conventional rules of the second group. But this is a distinction psychopaths are much less capable of drawing.[1] Crucially, it also turns out that psychopaths lack some of the basic emotions that normal people feel. And what Nichols claims is that this emotional lack is what explains psychopaths' non-recognition of the distinctive character that distinguishes moral rules from conventions. Violations of the harm-rule, for instance, typically cause normal people to feel emotional distress that they typically don't feel when considering license-less driving. Violations of the harm-rule (but not of the driver's license-rule) thus become associated in the minds of normal people with that feeling of distress. As a result, the harm-rule acquires a kind of psychological gravity. If, in contrast, a person did not feel emotional distress toward harm done to others, he'd fail to have the psychological response that, when associated with a certain rule, infuses that rule with the distinctive, significant character—even if his recitation of the rule and his ability to determine when it has been violated is otherwise unremarkable. The psychopath is just such a person: someone who does not feel emotional distress when others are harmed and so does not fully appreciate the difference between violations of the harm-rule and violations of the rule to carry a driver's license.

On Nichols' "sentimental rules" account, then, certain rules gain distinctive, non-conventional status because of their "affective resonance" with our basic emotions. When a rule resonates with a basic emotion, the latter infuses the former with a special gravitas, and this psychological process is essential to the origin of morality. Nichols argues that this account of morality's origins gains considerable confirmation from investigation into the cultural evolution of norms in general, but this is an area I will not go into here (Nichols 2004, 118–40; 2008, 269–72). What I want to call attention to are the pluralist implications. On Nichols' view, the rules that become moral are those that resonate with our basic emotional repertoire. Now if we had only one basic emotion, then perhaps our morality would have been monistic. (A crude egoist will hold, for instance, that we are at bottom purely and entirely self-interested, and that, consequently, all moral rules ultimately concern the promotion of self-interest.) But in fact we have a multiplicity of basic emotions—familial concern, distress at others' pain, disgust, and anger among them. There were compelling evolutionary reasons for us to develop these distinct emotions, and each "has a different functional role" (Prinz and Nichols 2010, 122). As a result, a variety of different kinds of rules have affective resonance, and so a variety of different kinds of rules have attained moral status. Because these rules do not all resonate with the same emotional base, moreover, there is no reason to expect that they will always converge on the same actions. Indeed, it is a fact of life that we sometimes face emotional conflict—that one of our basic emotions sometimes favors a course of action that another basic emotion does not favor. It should come as no surprise, therefore, that one moral rule, backed as it will be by one basic emotion, may sometimes come into conflict with another moral rule, backed as it will be by a different basic emotion. Such is Nichols' explanation of moral conflict.

Mikhail's Universal Moral Grammar

The views of Haidt, Prinz, and Nichols are far from uncontroversial. One of the most important criticisms of their sentimentalist approach has come from proponents of a Universal Moral Grammar (UMG).[2] The most prominent and well-developed version of the UMG view is John Mikhail's. On Mikhail's view, "humans possess an innate moral faculty that is analogous... to the language faculty that has been postulated by Chomsky and other linguists" (Mikhail 2007, 143). The faculty is innate in that its "essential properties are largely pre-determined by the inherent structure of the mind" (Mikhail 2007, 144). It's this faculty, not our emotions or sentiments, that is the origin of our moral judgments. As Mikhail explains, "[T]he properties of moral judgment imply that the mind contains a moral grammar: a complex and possibly domain-specific set of rules, concepts and principles that generates and relates mental representations of various types. Among other things, this system enables individuals to determine the deontic status of an infinite variety of acts and omissions" (Mikhail 2007, 144).

If UMG is correct, then the specifically sentimentalist aspects of the explanations of moral judgment developed by Prinz, Haidt, and Nichols must be wrong.

For Prinz, Haidt, and Nichols hold that emotion plays an essential causal role in our making of moral judgments while UMG holds that the innate moral faculty is what produces moral judgment, with emotion coming into the picture only after moral judgments have already been made (Huebner et al. 2008, 1). Certain emotions may be crucial in motivating us to do what we judge to be moral, and we may experience certain emotions when we contemplate violations (our own or others) of what we judge to be moral. But according to UMG, the judgments are prior to the emotions.

I believe contemporary sentimentalists have raised powerful objections to the UMG view.[3] But rather than enter the details of that debate, I want to address a different question. To what extent is UMG incompatible with Humean moral pluralism? There are two parts to this question. To what extent is the UMG view incompatible with pluralism? And to what extent is it incompatible with Humeanism? I'll address the pluralism question first, and then the Humean one. I'll discuss the second question in more detail, because it gives us the opportunity to discuss directly what is distinctive of "Humean" views of morality.

Mikhail's UMG is not a monistic theory, not a theory that has one fundamental principle from which all other principles can be derived. Mikhail argues that his findings show that our moral judgments are based on a multiplicity of distinct, independent principles that are "largely pre-determined by the inherent structure of the mind." These principles include: a prohibition on homicide, a prohibition on intentional battery, a rescue principle which "forbids one from failing to prevent an easily preventable death or other serious misfortune" (Mikhail 2011, 117), a self-preservation principle (Mikhail 2011, 137), and the principle of double effect (whose exact formulation is better left to an endnote[4]). It might initially seem that these principles could come into conflict with each other, insofar as we can imagine situations in which, for instance, one can prevent a death (as the rescue principle demands) only by violating the prohibition on intentional battery, or preserve one's own life only by violating the prohibition on homicide. But Mikhail's fuller construal of the rules of UMG also has prioritarian elements. In his description of the rescue principle, he says that one has a duty to prevent death or serious misfortune only "where this can be accomplished without risking one's own life or safety, or without violating other fundamental moral precepts" (Mikhail 2011, 117; see also 145). If we take that last phrase to be a part of the rescue principle, then it looks as though it would be impossible for the principle to conflict with the other deontic rules, which would be a prioritarian non-conflict or specificationist multiplist picture. Alternatively, we could take the last clause not as a specification built into the rescue principle but rather a statement of the principle's lexical subordination to the other deontic rules, which would suggest a prioritarian ordered multiplism.

Mikhail himself seems to lean toward this lexical interpretation at times (Mikhail 2011, 145–7; see also 152 and 162). As well, Mikhail says that the principle of double effect is a "second-order priority rule or ordering principle" (Mikhail 2011, 152) and that the various prohibitions of the deontic rules all fit together into a lexical ordering (Mikhail 2011, 162), which seem to be reasons to take Mikhail's UMG to be an ordered conflict multiplism. Either way—specificationist and without conflict between principles, or with conflict but also with a lexical ordering—the picture appears to be prioritarian.

On closer inspection, however, we find that Mikhail's account of the rules of UMG does not in fact speak against a non-prioritarian, pluralist view of morality. First of all, the priority of the other deontic rules over the rescue principle is not strict and absolute. If the harm that can be prevented by a rescuing action is severe or catastrophic, then the imperative to perform the rescuing action can override the prohibitions against battery, self-destruction, or homicide (Mikhail 2011, 146). And once we acknowledge this, we must acknowledge the need for pluralist judgment to decide when the rescue principle does or does not override one or another of the other deontic rules. (I discuss this issue concerning rescue principles and the prevention of catastrophic harms more fully in Chapter 8.) Secondly and relatedly, we can apply the deontic rules only if we also make comparative judgments about the goodness or badness of the effects of possible courses of actions (Mikhail 2011, 145, 150, 151). For instance, when trying to decide whether the principle of double effect justifies performing an action that has both morally good and morally bad results, we have to make a comparative judgment about whether the good results outweigh the bad (Mikhail 2011, 150, 162–7). Similarly, when trying to decide whether the harm that can be prevented by a rescuing action is bad enough to justify violation of some other deontic rule, we have to make a comparative judgment concerning the badness of the harm and badness of the violation. There is no reason to think these comparative judgments about goodness and badness will reduce to some monistic quantitative weighing rather than require pluralist judging of different kinds of goods and bads. But since our application of the deontic rules depends on value-judgments (or the deploying of an axiology), and since our value-judgments (or axiology) may very well be pluralist, it may also very well be the case that the resulting picture of moral judgment will contain ineliminably pluralist elements. Thirdly and most importantly, the rules of UMG are much too schematic and indeterminate to explain all the features of our actual activity of moral judgment. The interesting moral judgments we make in morally fraught real-world situations usually involve complexities that the deontic rules of UMG cannot fully explain. Should I break a promise or lie to a friend when doing so will make her significantly happier? How much of our personal resources may we devote to ourselves and our family, and how much are we obligated to donate to the desperately poor? What balance should we strike between environmental protection and conservation, on the one hand, and economic growth and property rights, on the other? There are many different ways of answering those questions that are all compatible with the rules of UMG (just as there are many different human languages, dialects, and poems that are all compatible with Chomsky's universal linguistic grammar). Our possessing those rules does not on its own account for what we decide to do in those situations (just as our possessing Chomsky's universal linguistic grammar does not on its own account for our specific uses of language). There are a great many elements that must be added to account for our actual moral thinking, and the evidence for UMG gives us no reason to believe that those added elements will all be prioritarian rather than pluralist. I do not intend this to be a criticism of UMG. Mikhail's goal is to describe the most general features of human morality, not to explain all the fine-grained features of persons' moral thinking. We shouldn't expect a Universal Moral Grammar to explain all the fine-grained features of anyone's moral thinking any more than we would expect Chomsky's universal linguistic grammar to explain the fine-grained features of our conversations and literary works. My point is just that the moral structure for which Mikhail argues is compatible with our moral thinking being pluralist. There are many different ways of making specific moral judgments—both prioritarian and pluralist—that are equally compatible with UMG's general rules.

Let us now turn to the question of whether Mikhail's UMG constitutes an objection to the *Humean* aspect of Humean moral pluralism. As I've mentioned, I will spend more time on this question as it affords the opportunity to explicate more fully what Humeanism about morality amounts to.

Mikhail presents his UMG view as a victory for at least one understanding of traditional moral rationalism, and thus a defeat for the non-rationalist followers of Hume (Mikhail 2011, 174). His position, he says, is a descendent of the "classical rationalism of philosophers such as Leibniz, Rousseau,[5] Kant, and Humboldt" (Mikhail 2011, 35), and the success of his project would establish that "the Enlightenment assumption that common moral knowledge 'depends upon demonstrations' (Leibniz 1996/1704, 92; cf. Locke 1991/1689, 549) would appear capable of being vindicated" (Mikhail 2011, 175). As Hauser sees it, Mikhail's findings show that "[w]e can explain how people manage to make the moral judgments they do by means of rational principles" (Hauser 2006, 125; see also Mikhail 2011, 97). They confirm the "classical rationalist idea, suitably interpreted, that certain basic moral and legal notions and precepts are engraved in the mind" (Mikhail 2011, 101).

To assess whether Mikhail's findings really do conflict with Humeanism and vindicate his rationalist opponents, we have first to distinguish between Hume's positive and negative claims. Hume's negative claim is that our moral judgments are not purely rational. What does this mean? Here are four possible construals of a moral judgment's being purely rational: (1) it tracks mind-independent features of reality (call this "mind-independence"), (2) it is rationally necessary, such as would have to be affirmed by any rational being whatsoever ("rational necessity"), (3) it is based on innate aspects of the human mind ("innate"), (4) it is "intuitive, stable, spontaneous, and impartial, and made with a high degree of certitude" ('intuitive, etc.') (Mikhail 2011, 97).

Humeanism denies (1) that moral judgments track mind-independent features of reality. On the Humean view, human moral judgment is at least partially determined by aspects internal to the human mind, and those aspects do not merely represent features that are external to the mind. That's the point to take away from the following passages:

Take any action allow'd to be vicious: Wilful murder, for instance. Examine it in all lights, and see if you can find that matter of fact, or real existence, which you call vice. In which-ever way you take it, you find only certain passions, motives, volitions and thoughts. There is no other matter of fact in the case. The vice entirely escapes you, as long as you consider the object. You never can find it, till you turn your reflexion into your own breast... (*T* 3.1.1.26)

While we are ignorant whether a man were aggressor or not, how can we determine whether the person who killed him be criminal or innocent? But after every circumstance, every relation is known, the understanding has no further room to operate, nor any object on which it could employ itself. The approbation or blame which then ensues, cannot be the work of the judgement, but of the heart; and is not a speculative proposition or affirmation. (*E* App 1.11)

Thus the distinct boundaries and offices of reason and of taste are easily ascertained. The former conveys the knowledge of truth and falsehood: the latter gives the sentiment of beauty and deformity, vice and virtue. The one discovers objects as they really stand in nature, without addition or diminution: the other has a productive faculty, and gilding or staining all natural objects with the colours, borrowed from internal sentiment, raises in a manner a new creation. (*E* App 1.21)

I do not take these Humean claims about the psychological causes of human moral judgment to imply anything in particular about the meaning of moral terms, or about what it is people take themselves to be doing when they make moral judgments. As I understand them, these Humean claims are compatible with an expressivist meta-ethics; with a dispositional or secondary-quality-like meta-ethics that takes moral judgments to be akin to judgments about objects' colors or jokes' funniness; and with an error theory that holds that our moral judgments lay claim to a kind of objectivity that they cannot live up to. They're also compatible with the meta-ethical view I myself favor, according to which the meaning of moral terms is more indeterminate and variable than most traditional positions in meta-ethics imply.[6] The Humean claim is just that, when making moral judgments, we are not describing mind-independent properties (whatever it is we might think we're doing).

Mikhail's universal moral grammar doesn't conflict with the Humean denial of mind-independence. Mikhail himself is perfectly clear that the principles of UMG do not represent mind-independent reality, any more than the grammar of our language does. He makes this point when explaining his "poverty of the stimulus" argument, writing: "Clearly the brain must be generating action representations of its own that go beyond the information given... [T]he stimulus here evidently consists merely of clues for the formation of an unconscious percept that the perceiver first constructs using her own internal resources and then projects back onto the stimulus, creating an illusion of qualities that the latter does not in fact possess" (Mikhail 2011, 114–16). In making moral judgments, we are not perceiving what is already there. "Instead, an intervening step must be postulated: a pattern of organization imposed on the stimulus by the mind itself" (Mikhail 2011, 310). To use Hume's metaphor, the UMG gilds and stains mind-independent reality rather than simply representing it. As we have already seen Hume put it, "The vice entirely escapes you, as long as you consider the object. You never can find it, till you turn your reflexion into your own breast..." (T 3.1.1.26). Hume goes on in this passage to make a positive claim about which internal aspects of human nature are operative in our moral judgment. But if we focus only on the negative, anti-rationalist part of the passage (as I have done by cutting it off in mid-sentence), Hume's claim and Mikhail's UMG are in perfect alignment. Both deny that human moral judgment represents mind-independent reality. Both maintain that human moral judgment is a pattern projected onto the world by the human mind.

Construal (2)—that a moral judgment is purely rational if it is rationally necessary, such as would have to be affirmed by any rational being whatsoever—is what Clarke and Kant held. That Clarke believed that moral judgments could be rational in this way is evident from his use of the analogy between morals, on the one hand, and mathematics and logic, on the other (see Clarke 1705/1738, 609, 613, 614, 626). Clarke didn't think morality was similar to math and logic in every respect. The crucial similarity for Clarke was that each of them was necessary, rationally inescapable, demonstrably certain, something that we were committed to simply in virtue of being rational beings and not because of any contingent features of human nature. Kant's account of morality differs from Clarke's in important ways, but he too believed that the fundamental principles of morality were necessary or demonstrable, such as could be shown to follow from considerations to which every rational being must assent (Kant 1785/2002, 200–3, 221–2, 229–30). This meant, for Kant, that all rational beings were committed to the same fundamental moral principle, regardless of whether they differed from each other in non-rational aspects—that the fundamental moral principle's place in our moral thinking was independent of any contingent features of human nature. As Kant put it,

[W]e must grant that its law is so broad in meaning that it must be valid not merely for human beings, but for all rational beings as such, and valid not merely under contingent conditions and subject to exceptions, but with absolute necessity...For by what right can we make something that is perhaps valid only under the contingent human conditions into an object of unlimited respect and view it as universally prescribed for every rational creature? And how could laws for determining our will be taken as laws for determining the will of rational beings in general—and only on that account laws for determining our will—if these laws were merely empirical and did not have their source completely a priori in pure, but practical, reason? (Kant 1785/2002, 209–10)

Ralph Cudworth, a seventeenth-century predecessor of Clarke and Kant, is another good example of this rationalist view. Cudworth too held that morality must be based on principles independent of any contingencies of human nature. He expressed this view by maintaining that fundamental moral principles are necessarily true in the same way logic is and thus will apply equally to us and "a world of men created either in the moon or elsewhere" (Cudworth 1731/1996, 140).

On Mikhail's UMG view, moral judgments are not rational in this sense of being rationally necessary. UMG is a contingent feature of human nature, not a necessary structure that we have reason to think would characterize every rational mind, human or not. We could not generate UMG from purely rational considerations alone. Indeed, one way to state the poverty-of-stimulus argument is precisely this: the capacity of (linguistic or moral) grammar cannot be rationally inferred from the available evidence. And the fact that the moral judgments we make can be derived from the principles of UMG constitutes no basis for claiming that those judgments are rational in any sense that would satisfy Clarke and Kant, for the way those principles were identified was by determining which principles were the best predictors of our actual moral judgments. That is to say, since UMG is formulated entirely on the basis of which principles will fit the moral judgments we happen to make, we cannot then claim that those judgments have some kind of independent-of-human-nature rational justificatory warrant because they can be derived from the principles. As Mikhail puts it in his discussion of the principle of double effect (PDE), "Our question here is not whether the PDE is a sound principle of normative ethics, but whether it is descriptively adequate, or at least captures the implicit logic of common moral intuitions to a useful first approximation" (Mikhail 2011, 148). Consider a parallel case of human reactions that no one thinks are rational in the sense of being rationally necessary, such as judgments of funniness or deliciousness. Imagine we did an exceedingly extensive study of the things humans find funny or delicious. We formulated principles that fit the data. We then used those principles to predict humans' judgments about what is funny or delicious. No one would think that we had therefore shown that those judgments are rational in the sense that Clarke and Kant wanted moral judgments to be. Just so, no one would think that our being able to describe general rules that identify grammatical English sentences shows that English grammar is rational in Clarke or Kant's rationally necessary sense.

Let's now turn to construal (3), according to which a moral judgment is rational if it is based on innate features of the human mind. To clarify the Humean position on (3), we have to draw a distinction. One idea that can be involved in claiming that some feature of a human is innate is (3a) that the presence of the feature cannot be explained by that human's interactions with the empirical world. The feature is explanatorily original to a human's nature, hard-wired into her, something that can be used to explain how other features develop but cannot itself be explained by her experiences. Another idea that can be involved in claiming that some feature is innate is (3b) that it delivers a priori knowledge of necessary, mind-independent truths. Seventeenth-century defenders of innate ideas, such as Descartes, Herbert of Cherbury, and Cudworth, affirmed both 3a and 3b. They maintained that our ideas of such things as geometry, morality, and God both are original (cannot be explained by our empirical interactions) *and* represent mind-independent, necessary features of reality. This was not mere coincidence, for underlying this strand of seventeenth-century thought was a theological conception of human nature that drew together 3a and 3b—a conception according to which those aspects of human nature that cannot be explained in any other way (3a) must be attributed to the original design of a Good and Truthful God (3b).

Hume does not deny that there are features of human nature that are innate in the sense of 3a, according to which the presence of a feature cannot be explained by a human's interactions with the empirical world. Indeed, Hume clearly believes that human beings are hard-wired with certain original mental tendencies—such as the empiricist copy principle of impressions and ideas, various principles of mental association, and motives of self-love, parental concern, and sexual desire. His positive project is an attempt to explain observable phenomena of human life on the basis of these original tendencies and our interactions with the empirical world. But while Hume takes certain features of human nature to be original, affirming the 3a sense of innate, he does not think those features deliver knowledge of necessary truths about mind-independent reality, which is the denial of the 3b sense of innate. Hume rejects the theological conception of human nature that drew together 3a and

3b. He thinks the aspects of human nature that are original do not on their own produce necessarily true beliefs. This is why Hume uses the word "original" to describe the inherent, hard-wired features of human nature rather than "innate"—because in that period, the word "innate" brought with it a theology that led to the idea of being representative of the necessary structure of reality. ("Innate" has lost its association with that idea in the contemporary era, and as a result, people today may sometimes fail to note the difference between a seventeenth–eighteenth-century affirmation of something's being innate and a twenty-first-century affirmation of it.)

If there is a Universal Moral Grammar, as Mikhail argues, then there are important parts of morality that are innate in the sense of 3a (i.e. original, not explained by a human's interaction with the empirical world). Hume argues that morality is not innate in the sense of 3a but rather develops out of other, more basic mental mechanisms.[7] So here we do have a real incompatibility between UMG and Humeanism, a disagreement about whether morality is original, not to be explained by a human's interaction with the empirical world (although, as I shall explain, this disagreement is less significant than it might initially appear). But UMG and Humeanism agree with each other about 3b, whether moral judgments deliver a priori knowledge of necessary mind-independent truths. As we have seen in our discussion of mind-independent construal (1), the universal moral grammar does not represent mind-independent reality any more than Humean sentiments do, or, for that matter, any more than Chomskean linguistic grammar does. Mikhail's account of UMG does not include the seventeenth-century theological underpinnings that would imply an isomorphism between the hard-wired features of the human mind and the necessary structure of reality. Rather than attribute those hard-wired features to the will of the perfectly good and truthful Mind that designed reality, they are now attributed to evolutionary and other empirical forces (Mikhail 2011, 172). Hume's rationalist opponents sought to vindicate our moral judgments by showing that they were based on principles that were as rationally inescapable as logic and mathematics and that represented accurately the structure of a God-created reality that was independent of our minds; Hume's rationalist opponents wanted to show that our moral judgments were *TRUE* in as robustly a capitalized sense as one could hope for.[8] Mikhail's UMG, like the sentimentalist theories of Prinz, Haidt, and Nichols, is squarely on the Humean side of this debate about the fundamental metaphysics of morality.

Let's now turn to construal 4, according to which a moral judgment is rational if it is "intuitive, stable, spontaneous, and impartial, and made with a high degree of certitude" (Mikhail 2011, 97; see also 83). This is the description Mikhail gives of the "considered moral judgments" on which he bases his development of the principles of UMG. This is a much weaker sense of "rational" than Hume's rationalist opponents sought, and it is a sense that Hume himself could embrace. Moral judgments as the Humean understands them can very well be intuitive and spontaneous, given that what Mikhail means by those terms is "not determined by the systematic and conscious use of ethical principles" (Mikhail 2011, 83; see also 243). A judgment is stable if "it endures through a period of [a person's] personal history, and is shared by" the group the person is a part of (Mikhail 2011, 243). That a judgment is based in part on sentiment does not preclude this kind of stability: my judgment that vanilla ice cream is better-tasting than cod liver oil, and that the sonatas of J. S. Bach are superior to the albums of the 1970s easy listening group America, certainly meet these criteria of stability while also pretty clearly having non-rational origins. What of impartiality? Hume and Adam Smith go into great detail developing rich accounts of how sentimental bases can produce moral judgments that are impartial, Hume by means of the "general point of view" and Smith by means of the "impartial spectator." Hume and Smith's notions of impartiality are, moreover, quite similar to the Rawlsian conception Mikhail endorses—which is, explicitly, not a conception in which emotion plays no role but rather one in which no "distorting" emotion plays a role (Mikhail 2011, 244–5). As far as a judgment's being "made with a high degree of certitude," note that this is not "certainty, strictly speaking," where that is a "logical relation between a proposition and its evidence" (Mikhail 2011, 243). Rather, the certitude Mikhail has in mind is a *feeling*—"the psychological state of feeling confident or certain about the truth of a given proposition," a "feeling of conviction [that] is not temporary, but remains with us after criticism" (Mikhail 2011, 243–4). But this is also something that could characterize judgments that are sentimentally based, such as my judgment about the relative merits of ice cream and cod liver oil, Bach and America.

Mikhail refers in passing to Brandt and Hare's view that judgments "qualify as *rational* [if] they survive maximum criticism of facts and logic" (Mikhail 2011, 97), which we can call construal 4a. But once again, there is no reason to think that a Humean judgment cannot qualify as rational in this sense. Some non-moral judgments that uncontroversially involve sentiment can survive maximum criticism of facts and logic. (Consider again the Bach-America judgments, or someone's decision to marry.) This is because some of our sentimental dispositions are deep and stable enough to ground judgments that continued further reflection will not unseat. Indeed, Hume's moral judgments are supposed to be grounded in just those sorts of sentimental dispositions. So to the extent that 4a is Mikhail's construal of rational, we find once again that there's no reason to think that his account is incompatible with Humeanism.

As a Rawlsian, Mikhail believes that the moral judgments that are normatively justified are those to which we hold in a state of reflective equilibrium (Mikhail 2011, 202–13). The extensive data on considered moral judgments on which he builds his UMG are merely the normative starting points. To determine how we ought to live we must reflect on each of those judgments in light of each other as well as in conjunction with a myriad of other beliefs. As a result of such reflection we will shed some of the judgments we started with and adopt new ones. Now we can say that the judgments we hold in reflective equilibrium are reasonable and perhaps call this construal (5) of rational. But this reflective equilibrium construal of the way in which moral judgments can be rational is, once again, not something the Humean needs to deny, as it implies neither correspondence to any mind-independent reality nor mathematical-like necessity.[9] Nor is this sense of rational one that the rationalists of Hume's day would have accepted as sufficient to vindicate morality and defeat Hume.

There is, therefore no important sense in which Mikhail's UMG conflicts with Hume's negative project, where the latter is a denial that moral judgments represent necessary features of mind-independent reality or can be derived from rationally inescapable, logic-like reasoning. Indeed, it seems to me that if Mikhail's UMG had been proposed in the eighteenth century, rationalists of the day would have taken it to be just as much a threat to the validity of morals as they took Humeanism to be. On the fundamental questions separating Hume and the rationalists—whether the world has an intrinsic moral structure that our moral judgments reflect and whether our moral judgments can be shown to have a mathematical-like necessity—Mikhail agrees with Hume.

Let's now turn to the positive part of Hume's moral project. Hume tries to show that almost all the phenomena of human moral judgment can be explained by the empiricist copy principle of impressions and ideas, the principles of mental association (with the associative mechanisms of sympathy and our addiction to general rules shouldering much of the explanatory burden), and a small handful of original motives, such as self-interest, parental concern, and sexual desire. This is a very short list of original ingredients. Each of the accounts of contemporary moral psychologists we've examined in this chapter starts with considerably more. Mikhail argues that numerous moral principles are psychologically original. Haidt, Prinz, and Nichols recognize more basic emotions as being original to human nature than Hume. Nichols also relies on humans having a robust inborn capacity to grasp rules (Nichols 2005). I label Haidt, Prinz, and Nichols "Humean" because emotions play an essential role in their accounts, but the details of their explanations of moral judgment differ from the details of Hume's account in a similar way to Mikhail's. All these contemporary thinkers believe that human beings come into the world with more extensive hard wiring than Hume supposes. And I think there is good reason to believe these contemporary accounts are more accurate— that humans do have a richer original endowment than Hume allowed. Let me illustrate this by pointing to two parts of Hume's positive account that look to be weaker precisely because of Hume's reliance on an excessively thin original endowment.

First, there is Hume's explanation of the distinctions between different kinds of virtues. I argued in previous chapters that Hume does a marvelous job of describing the multifarious phenomena of our positive moral judgments of many different kinds of virtue. He tries, however, to show that all those judgments are based in the single morally judging sentiment of approbation. The problem with this account is that the positive emotional response we have to, say, kindness toward children does not seem to be the same as the positive emotional response we have to, say, courage in battle. Hume realizes there is this difference in our moral emotional responses. But because he has only the single moral sentiment of approbation, he struggles to explain why we think of both traits as virtues. As we have seen Hume say, "Each of the virtues, even benevolence, justice, gratitude, integrity, excites a different sentiment or feeling in the spectator. The characters of *Cæsar* and *Cato*, as drawn by *Sallust*, are both of them virtuous, in the strictest sense of the word; but in a different way: Nor are the sentiments entirely the same, which arise from them. In like manner, the approbation, which attends natural abilities, may be somewhat different to the feeling from that, which arises from the other virtues, without making them entirely of a different species" (*T* 3.3.4.2). There is a tension here. On the one hand, Hume wants to say that every trait that is a virtue is so because it elicits the single morally judging sentiment of approbation (so long as it's approbation that would be felt when considering the object of evaluation from the general point of view). On the other hand, he also wants to say that we feel differently about different traits we judge to be virtues. Hume's solution to this problem is to say that one feeling of approbation can feel "somewhat different" from another feeling of approbation "without making them entirely of a different species." But this leaves unexplained why different traits elicit different flavors of approbation, and when a difference in feeling would or would not constitute a difference in species. There may be elements of Hume's psychology that we can draw on to try to interpolate a fuller explanation, but the alternatives offered by the contemporary accounts look to be simpler and more powerful. On those contemporary accounts, the differences are explained as resulting from our possessing a number of different basic moral emotions or a number of different basic moral rules. These contemporary accounts can, moreover, offer evolutionary explanations of how we came to be hard-wired with a number of distinct basic moral elements instead of the single morally judging sentiment of approbation.

Consider, second, how Hume argues for the claim that justice is not a natural virtue. If justice were a natural virtue, according to Hume, there would have to be an original sentiment that motivates us to perform just acts (T 3.2.1.1–9). Hume examines three sentimental candidates for this role: self-interest (T 3.2.1.10), general benevolence or a regard to public interest (T 3.2.1.11–12), and private benevolence or a regard to the interest of the particular person to whom justice is owed (T 3.2.1.13–14). He finds that none of these three sentiments, as they exist in their original condition, could be the cause of our motive to perform just acts. He thus concludes that justice is not a natural virtue—that justice must originate in an artificial or conventional alteration of our original sentimental make-up. The problem with this argument is that the list of sentimental candidates that Hume canvasses is so blunt and short. He does not consider, for instance, the emotion of anger or resentment and how it might naturally manifest in cases in which one person takes something that another person had possessed. Nor does he consider the possibility that we have hard-wired instincts that lead us to negatively respond to unfairness or violations of reciprocity. Hume does go on to develop an astute diachronic account of the development of our ideas of property, and I think there are real insights there—all the more remarkable for Hume's having arrived at them centuries before the emergence of many of the techniques (such as cross-cultural studies, developmental psychology, behavioral economics, and primatology) we currently use to study human nature. But the richer emotional bases of Haidt, Prinz, and Nichols, Nichols' natural facility with rules, and Mikhail's innate universal moral principles—along with the evolutionary advantages the four of them can draw on to explain why such features might be original to human nature—all seem explanatorily more promising than the starting point of Hume's argument for the artificiality of justice.

At least part of the explanation for Hume's shorter list of original ingredients is that he was writing before Darwin. Before Darwin, there were two things to say about hard-wired features of human nature: they were designed by God, or they were brute facts, unexplained explainers. Hume wanted to provide the richest explanations possible while also holding that appeals to God pulled no explanatory weight.[10] This led to his trying to produce an account that relied on as small a number of original ingredients as possible, minimizing his account's unexplained explainers. But Darwin gave us a third thing to say about our hard-wired features: that evolutionary pressures over generations helped build them into human nature. Given this Darwinian option, I expect Hume would have been very amenable to admitting into his account of human nature a longer list of original ingredients. For after Darwin, he would not have had to take those original ingredients to be unexplained explainers but could have drawn on evolutionary explanations of them. Instead of having to restrict his focus to the changes that can be wrought on an individual by the interactions with the empirical world she has in her own lifetime, Hume would now be able to consider the changes that can be wrought on a species by the interactions with the empirical world its members have over generations. This would fit perfectly with Hume's non-theological empiricism, allowing him to acknowledge a much larger hard-wired emotional repository without having to include many more unexplained explainers.

There are three things we could mean when we say that an account of morality is "Humean." It is (A) Hume's own account, the view developed mainly in books 2 and 3 of A Treatise of Human Nature.[11] It is (B) an account that follows Hume in holding that sentiment plays an essential causal role in the origin of morality but does not cleave to the specifics of the mental mechanisms and social conventions Hume uses in the Treatise. It is (C) an account that gives a naturalist, empirical explanation of observable human behavior and does not suppose that morality can be fully explained by a priori rationalization and introspection. In Chapters 2 and 3, I explored (A) Hume's own account. In the first part of this chapter, I sketched Haidt, Prinz, and Nichols' accounts, which are (B) sentimentalist but differ in detail from Hume's own. Hume's broadest contribution, however, was his role in the creation of what we think of today as scientific psychological inquiry, the result of his pioneering of type (C) accounts (of which Haidt, Prinz, Nichols, and Mikhail are recent examples).

6

Rossian Non-Naturalist Pluralism

All the views I discussed in the previous chapter can be called "naturalist." But some of the most prominent pluralist views of the recent past have been non-naturalist. Why prefer the naturalist pluralism of Hume to non-naturalist alternatives? Answering this question is difficult because the distinction between naturalism and non-naturalism is highly contested.[1] I will not try to canvass all the pluralisms that could plausibly be taken to be non-naturalist alternatives to Humean pluralism, let alone take on the daunting task of showing that Humeanism can defeat all comers. Instead, I will limit myself to explicating the reasons for preferring the Humean naturalist version of pluralism to the prominent non-naturalist pluralism advanced by Ross.

There are two parts to Ross's account of our experience of making moral judgments: his view of our general judgments concerning prima facie duties, and his view of specific judgments concerning our actual duty. Let's start by examining his view of our general judgments of prima facie duties—of our judgments that it is generally right to keep promises, not to cause injury, to be just, and the like (as distinct from the judgment that one ought to keep this particular promise at this particular time, or one ought not cause that particular injury at that particular time, or one ought to deliver a certain specific punishment to a specific person). Ross believes that our general moral judgments of prima facie duties are non-inferential, certain, and self-evident. Because our general moral judgments have these features, Ross argues, we should conclude that they are based in reason and reflect necessary features of reality—features of reality that are independent of our mental reactions as a whole and of our sentiments more specifically. "[W]e *know* them true," Ross asserts (Ross 1930, 20–1; his italics), and we know them to be true because our judgments about them have the same qualities as our judgments about mathematics. As Ross puts it:

That an act, *qua* fulfilling a promise, or *qua* effect a just distribution of good, or *qua* returning services rendered, or *qua* promoting the good of others, or *qua* promoting the virtue

or insight of the agent, is *prima facie* right, is self-evident . . . It is self-evident just as a mathematical axiom, or the validity of a form of inference, is evident. The moral order expressed
in these propositions is just as much part of the fundamental nature of the universe (and,
we may add, of any possible universe in which there were moral agents at all) as is the spatial or numerical structure expressed in the axioms of geometry or arithmetic. In our confidence that these propositions are true there is involved the same trust in our reason that
is involved in our confidence in mathematics; and we should have no justification for trust-
ing it in the latter sphere and distrusting it in the former. In both case cases we are dealing
with propositions that cannot be proved, but that just as certainly need no proof. (Ross
1930, 29–30)

Or as Ross put it in *Foundations of Ethics*, the prima facie duties

seem not to express mere brute facts, but facts which are self-evidently necessary. For
instance, the very object of a promise being to encourage some one to believe that one will
act in a certain way, it is self-evident that he has a moral claim to our behaving in that way if
he wants us to do so. If we now turn to ask how we come to know these fundamental moral
principles, the answer seems to be that it is in the same way in which we come to know the
axioms of mathematics. Both alike seem to be both synthetic and a priori; that is to say, we
see the predicate, though not included in the definition of the subject, to belong necessarily
to anything which satisfies that definition. And as in mathematics, it is by intuitive induction that we grasp the general truths. (Ross 1939, 320)

To assess Ross's analogy between judgments of prima facie duties and mathematics—
his contention that we can conclude that the former are rational and reflect necessary
features of reality because they share certain features with the latter—let us distinguish two different elements of mathematical judgments: their being necessarily true,
and our phenomenology when making them.[2]

Let's grant that our judgments of simple mathematical claims (such as our judgment that two plus two equals four) are necessarily true—such that it is not even
sensible to deny them, such that we cannot conceive of their being false. The question is whether our judgments of prima facie duties are necessarily true in the
same way. There is a sense in which they may be said to be necessarily true, but it's
not a sense that will help Ross. Judgments of prima facie duties may be said to be
necessarily true when they are construed analytically. We can, for instance, take
the term "promise" to analytically contain the idea that a promise is something
that it is (ceteris paribus) right to keep. We can take the term "just distribution" to
analytically contain the idea that it is (ceteris paribus) right to justly distribute. We
can take the term "the good of others" to analytically contain the idea that the good
of others is something it is (ceteris paribus) right to promote. But if we take the
terms in this way, then assent to Ross's statement of the prima facie duties reveals
something only about the way we use certain terms—e.g. when we call something
a promise, we mean that it is something that (ceteris paribus) ought to be done;

when we call a certain distribution just, we mean that it is a distribution that (ceteris paribus) ought to be followed; when we say a course of action will promote the good of others, we mean that it is something that (ceteris paribus) ought to be done. It does not reveal anything about the "fundamental nature" of "any possible universe." Now Ross himself wants to claim that "the fundamental moral principles" are like the "axioms of mathematics" in being "synthetic and a priori" (Ross 1939, 320). The Humean view is that if Ross's prima facie duties are construed so as to be necessarily true, that will be because they are being understood in an analytic sense; and if they are construed synthetically, then they will not be necessarily true.

This charge of analyticity is one that Hutcheson and Hume leveled at the moral principles that the rationalists of their day claimed were rational and necessarily true. Clarke, for instance, offered as examples of necessary moral principles the following:

'Tis evidently more *Fit*... that Men should deal one with another according to the known Rules of *Justice and Equity*; than that every Man for his own present Advantage, should without scruple disappoint the most *reasonable and equitable Expectations* of his Neighbours, and *cheat* and *defraud*, or *spoil by violence*, all others without restraint... 'tis without dispute more *Fit* and reasonable in itself, that I should *preserve the Life* of an innocent Man... than that I should suffer him to perish, or *take away his Life*, without any reason or provocation at all. (Clarke 1705/1738, 609)

Hutcheson and Hume can grant that we can take these principles to be making claims that we cannot conceive of as being false. But that is because each principle contains terms that may be construed so as to analytically contain a moral evaluation. To say that a course of action is in accord with "Justice and Equity" may be construed so as to analytically imply that there is a moral reason to take that course. To say that a course of action will disappoint "reasonable and equitable expectations" or "cheat and defraud, or spoil by violence" may be construed so as to analytically imply that there is a moral reason not to take that course. To say that someone is "innocent" may be construed so as to analytically imply that he ought not to be killed "without any reason or provocation at all." This is the point Hume has in mind when he says that people mistakenly believe that there is universal moral agreement because they fail to realize the merely verbal nature of our assent to some judgments. "Certain terms," he writes, "import blame, and others praise" (*Essays*, 227). It thus seems absurd to blame someone for virtue and praise someone for vice. But that is only because the "word *virtue*, with its equivalent in every tongue, implies praise; as that of *vice* does blame" (*Essays*, 228). That this seeming agreement is merely verbal becomes clear when we realize that the same people who all agree in praising virtue can nonetheless disagree wildly about which conduct is in fact virtuous. Similarly, it is perfectly "obvious" that "writers of all nations and all ages concur in applauding justice, humanity, magnanimity, prudence, veracity; and in blaming the opposite qualities" (*Essays*, 228). But this "seeming harmony in morals may be accounted for from the very nature of language," as we can see when we note that these same writers disagree wildly about who is just, humane, magnanimous, prudent, and veracious (*Essays*, 228). The descriptions of actions that are universally agreed to be virtuous contain morally thick terms, which include not only non-evaluative descriptions of action-types but also the positive evaluative component of praiseworthiness. Hutcheson makes the same point about the following principle, which Clarke presented as an example of a necessary moral truth: "[W]hoever first attempts, without the *consent* of his Fellows, and except it be for some *publick Benefit*, to take to himself more than his *Proportion*, is the Beginner of Iniquity" (Clarke 1705/1738, 631). The crucial term here is "take to himself more than his proportion." Yes, Hutcheson allows, everyone might assent to this as being something necessarily true. But that is only because the term "to take to himself *more than his proportion*" analytically contains the idea that the person in question is doing something he ought not. As Hutcheson puts it, "It were to be wished that writers would guard against, as far as they can, involving very complex ideas under some short words and particles which almost escape observation in sentences . . . Some writers treat the pronoun 'his' as if it were the sign of a simple idea and yet involve under it the complex ideas of property and of a right to natural liberty, as the Schoolmen made space and time to vanish into nothings by hiding them in the adverbs 'when' and 'where' or by including them in the compound words 'coexistent,' 'corresponding,' etc." (Burnet and Hutcheson 1725/1971, 213–14).

I think Hume and Hutcheson's diagnosis of the eighteenth-century rationalist claims about fundamental moral principles—that they seem necessarily true only because they include terms that can be taken to analytically include a certain moral evaluation—can also be applied to Ross's claims about prima facie duties. When the prima facie duties seem necessarily true, it's because parts of them are being construed analytically, because we are taking terms like 'promise' and 'promoting the good of others' and 'just distribution' to analytically contain the idea that there is a moral reason in favor of the actions so described. It's not because they're purely rational apprehensions of mind-independent truths.

But isn't it possible to consider Ross's prima facie duties in a non-analytic way? Can't the evaluative aspects of Ross's statement of the prima facie duties be shaved off, leaving us only with claims about the rightness of certain action-types described entirely in non-evaluative terms? Yes. But when we eliminate the evaluative element of our statement of prima facie duties and consider the relevant action-types entirely non-evaluatively, they are no longer necessarily true in the way that mathematical claims are. If we describe promises in strictly non-evaluative terms, a person can then deny that one has reason to perform the action that is called a promise without being guilty of the kind of non-sensibility that afflicts $2 + 2 = 5$. If we describe a distribution of benefits and burdens in strictly non-evaluative terms, a person can then deny that there is a reason to follow a distribution of that without being guilty of an offense that is rationally equivalent to that of denying that $2 + 2 = 4$. I am not claiming that a normal person would sincerely believe that there is no moral reason at all to keep promises or to oppose certain distributions. My point is just that her beliefs that there are general moral reasons to keep promises and act justly (where those are construed entirely non-evaluatively) are not impossible to intelligibly deny in the same way her belief that $2 + 2 = 4$ is. Ross says that our judgments of prima facie duties describe a "moral order [that] is just as much part of the fundamental nature of the universe (and, we may add, of any possible universe in which there were moral agents at all) as is the spatial or numerical structure expressed in the axioms of geometry or arithmetic." But if the feature of geometry and arithmetic that is crucial is their being synthetic and impossible to conceive of as being false, then Ross's analogy breaks down.

It might be thought, however, that the key similarity between our judgments of prima facie duties and mathematics is not necessary truth but rather the phenomenology of non-inferential certainty or self-evidence that characterizes both. $2 + 2 = 4$ is something we find to be certain, and we do not need to follow any inferential steps to reach that conclusion; our apprehension of $2 + 2 = 4$ and our conclusion that it is true are one and the same mental event. But the same certainty and self-evidence characterizes our moral judgment that it is right to keep promises, or justly distribute rewards and punishment, or promote the good of others. As Ross explains, "[A]ttention to our state of mind when we express approval of conscientiousness, say, or of benevolence shows that what we really think about them is that they are good in themselves. No one can prove that they are, but then nothing could be proved unless there were truths which are apprehended without proof; and we apprehend that conscientiousness or benevolence is good with as complete certainty, directness, and self-evidence as we ever apprehend anything" (Ross 1939, 262). According to Ross here, the phenomenology of apprehending prima facie duties is crucially similar to the phenomenology of apprehending mathematical truths. And this phenomenological similarity gives us grounds for holding that the moral judgments are rational and reflect mind-independent truth in the same way the mathematical judgments do.

There are three reasons this phenomenological argument is not convincing.

First, even if the phenomenology of the certainty of our judgments of prima facie duties and of basic mathematics were the same, that would not ensure that the former reflect the same kinds of truths as the latter. If something is truly unintelligible to deny, we might have grounds for concluding that it captures necessary truth. But the experience of non-inferential certainty (where that is different from being unintelligible to deny) does not on its own give us the same grounds. The phenomenology of certainty does not guarantee necessary truth.

Second, there is reason to think that Ross overstates the phenomenological similarity between morals and mathematics. Ross claims that when he introspects, he finds that his general moral judgments have some crucial phenomenological similarity to mathematics. But other people, such as sentimentalists like Hutcheson and Hume, claim that when they introspect they find that moral judgment has a more sentimental phenomenology. Still others claim that they find that moral judgment has yet a different phenomenology, one that has theological or egoistic implications. This raises the possibility that there do not exist phenomenological features of moral judgment that are both universal and robust enough to support Ross's meta-ethical theory over any other. Indeed, it may be that moral phenomenology cannot serve as a pre-theoretical starting point or anchor for debates between naturalists and non-naturalists (or sentimentalists and rationalists, or egoists and altruists, or divine command theorists and atheists), because one's moral phenomenology may itself be infected by one's meta-ethical position on those debates. Our moral phenomenology simply may not contain introspectable evidence that is dispositive for some of our metaphysical questions.[3]

Third, the Humean position can mount a plausible explanation of what Ross claims our phenomenology to be without having to invoke any purely rational apprehensions of necessary truth. This Humean explanation has two parts. First, we may experience our judgments of prima facie duties as non-inferential, self-evident, and certain partly because we are responding to the (previously discussed) analytic connection between evaluatively loaded construals of, on the one hand, "fulfilling a promise," a "just distribution," and "promoting the good of others," and, on the other hand, "being (ceteris paribus) right." Second, we may experience moral judgments as being non-inferential, self-evident, and certain partly because of sentiments' role in forming those judgments. Prinz articulates well this aspect of the sentimentalist explanation when he writes: "I think sentimentalism can explain this phenomenology [of moral judgments' seeming self-justifying]. Sentimental judgments generally seem self-evident. It is evident to me that Buster Keaton is funny, because he makes me laugh. It is evident to me that chocolate is delicious, because it induces pleasure when I taste it. It would be somewhat perverse to demand more evidence than this. Likewise, emotionally grounded moral judgments have a kind of perception-like immediacy that does not seem to require further support. We can feel that killing is wrong… The judgment

that something is funny is justified by our amusement, because causing amusement is constitutive of being funny. If moral judgments are sentimental, and they
refer to response-dependent properties, then the judgment that killing is wrong
is self-justifying because killing elicits the negative sentiment expressed by that
judgment and having the power to elicit such negative sentiments is constitutive
of being wrong. Sentimentalism explains the phenomenology driving intuitionism..." (Prinz 2006, 37).[4] I do not need to make any inferences or appeal to any
evidential support to think I am justified in judging that the Buster Keaton movie
I'm watching is funny or the chocolate I'm eating is delicious. My experience of
the movie can itself be justification for my judgment that it is funny; my experience of the chocolate can itself be justification for my judgment that it is delicious.
Similarly, according to the moral sentimentalist, my negative reaction to something may be both the basis of my judgment that it is immoral and the justification
of the judgment—and this is why I experience the judgment as self-justifying.[5] To
put the point in Humean terms, because eliciting approval from the general point
of view is constitutive of my judgment that a trait is virtuous, I can experience my
approval of a trait from the general point of view both as the basis of my judgment
that the trait is virtuous and as the justification for that judgment.

There are similar reasons to reject a related argument Ross gives for the
mind-independence of moral properties. Ross argues against "interest" or "relational" theories, or theories that claim that something's moral status is based in
part on a certain kind of reaction we have to it, by claiming (1) that we all think
that a thing's moral status is independent of the reaction anyone has to it, and
(2) the best explanation of our thinking (1) is that a thing's moral status *is* independent of the reaction anyone has to it. He writes, "It is surely clear that when we
call something good we are thinking of it as possessing in itself a certain attribute and are not thinking of it as necessarily having an interest taken in it... What
the relational theory must maintain [is] that whereas most people think that certain things have a characteristic, goodness, distinct from that of being objects of
interest, nothing has any such characteristic. And then the question arises, what
could have led mankind to form this quite superfluous notion to which nothing in reality corresponds?" (Ross 1930, 81–2). According to Ross here, we think
that what makes something moral is its possessing a certain mind-independent,
non-natural property; and the most reasonable explanation of our thinking is that
this mind-independent non-natural property actually exists.[6] Once again I think
there are three reasons not to be convinced.

First, even if we did all always think that a thing's moral status is independent
of any interest or relation to ourselves, that would not guarantee that there is any
mind-independent property that vindicates such a thought.[7] Perhaps we must trust

our judgments concerning propositions that we apprehend to be necessarily true, but we do not apprehend substantive moral judgments as being necessarily true. Moreover, the issue here is not whether certain moral judgments are true; it's whether the judgments are made true by a mind-independent property. And even if we cannot seriously consider the possibility that certain kinds of actions (such as killing innocent people or breaking promises when there are no other relevant moral considerations) are morally correct, we can seriously consider the possibility that what makes those actions morally incorrect is, partly, our reaction to them.

Second, Ross overstates the extent to which we all think that what gives something its moral status is a mind-independent property. Some people claim to think of morality as mind-dependent, or culturally determined, or based on divine commands. Ross says that it "is surely clear that when we call something good we are thinking of it as possessing in itself a certain attribute and are not thinking of it as necessarily having an interest taken in it," but that is not so surely clear at all.[8] There is no universal pre-theoretical thought about what we are doing when we make moral judgments that can successfully anchor the argument Ross is trying to make.

Most important is the third reason to resist Ross's claim that our experience of moral judgment comports best with mind-independent non-naturalism, which is that there is an alternative, Humean explanation of our moral experiences that is superior to Ross's mind-independent non-naturalist one. Why think the Humean explanation is superior? Because it does as good a job of accounting for the phenomena of our moral judgment as Ross's, and it does so much more parsimoniously. Humeanism explains the phenomena on the basis of the natural facts of the external world and our psychological reactions to it, facts that science already countenances and that play a role in our best explanations of other phenomena, while Rossianism must include an additional category of mind-independent, non-natural, causally inert properties and some means for our minds to access them. Humeanism can parsimoniously explain the conspicuous motivational influence morality has on us, as it holds that morality originates in a motivationally effective sentimental base, while Rossianism, which tells us that moral properties are independent of our motives, will struggle to account for the strong connection between motivation and moral judgment. Rossianism will also struggle to explain how and why its non-natural moral properties supervene on natural properties, while the thoroughly naturalistic Humean picture has no difficulty explaining this at all.

Of course, the statements I made in the previous paragraph about the superiority of Humean naturalism to Rossian non-naturalism are highly contentious. Non-naturalists have contested each of them at great length and with great ingenuity, and it would take another book (at least one) to do full justice to their positions. I want to maintain, however, that pluralism creates special problems for non-naturalism. If you accept the pluralist view of the content of morality, you will have additional reason (additional to the much-discussed objections to non-naturalism I mentioned in the previous paragraph) to favor a Humean naturalist account over a non-naturalist one. This might seem surprising, given that Ross is so closely associated with both pluralism and non-naturalism. What I want to suggest in the remainder of this chapter is that Ross's pluralism and non-naturalism do not comport well with each other. His two main positions are actually in tension. Or to put it another way, Ross's pluralism is an added cost to his non-naturalism. His pluralism makes his non-naturalism even more explanatorily expensive (which makes the Humean, naturalist pluralism all the more attractive).

Ross's arguments for non-naturalism rely on the self-evident, a priori, necessary character of prima facie duties. Ross's arguments for pluralism rely on the existence of incompatibilities between the actions different prima facie duties would have us perform. But the idea of two things that are a priori and necessary having incompatible implications should strike us as queer. Outside of morality, principles that are a priori and necessary fit together with each other perfectly. Clarke and Kant reasonably thought that the same thing was true of moral principles: that given their purely rational status, it was impossible for such principles to come into conflict. Ross, in contrast, has to ask us to take on board not only non-natural moral properties but also a category of a priori, necessary principles that do not exist anywhere else—namely, a priori, necessary principles that have incompatible implications.

Perhaps the Rossian will reply that the prima facie duties do not contradict each other insofar as each prima facie duty is a statement merely of a moral reason, and insofar as there is no contradiction in holding that there is both a reason to perform an action and a reason not to perform the same action. The physical laws describing the behavior of middle-sized dry goods provide a model of this. An object's velocity and direction of motion are determined by various forces, some of which may push in opposite directions. But we don't then say that the physical laws contradict each other. We say, rather, that each law tells us what would happen if there were no other forces at work and that the final result is the interaction of the multiple forces that in fact are at work in this particular instance. As Ross puts it, "*Qua* subject to the force of gravitation towards some other body each body tends to move in a particular direction with a particular velocity; but its actual movement depends on *all* the forces to which it is subject. It is only by recognizing this distinction that we can preserve the absoluteness of laws of nature, and only by recognizing a corresponding distinction that we can preserve the absoluteness of the general principles of morality" (Ross 1930, 28). So why not think of prima facie duties as akin to the physical laws, telling us what would be right to do if there were no other moral considerations in play, and actual duty as akin to the velocity and direction of the particular object, the result of the interaction of the various moral considerations that are in fact in play? There are several reasons why the example of physical laws does not help Ross.

First, Ross himself acknowledges that the a priori, necessary principles of morality are unlike the a posteriori, contingent physical laws. Most importantly, we experience the former but not the latter as a priori, necessary, and certain; and it's just those features that are the basis of Ross's arguments. Moreover, the physical laws are causal while the former are logical, which difference further undermines the analogy between the interaction between moral principles and the interaction between physical laws. As Ross explains, "But an important difference between the two cases must be pointed out. When we say that in virtue of gravitation a body tends to move in a certain way, we are referring to a causal influence actually exercised on it by another body or other bodies. When we say that in virtue of being deliberately untrue a certain remark tends to be wrong, we are referring to no causal relation, to no relation that involves succession in time, but to such a relation as connects the various attributes of a mathematical figure" (Ross 1930, 29). The feature of natural laws that makes sense of their exerting contrary forces on a single object is their having different causal tendencies. But it's that very feature that Ross's moral principles lack. It's precisely because they lack causal tendencies—or, really, "tendencies" of any kind—that Ross's moral principles are like mathematics, and this is why pointing to how contingent causal laws interact doesn't minimize the queerness of necessary non-causal principles' having contradictory tendencies. Of course it is open to Ross to say that moral principles are *sui generis*, unlike any other kinds of laws we know of: necessarily true (like mathematics) and yet capable of having opposing tendencies (like physical laws). My point is that this is an additional explanatory cost. Because he is both a non-naturalist and a pluralist, Ross has to purchase not only non-natural entities that are not part of our picture of the rest of the world but, in addition, a certain class of (necessary and yet capable of having opposing tendencies) principles that are also not part of that picture.

Another reason the analogy between prima facie duties and physical laws breaks down is the different ways induction operates in the learning of each. The induction that produces belief in physical laws is based on observations of actual occurrences. But we don't come to prima facie duties by induction in the same way. We have certain, self-evident apprehensions of prima facie duties in particular cases and then generalize from them (which would be analogous to our apprehending a physical law in one particular case). "[W]e see the *prima facie* rightness of an act which would be the fulfillment of a particular promise, and of another which would be the fulfillment of another promise, and when we have reached sufficient maturity to think in general terms, we apprehend *prima facie* rightness to belong to the nature of any fulfillment of promise. What comes first in time is the apprehension of the self-evident *prima facie* rightness of an individual act of a particular type" (Ross 1930, 33). On Ross's story, we apprehend in a particular case that the fact that an action is the keeping of a promise or the reducing of suffering is a prima facie reason to perform it (*not* that that action is our actual duty). Then we apprehend in a second particular case that the fact that an action is the keeping of a promise or the reducing of suffering is a prima facie reason (*not* an actual duty) to perform it. Then we apprehend the same thing in a third particular case. And so eventually we come to the general conclusion that, in all particular cases, the fact that an action is the keeping of a promise or the reduction of suffering is a prima facie reason to perform it. But this story doesn't *explain* our certain, self-evident apprehension of prima facie duties in particular cases. This story *presupposes* that we have those apprehensions; it takes those apprehensions *as givens*, and then uses them to explain our assent to generalizations about when those reasons obtain.[9] But this is significantly disanalogous to the story of how we come to believe in physical laws, for in the case of physical laws, our observations of numerous actual events (whose counterpart in the moral case would be our awareness of numerous actual duties) explains our belief in the existence of ceteris paribus forces. Moreover, it's just our belief that there is a moral reason to keep a promise or reduce suffering that Humeanism does offer an explanation of (having to do with how psychological mechanisms and contingent circumstances combine to produce moral sentiments in favor of certain things), rather than simply presupposing. It's the Humean picture, not the Rossian, which is more analogous to the picture of physical laws on this score.

A final reason the analogy to physical laws doesn't make Ross's mind-independent non-naturalist account of moral principles any less queer is this: there are laws that describe how physical laws interact with each other. There is a uniformity or pattern to how the forces on middle-sized dry goods jointly cause events. The mind-independent world that science seeks to describe is lawful. Ross's pluralism, in contrast, requires that he deny that moral principles interact in lawful ways. His pluralism commits him to holding that the interactions between prima facie duties are not just difficult to subsume under general laws but impossible.[10] That's what makes his view pluralist rather than some form of prioritarianism. Ross thus also has to include in his ontology a special kind of interaction between mind-independent principles—a kind of interaction that is not just difficult for us to lawfully describe but is itself objectively unlawful.

The problem here results from the combination of the two different aspects of Ross's account of moral judgment. Our general moral judgments provide us mind-independent facts about right-making moral principles. Our particular moral judgments provide us mind-independent facts about which particular acts are right. But the mind-independent facts of which particular acts are right do not follow in law-like ways from the mind-independent facts of right-making principles. This disconnect between the general and the specific—a disconnect that is metaphysical, not merely epistemic—does not exist in other realms of mind-independent fact. This disconnect is a queerness that arises from Ross's attempt to marry pluralism to non-naturalism. We can see the queerness in Ross's abrupt pivot from his assertion of the absolute, mathematical-like, "self-evidently necessary" certainty of our judgments of prima facie duties to his admission of our never having "intuitive or any other kind of certainty as to the actual (or resultant) rightness of particular acts" (Ross 1939, 320).

The queerness also manifests in the jarringly mismatched analogies Ross uses to illustrate our experience of the two different aspects of moral judgment. We have seen that Ross emphasizes the analogy between mathematics and morality when explicating prima facie duties. That analogy is supposed to impress on us the non-inferential self-evidence and certainty of the prima facie duties—of their being a priori apprehensions of the necessary structure of reality, true not only of our world but of any possible world. Ross acknowledges, however, that our judgments of actual duties have a significantly different mental character from our judgments of prima facie duties. As he writes, "Something should be said of the relation between our apprehension of the *prima facie* rightness of certain types of act and our mental attitude towards particular acts. It is proper to use the word 'apprehension' in the former case and not in the latter" (Ross 1930, 29). Immediately following this, Ross presents the description of prima facie duties we have already looked at, in the passage in which he relies on the analogy to mathematics. Then, right after that passage, he presents his description of the different "mental attitude" of our judgments of our actual moral duties. In this passage, he relies on a very different analogy—namely, to beauty. He writes:

Our judgments about our actual duty in concrete situations have none of the certainty that attaches to our recognition of the general principles of duty. A statement is certain, i.e., is an expression of knowledge, only in one or other of two cases; when it is either self-evident, or a valid conclusion from self-evident premises. And our judgements about our particular duties have neither of these characters. (1) They are not self-evident...[and] (2) ...there is no principle by which we can draw the conclusion that [any particular action] is on the whole right or on the whole wrong. In this respect the judgement as the rightness of a particular act is just like the judgement as to the beauty of a particular natural object or work of art. A poem is, for instance, in respect of certain qualities beautiful and in respect of certain others not beautiful; and our judgement as to the degree of beauty it possesses on the whole is never reached by logical reasoning from the apprehension of its particular beauties or particular defects. (Ross 1930, 30–1)

It's the transition from the math-analogy to the beauty-analogy that jars. It jars because it reveals that Ross's view implies that the relationship between necessarily true general moral principles and particular moral truths is radically different from the relationship of any other system of necessarily true principles and particular truths. Ross is right that the beauty of a natural object or poem is not a logical implication. It's not merely that we think we are epistemically incapable of discerning the logic of what makes objects and poems beautiful or unbeautiful. We don't think there's a strict logic to it at all. But we do think there's a logic to how mathematical (and other systems of self-evident a priori) principles combine with each other. There are mathematical claims whose truth we are uncertain of, but that is because of our epistemic limitations. It's true that Gödel showed that within powerful and consistent logical systems there will be truths that are unprovable. Gödel did not show, however, that *every* truth in a powerful and consistent system is unprovable. Yet that is just what Ross is claiming about morality: that it is based on logic-like axioms that are incapable of proving a single actual thing. And this is queer, for being bases of proofs seems to be the raison d' être of the axioms of every other system of a priori necessary truths.

Don't some mathematical and logical theorems strike us as beautiful? Yes, but in such cases our experience of beauty is a response to our understanding of the theorems, a response to our apprehension of why they are true. The experience of the beauty of a theorem is essentially linked to (at least an inkling of) the theorem's rational necessity, of how it follows from things of which we are certain. Not so for our experience of the beauty of a natural object or poem. Awareness of why an object or poem's particular features and overall design affect us as they do can enhance our appreciation, and sometimes bring us to see as beautiful what before we had not so seen. But that kind of awareness is not essential to the experience of a natural object or poem's beauty in the same way discursive understanding of a theorem (or at least an inkling of that discursive understanding) is to our experience of its beauty. Ross acknowledges this difference himself when he says that "our judgement as to the degree of beauty [a natural object or poem] possesses on the whole is never reached by logical reasoning from the apprehension of its particular beauties or particular defects." But there is no such severe discontinuity between the apprehension of mathematical or logical axioms and our judgment as to the truth of a particular theorem. (There is, as well, something curious and strained about Ross's phrase, "the apprehension of its particular beauties or particular defects." Previously Ross restricted the use of "apprehension" to our understanding of necessary general truths, but we do not have such an understanding of general features that make objects and poems beautiful. There are no aesthetic prima facie principles that have the necessity that characterizes mathematical and logical axioms. The strain here comes from Ross's statement's being a somewhat desperate attempt to hold together the disparate math and beauty analogies.)

I have been focusing on what Ross says about our experiences of moral judgment because Ross himself bases his meta-ethical arguments on those experiences. He claims that non-naturalism best accounts for those experiences. What I have been trying to show is that the alternative Humean explanation is much more smooth and natural. According to the Humean alternative, the situation Ross describes as certainty about relevant prima facie duties and uncertainty about an actual duty is actually one in which we care about incompatible things and are uncertain about how to resolve the conflict. The certainty that Ross takes to be our apprehension of prima facie duties is just our awareness that we care about certain things—an awareness that we sometimes experience as self-evident and non-inferential. The uncertainty that Ross takes to be our struggle to discern a mind-independent actual duty is just a reflection of the difficulty we sometimes have in prioritizing the things we care about and the reluctance we sometimes feel in acting against one of those things.[11] The Humean will not deny that there are scientific laws that explain entirely all of these moral experiences of ours. There is no scientific disconnect between general and specific. But there can be a significant experiential difference between our awareness of the various things we want to do and our uncertainty about what to do when some of those things conflict.

In both *The Right and the Good* and *Foundations of Ethics*, Ross distinguishes between an "objective" and a "subjective" understanding of actual duty. On the objective understanding, one's actual duty is a mind-independent feature of the situation in which one has to act, something made true by facts independent of whether or not one believes them. These objective facts are of two sorts: non-evaluative empirical facts about causes and effects and other states of the natural world, and the non-natural moral fact of what is "suitable, in a unique and indefinable way" (Ross 1939, 146). On the subjective understanding, one's actual duty is to do what one *thinks* is morally suitable given what one *thinks* are the empirical facts. The subjective understanding thus admits a "double dose of subjectivity into the answer to the question 'what is my duty?', by making it depend on my *opinion* as to what is morally suitable to what is in my *opinion* the state of the facts" (Ross 1939, 164). Ross acknowledges that both understandings make appearances in our thoughts and speech, but he wants to determine which of the two describes our duty in "the most important sense," "which of the characteristics—objective or subjective rightness—is ethically the more important: which of the two acts is that which we ought to do" (Ross 1939, 147). In *The Right and the Good*, he contends for the objective sense. The right act for me, he says there, is not that "which on all the evidence available to me I should think to be my duty" but rather "that which if I were omniscient I should see to be my duty" (Ross 1930, 32). This is why there is "much truth in the description of the right act as the fortunate act. If we cannot be certain that it is right, it is our good fortune if the act we do is the right act" (Ross 1930, 31). This objective understanding of duty is all the more noteworthy given that in *The Right and the Good* Ross allows that beauty may be a response-dependent property—i.e. he allows that what makes an object beautiful may be its possession of certain features towards which we have certain positive reactions (Ross 1930, 127–30). Even though he says this about beauty, Ross remains adamant that morality is *not* dependent on our responses in the same way—that our moral judgments are attempts to get at truths that are independent of our reactions.

In *Foundations of Ethics*, however, Ross gives a different answer to the question of whether the subjective or objective understanding is more important.[12] He acknowledges that there is much that can be said for the objective answer but goes on to say he has come to believe there are decisive reasons to hold "that it is the subjectively right act that is obligatory" (Ross 1939, 148). "One who does what seems to him to be right is doing what in another sense *is* right, and is doing an action of moral worth" (Ross 1939, 321). Ross explicates in detail a number of subtle considerations that led him to this new position. I won't trace his arguments here. But in closing, let me note how significant a step this change is toward Humeanism (even if Ross himself would not have been amenable to such a characterization). Ross seems to have been led to concede that we can explain the most important aspect of what it is right for a person to do by referring entirely to that person's response to the world. Perhaps the person thinks she is responding to non-natural moral facts; perhaps not. But it's how the person responds that is crucial. It's the person's response that is the origin of the content of her duty.

7

Formal Monism

A Humean pluralist view captures deep and pervasive aspects of our moral think-ing. But our moral thinking is not exclusively pluralist. In this chapter, I explain what I take to be the most powerful reason for holding that commonsense moral-ity includes non-pluralist aspects as well. I look, specifically, at one of the chief motivations behind the grand monistic theories of Kant and the utilitarians.[1]

Arguments for moral monism can be formal or substantive. A formal argument attempts to show that there is one and only one ultimate moral end but is neutral on what that end is. A substantive argument attempts to show that some single identifiable end is the one and only ultimate moral end.

Mill and Kant are two-step monists (at least at certain times and in certain respects). Each advances formal monism, the first step, maintaining that we are committed to there being a single ultimate moral end, without initially making a claim about what that end is. Each then advances his own version of substan-tive monism, the second step, arguing that something in particular is the ultimate moral end.

Mill and Kant's substantive arguments end in different places, of course—Mill's at utility and Kant's at the Categorical Imperative. But what I want to focus on is the similarity of their formally monistic views. I will first point to the passages that indicate their formal monism. I will then fill out the formally monistic position suggested by those passages (without claiming that that filled out position is neces-sarily the only one that is consistent with Mill and Kant's texts) and connect that position with how other thinkers have viewed morality.

Mill puts forward his formally monistic view in a section of *A System of Logic* titled "Necessity of an ultimate standard, or first principle of Teleology."[2] He writes:

There is, then, a Philosophia Prima peculiar to Art... There must be some standard by which to determine the goodness or badness, absolute and comparative, of ends, or objects of desires. And whatever that standard is, there can be but one: for if there were several ultimate principles of conduct, the same conduct might be approved by one of those princi-ples and condemned by another; and there would be needed some more general principle, as umpire between them. Accordingly, writers on moral philosophy have mostly felt the necessity not only of referring all rules of conduct, and all judgements of praise and blame, to principles, but of referring them to some one principle; some rule, or standard, with which all other rules of conduct were required to be consistent, and from which by ultimate consequences they could all be deduced. (Mill 1843/1904, 657–8)

There can be "but one" ultimate principle of conduct, Mill tells us here. There must be "one principle" or "rule, or standard" at the base of our practical reasoning. Mill does go on in this section to express his belief that utility is "the ultimate principle of Morality." But it's clear that he thinks that that substantive position can be distinguished from the position of formal monism. He writes, "Without attempting in this place to justify my opinion…I merely declare my conviction that the general principle to which all rules of practice ought to conform, and the test by which they should be tried, is that of conduciveness to the happiness of mankind, or rather, of all sentient beings…" (Mill 1843/1904, 658). Note the contrast between the surety of the claim that there must be a single standard ("There must be some standard…[a]nd there can be but one") and the provisionality of the claim that conduciveness to happiness is that standard ("Without attempting…to justify my opinion…I merely declare my conviction…"). Mill takes the formal claim of monism to be firmly in place, and is only gesturing toward his substantive view while acknowledging that it has not yet been established. The formal step comes first; the substantive step second.[3]

Kant does not separate the formal and substantive steps of monism as explicitly as Mill does in the *Logic*. But there are places in the *Groundwork of the Metaphysics of Morals* where he proceeds as though morality's having a single ultimate end has already been established and that the philosophical task at hand is to figure out what exactly that end is. When he tells us in the preface that the "present groundwork…aims only to seek out and establish *the supreme principle of morality*" (Kant 1785/2002, 193), he is proceeding on the idea that the question to be answered is what *the* ultimate principle of morality is, not whether there is only one such principle. Kant later contends that the worth of relative or material ends can "provide no universal principles, no principles valid and necessary for all rational beings and for every act of will—that is, it can provide no practical laws. Consequently all these relative ends are only the ground of hypothetical imperatives. Suppose, however, there were something *whose existence in itself* had an absolute worth, something that, as an end *in itself*, could be a ground of definite laws. Then in it and in it alone, would the ground of a possible categorical imperative, that is, of a practical law, reside" (Kant 1785/2002, 228; see also 217). Note how he pivots from the plural to the singular when making the transition from material, relative *ends* to an *end* that can be the ground of a practical law or categorical imperative. Immediately following this passage, Kant argues that humanity or rational nature is the end that grounds the practical law and categorical imperative. That argument is powered by the idea that morality requires one and only one thing with unconditional worth, one thing that is an end in itself. The formal aspect of monism—the notion that morality requires a single ultimate (unconditional, absolute, supreme) end—is already in place. What Kant's engaged in is the subsequent task of presenting the substantive content of the monistic view. Or as he puts it when discussing the first formulation: "There is therefore only one categorical imperative" (Kant 1785/2002, 222).[4]

Between this emphatic monism of Kant and Mill and the explicit multiplism of earlier moralists the contrast is striking. *The Whole Duty of Man*, Whichcote, Clarke, and Carmichael all took a three-part moral multiplism to be commonsensically and philosophically confirmed. Butler, Hume, Reid, Price, and Smith were equally confident that there were multiple ultimate moral ends, that Hutcheson was wrong to claim that there was only one. When we arrive at Kant and Mill, something has changed.

I believe this change was driven by justificatory concerns, not by metaphysical ones. Mill and Kant's monism grew out of the idea that our notions of moral justification commit us to there being a single ultimate moral end; it was not based on metaphysical commitments that tell for or against a meta-ethics that is rationalist, constructivist, sentimentalist, mind-independent realist, etc.

What I think Mill and Kant took to be the insurmountable problem for pluralism is that it is not able to account properly for moral justification in cases in which ultimate moral ends come into conflict with each other—a problem that did not arise when it was assumed that all the multiple ends fit together perfectly (non-conflict multiplism) but did arise when the prospect of such conflict started to become apparent (conflict multiplism). If pluralists hold that both of two ultimate ends are on the bottom floor of moral justification, they will also have to hold that there is no more fundamental moral end that tells us why we ought to act on one of those moral ends rather than the other when they conflict. If pluralists hold that two truly basic moral reasons require incompatible actions, then they must also hold that there is no more basic moral reason for acting on one of those reasons rather than the other. Of course there may be a third ultimate moral end that requires the same course of action as one of the first two, but that third end will not add anything more justificatorily fundamental to the mix. There will then be the same kind of conflict between ultimate ends, except that now there will be two ends on one side of the conflict and one end on the other. (The pluralist will surely not want to say that two moral ends have invariable moral justificatory superiority to one simply because the number two is larger than the number one.) Pluralism implies, therefore, that whether the agent acts on the first end or the second is a morally arbitrary matter. Pluralists are committed to denying that any moral justification can be given for such a choice. They can allow aesthetic or self-interested or etiquette-based reasons for acting one way rather than the other. But they will not be able to accommodate a *moral* reason to do so, and that's because they have to say that the moral reasons are still in a state of conflict after having exhausted all of their justificatory force.

According to the monists, however, it's part of our concept of morality to think that moral justification comprehends more than that—that moral justification doesn't give out where pluralism must leave it. When arguing for the superiority of his pluralist view over monistic versions of Kantianism and utilitarianism, Ross says, "[I]t is more important that our theory fit the facts than that it be simple, and the account we have given above corresponds (it seems to me) better than either of the simpler theories with what we really think..." (Ross 1930, 19). But the claim we are examining here is that "what we really think" about moral justification corresponds better with monism. This pressure toward monistic moral theory does not come from outside commonsense moral thinking but from within the everyday practice of moral justification. The concern about the arbitrariness of pluralist judgment in cases of moral conflict is (according to monists) part of "ordinary moral consciousness" itself.

Monistic accounts meet these commonsense concerns about moral justification. Monistic accounts tell us that there is only one fundamental moral end. Thus, according to monism, if there is a conflict between two moral ends, then one of three things will be the case. First, one of those ends is ultimate and the other is derivative, in which case there will be a moral justification to act on the ultimate end. Second, both ends are derivative on the single ultimate end but one derivative end will more effectively promote or more fully accord with the ultimate end than the other, in which case there is a moral justification to act on that first derivative end. Or third, both derivative ends promote or accord with the ultimate end to an equal extent, in which case there is a moral justification to act on either of the derivative ends (i.e. the agent's duty will be disjunctive). Pluralist theories tell us which factors to consider when making moral judgments, but they cannot adjudicate between those factors when they pull in opposite directions. Monistic theories, in contrast, hold out the promise of justificatory finality—of filling the justificatory gap between principle and judgment (Seung and Bonevac 1992).

We can illustrate this monistic argument by considering how a simple kind of pluralism handles a couple of stock scenarios. (We'll look later at more complex pluralisms and ask whether the monistic charge sticks to them; right now our goal is just to understand the charge.) The simple pluralism holds that we have an ultimate moral end to keep our promises and that we have an ultimate moral end to prevent the suffering of innocent people. In the first scenario, the only way you can prevent an innocent person from losing both her legs is by breaking your promise to help a friend move furniture from one apartment to another. In the second scenario, by breaking your promise to help a friend move furniture you will prevent someone else from getting a scratch on his little finger. Now it's commonsensical to hold that breaking your promise is the right thing to do in the first scenario and the wrong thing to do in the second scenario. But the simple pluralism cannot accommodate a moral justification for the difference between these two judgments—or, perhaps I should say, cannot accommodate a justification for the judgment that there is a difference between these two cases. It tells us that the agent has a basic moral reason to keep promises and a basic moral reason to prevent suffering, and that's the end of its justificatory story. It hasn't any further resources it can marshal to show that in these sorts of scenarios one of those moral reasons is justificatorily superior to the other. Those who hold the simple pluralist view will want to say that in the first scenario the end of preventing suffering overrides the end of keeping promises and that in the second scenario the end of keeping promises overrides the end of preventing suffering. But they won't be able to provide a justification for this judgment of overridingness. Simply saying that in this particular situation one end overrides another is not the same thing as giving a justificatory reason for that overridingness. "Overrides" here is a justificatory placeholder that the pluralist cannot fill.[5]

So the pluralist story has moral justification give out sooner than we think it actually does. The monist, in contrast, has a perfectly fitting justificatory tale to tell. According to the monist, there is one and only one ultimate moral end underlying both the keeping of promises and the prevention of innocent suffering. And that single moral end will fund a justification for acting one way rather than another in the two scenarios. Mason expresses well this monistic criticism when she writes: "On [the pluralist] picture then, when reasons have run their course, we are choosing without reasons. It doesn't matter hugely whether we call that 'rational' (it is not rational in the strong sense, but it is in the weak sense)—what matters is whether this weak sense of rational is sufficient to satisfy our concept of moral choice as being objectively defensible. The problem is that choosing without reasons looks rather like plumping. Plumping may be an intelligible form of choice, but it is questionable whether it is a satisfactory account of moral choice" (Mason 2011).[6]

This argument does not saddle the monist with any particular position on strict moral dilemmas. Maybe there truly are moral dilemmas and maybe there aren't. Maybe moral monism can accommodate true moral dilemmas and maybe it can't. But commonsense does not take the two scenarios just discussed to be moral dilemmas. It is commonsensical to think that one option clearly does morally override the other—that it is morally right to break a promise in order to prevent extreme suffering, and that it is morally wrong to break a promise to prevent a very small annoyance. And it is commonsensical to think that there is some moral justification for those judgments—that those judgments do not outstrip our moral justificatory resources. Maybe moral justification does give out in the case of true moral dilemmas, but simple pluralism does not seem to be able to avoid the implication that moral justification gives out well before that. Or, put another way, simple pluralism does not seem to be able to avoid the implication that those two scenarios are moral dilemmas, despite commonsense's taking them not to be dilemmatic. So insofar as monism and pluralism aim to capture commonsense moral thinking, monism is superior.

An important feature of this argument for monism is that it doesn't rest on any commitment to mind-independent moral facts, or indeed to any particular metaphysical position on moral entities at all. The central idea is that essential to the function of moral judgment is its role in resolving practical quandaries. Moral judgment meets our critical need for some method for making justifiable rather than merely arbitrary decisions. This is a metaphysically neutral motivation for monism.

The monistic argument has an analogical resemblance to a Hobbesian argument for a single absolute sovereign.[7] On this Hobbesian view, if there are two members of a single commonwealth with equal authority and those two members come into conflict with each other, then neither member will be able to resolve the conflict by exercising his authority. That's because, by hypothesis, neither member's authority is superior to the other's. The two members will thus be in a state of nature *vis-à-vis* each other—unless there is a third party who has an authority superior to both of them who can adjudicate their dispute. By hypothesis the two are members of a single commonwealth, not in a state of nature, so there must be a third party with superior authority. But what if there is a fourth member who has an authority equal to the third member? Then when the third and fourth members come into conflict with each other, there must be a fifth member with an authority superior to both of theirs, else those two find themselves in a state of nature *vis-à-vis* each other, contrary to our hypothesis. Thus, if there truly is a commonwealth—a state in which all conflicts are resolved by authority—there must be a single supreme sovereign. For if supreme authority is shared between two or more members, then those members will be in a state of nature *vis-à-vis* each other, not in a commonwealth.

The soundness of this Hobbesian argument concerning political sovereignty need not concern us here. My point is that Mill and Kant thought the

Hobbesian-like requirement of an authoritative way of resolving conflict applies to the moral realm, albeit with the authority inhering in practical principles instead of people. As Hill puts it in his commentary on Kant's *Groundwork*:

Assuming that two or more allegedly supreme executive authorities in a state can issue conflicting orders, then neither one would really be the supreme authority. Either there would be an unsolvable dilemma in the system or there must be a higher authority who can settle the conflict. Kant thought the first alternative intolerable in both law and morals, and he no doubt thought it obvious that conflicting prescriptions cannot come from the highest authority if they must be reconciled by appeal to a higher authority. For similar reasons, assuming that consistency is a hallmark of rationality, the most basic unconditional standards of rational choice cannot fall into irreconcilable conflict. If there is a Categorical Imperative, then, it seems to follow that there can be only one or, if several, they cannot prescribe incompatible courses of action. (Hill 2002, 121)

Here's a passage from Kant's *Metaphysics of Morals* that suggests that idea that the concept of morality forbids conflict between ultimate moral ends, in a way analogous to the way that the concept of a Hobbesian commonwealth forbids conflict between those with supreme authority: "A *conflict of duties* would be a relation between them in which one would cancel the other (wholly or in part). But since duty and obligation are concepts that express the objective practical *necessity* of certain actions and two rules opposed to each other cannot be necessary at the same time, if it is a duty to act in accordance with one rule, to act in accordance with the opposite rules is not a duty but even contrary to duty; so a *collision of duty and obligations* is inconceivable" (Kant 1797/1991, 50). Kant puts the point here in rational terms of "objective practical necessity," but the basic idea that the concept of morality forbids irresolvable conflict can be abstracted from Kant's rationalist commitments. For the basic idea is that there has to be a way of resolving conflict that is non-arbitrary, morally principled. And one can subscribe to that idea without having to hold that the concept of morality or the principles that resolve conflict need be purely rational.

Indeed, a non-rationalist version of Kant's idea that a conflict of moral duties is conceptually incoherent is just what we have already seen in Mill's *Logic*, wherein he writes: "There must be some standard by which to determine the goodness or badness, absolute and comparative, of ends, or objects of desires. And whatever that standard is, there can be but one: for if there were several ultimate principles of conduct, the same conduct might be approved by one of those principles and condemned by another; and there would be needed some more general principle, as umpire between them" (Mill 1843/1904, 658). Mill draws on similar monistic ideas in *Utilitarianism*:

There exists no moral system under which there do not arise unequivocal cases of conflicting obligation ... If utility is the ultimate source of moral obligations, utility may be invoked to decide between them when their demands are incompatible ... while in other systems, the moral laws all claiming independent authority, there is no common umpire entitled to interfere between them; their claims to precedence one over another rest on little better than sophistry, and unless determined, as they generally are, by the unacknowledged influence of considerations of utility, afford a free scope for the action of personal desires and partialities. (Mill 1861/2001, 25–6)

Mill takes the "moral obligations" or "moral laws" concerning non-deception, gratitude, promise-keeping and the like to be "secondary principles." He points out here that these will inevitably come into conflict with each other. He then maintains that there must be a single "first principle" to adjudicate or "umpire" such disputes. For if there were no such first principle—as pluralist views (which he here calls "other systems") imply—our decisions about what to do in such cases would be morally arbitrary, unjustified, based on nothing but "sophistry," or "personal desires and partialities."

The background requirement that morality provide principles for resolving any potential conflict—the rejection of moral pluralism on formal grounds—is also apparent in Sidgwick. Sidgwick surveys commonsense moral thinking. He finds that it involves moral principles that sometimes come into conflict with each other. But Sidgwick takes it to be a given that the true account of morality cannot involve such conflict. As Sidgwick puts it:

[I]t is obvious that any collision between two intuitions is proof that there is error in one or the other, or in both. Still, we frequently find ethical writers treating this point very lightly. They appear to regard a conflict of ultimate rules as a difficulty that may be ignored or put aside for future solution, without any slur being thrown on the scientific character of the conflicting formulae. Whereas such a collision is absolute proof that at least one of the formulae needs qualification: and suggests a doubt whether the correctly qualified proposition will present itself with the same self-evidence as the simpler but inadequate one; and whether we have not mistaken for an ultimate and independent axiom one that is really derivative and subordinate. (Sidgwick 1907, 341)

Sidgwick then goes on to argue that utilitarianism is most successful at resolving the conflicts between our moral intuitions—that utilitarianism does the best job of accommodating commonsense morality while also eliminating all moral conflict. This necessarily requires revising commonsense morality to some extent, as commonsense morality involves moral conflict. But Sidgwick's point is that utilitarianism retains the most of commonsense morality that is possible while also eliminating conflict. As he puts it, "[I]t must be observed that Utilitarianism furnishes us with a common standard to which the different elements included in the notion of Justice may be reduced. Such a standard is imperatively required: as these different elements are continually liable to conflict with each other" (Sidgwick 1907, 447). The point I want to draw attention to is that Sidgwick does not even consider the possibility that the true account of morality is pluralist—i.e. such as involving conflict between truly ultimate moral ends. For Sidgwick the question is: which account that eliminates all ultimate moral conflict is best? He does not consider the question: is an account that eliminates all moral conflict or an account that allows for such conflict best?

The Hobbesian-like argument for formal monism has been common in recent moral philosophy as well. Ronald Dworkin maintains that since a pluralist view implies that we are "subject to two sovereigns" and that "the command of each counts for nothing in the eyes of the other," pluralism is committed to holding that we can be placed in a "tragic difficulty" in which we "must choose, and each choice is a final and terrible disloyalty" (Dworkin 2001, 82). Our actual moral situation is, however, "very different" from that. We take our moral commitments not to originate in "two independent" principles. "On the contrary, we are drawn to each of the rival positions through arguments that, if we were finally to accept them as authoritative, would release us from the appeal of the other one" (Dworkin 2001, 82). Dworkin is focused in this essay on the principles of liberty and equality, but his point here is more general. He is arguing for the view that our moral concepts forbid us from thinking that we have independent ultimate moral ends that can come into conflict with each other—and that's because our moral concepts imply that there is always a single justificatory sovereign that can resolve all moral disputes.

Lawrence Kohlberg built the same prioritarian commitment into his influential psychological theory of moral development. According to Kohlberg, there are six stages of moral development. Few people ever reach the sixth stage, but it is the conception of morality that sixth stagers attain that is the highest, most correct. The sixth stage is true moral understanding. And one of the essential features of the sixth stage is belief in a single supreme principle that resolves all moral conflict, that eliminates any "unresolved conflicting claims" (Kohlberg 1981, 194). The highest stage of moral thinking is reached only by those who realize that their moral obligations are "directly derived from a substantive moral principle that can define the choices of any person without conflict or inconsistency. This, of course, was the original intent of Kant's categorical imperative as well as the intent of the earlier act utilitarianism" (Kohlberg 1981, 162). Sixth stagers recognize a single supreme principle as "unconditional" (164), "basic" (175), "central" (176), as "higher" (164) than and "taking precedence" over any other (120). People at lower stages of moral development recognize a number of potentially conflicting moral rules, but those

at the highest stage understand that there must be a fundamental principle that
tells us what to do when those rules conflict. "A moral principle has some of the
properties of a moral rule, but a principle is different from a rule... *A moral principle is a rule or method of choosing between legitimate alternatives.* A rule says,
'Don't do that' or 'Do that'—it prescribes an action. A principle is some rule that
tells us how to make a choice between two more-or-less legitimate or ruleful alternatives. A rule tells us we must not steal and a rule tells us we must maintain the
lives of others in our family, but there is no set rule that tells us which to prefer
if we must choose one... [A principle] must be general: it must order all the relevant decisions, or it will lead to inconsistency or conflict" (220). Kohlberg's view
that pluralism is a lower stage and monism the highest is evident in his discussion
of "Richard." Richard, according to Kohlberg, is advancing in moral development
when he moves from responding to moral dilemmas by irresolutely describing
reasons for acting in two incompatible ways ("Given the... responsibility to save
human life... he probably shouldn't, but there is another side...") to resolutely
deploying a single, invariable principle of resolution ("Yes. A human life takes
precedence over any other moral or legal value, whoever it is.") (119–20). Those
who respond to moral dilemmas by ruminating on how different values pull in
opposite directions still have some moral growing up to do. Those who deploy a
single principle that cleanly and decisively settles the matter have achieved full
moral maturity.[8]

Attfield presses a similar criticism of pluralist theories, arguing that any successful moral theory must "supply a priority rule for conflicts between rules or
between practices" (Attfield 1987, 105–6). A pluralist view that identifies multiple
basic duties (of which Attfield takes Ross to be the exemplar) "is no help at all: for
we still lack a criterion for discovering, when *prima facie* obligations conflict, what
is our real obligation" (Attfield 1987, 106). Attfield goes on to say: "It may, of course,
seem to be a possibility that there just is no such rational criterion... Yet... it is difficult to credit that the unavailability of such a criterion is even possible. Nor does
experience confirm the pervasiveness of moral deadlock with a pluralistic deontological theory (involving a plurality of rules between which conflicts cannot be
resolved) would lead us to expect" (Attfield 1987, 106). Attfield's charge that pluralism fails because it does not provide principled guidance in cases of moral conflict
can also be found in H. W. B. Joseph, who argues that actions "which we judge that
we ought to do must have some common character to be a ground why we ought to
do them. It is not enough to say that we ought to do each on the ground of its own
specific nature; our obligations are not a heap of unrelated obligations" (Joseph
1933, 92).[9] This supposedly fatal objection to pluralism has been directed specifically at Ross.[10] But if there's a problem here, it will afflict Humean pluralism as well.

This belief in the inadequacy of pluralism is also prevalent in the field of bioethics, most notably in arguments against the principlist approach of Beauchamp and Childress (2009). Beauchamp and Childress's principlism is a form of moral pluralism, consisting of a multiplicity of potentially conflicting fundamental moral principles and no strict priority ordering for resolving such conflicts when they occur. Critics such as Gert et al. (1997) maintain that such a view fails to meet an essential requirement that we place on any moral theory, which is to provide determinate guidance about what to do when moral reasons appear to be in conflict. Gert et al. also affirm a multiplicity of moral rules, but they go on to insist that "[i]t is a philosopher's job to explicate, clarify, and organize these rules. More importantly, a philosopher must show how these rules fit within a system, so that conflicts between the rules can be resolved" (Gert et al. 1997, 5). Because the pluralist approach of Beauchamp and Childress has no underlying organizational rule for resolving moral conflict, according to Gert et al., "its 'principles' are really misnomers, since … they are not action guides at all" (Gert et al. 1997, 75). Pluralism, on this view, does not accurately describe morality because it simply gives us "a number of conflicting principles without being told how to rank them or how to resolve the conflicts between them" (Gert et al. 1997, 86). Gert et al. take to be a decisive general objection to pluralism that it implies that "even if the individual principles are interpreted as action guides, they often conflict with each other. [But] there is no agreed-upon method for resolving these conflicts… [T]here is no underlying theory to appeal to for help in understanding or resolving conflicts" (Gert et al. 1997, 87).

I think it is undeniable that these concerns about moral pluralism do capture an aspect of commonsense views of moral justification and that they do have monistic implications. The drive toward a single supreme moral principle that Kant, Mill, Sidgwick, and contemporary thinkers describe is present in ordinary moral thinking. But ordinary moral thinking also includes ultimate rules and goals that sometimes exert conflicting demands. If our purpose is simply to chart the contours of our pre-reflective moral thinking, this is a tension we must admit.

But what if we want to bring to our moral thinking more conceptual coherence? Of the pluralist and monistic aspects of commonsense morality, which would we do better to keep and which jettison?

I think this is a question worth asking because I don't think it's entirely unrealistic to consider winnowing our fundamental moral ends down to a single one, or to a hierarchically ordered set. Certain people do seem to be less pluralist than others, and while we may not be able to predict that a particular person is capable of ridding herself of all pluralist tendencies, some of us may be capable of significant change on this score. We have seen that Haidt and Bjorklund maintain that there are five sentimentally grounded fundamental moral ends (Haidt and Bjorklund 2008). But Haidt and Graham deny that all of these five ends get a grip on everyone's moral thinking (Haidt and Graham 2007). The moral thinking of some people, according to Haidt and Graham, is based on only two fundamental ends. (Specially, they claim that the moral thinking of conservatives is built on concerns about harm, reciprocity, group loyalty, hierarchy, and purity, while the moral thinking of liberals is built only on concerns about only harm and reciprocity.) And it doesn't seem to me unlikely that there are still other people whose moral thinking is based on only one fundamental end, or on a strict hierarchical moral structure. Certain extremely observant religious people may be this way, as may be those whose lives are consumed by a single cause (whether Marxist, feminist, libertarian, environmental, Kantian, utilitarian, or whatever). While we may not be able to alter the deep patterns of our moral thinking all at once by a snap of the fingers, we probably can, if we put in the effort, effect some significant change over time—by comporting with certain kinds of people rather than others, by controlling carefully our reading and viewing diet, by consciously bringing our intellectual attention back to certain ideas. It seems reasonable to ask, therefore, whether prioritarian ways of life are superior to pluralist, and thus whether we ought to make such efforts. Maybe many of us have pluralist tendencies right now. But should we work on ourselves to try to become prioritarian? In the next two chapters I'll explain why I think we should not—why prioritarianism isn't superior after all.

8

Humean Pluralism and Moral Justification

The monistic view we examined in the previous chapter holds that we must reject pluralism because it cannot accommodate moral justification, that pluralism implies that our moral judgments are arbitrary. In this chapter, I will argue to the contrary that Humean pluralism can accommodate moral justification—up to a point. It cannot accommodate all of the moral justification that some kinds of monistic theories can, but that does not mean it cannot accommodate any moral justification at all.

If there is only one ultimate moral end implicated in a certain situation (if in this situation the other moral ends simply don't come to bear), then the pluralist can hold that whichever course of action best accords with that one moral end is the morally justified one. If there are two or more ultimate ends implicated in a situation but all of them require the same course of action, then the pluralist can once again hold that that course of action is completely morally justified. If in a particular situation an agent has many different courses of action available to her but only two of those courses of action accord with the relevant ultimate moral ends, the pluralist has the resources to say that the agent is justified in following one of those two courses rather than any others; the pluralist can explain why all those other courses of action are wrong, significantly narrowing the morally legitimate choices even in those cases in which it does not uniquely select one (Wolf 1992).

I now want to argue, moreover, that even in cases in which they hold that ultimate moral ends do conflict, pluralists can still accommodate certain kinds of justification for acting on one end rather than the other. And while pluralism is not able to provide everything monists want from moral justification, versions of monism either fail to provide that as well (see Hill 1992), or provide it at prohibitive cost to the rest of the theory. To get this argument going, let's start by developing our scenarios from the last chapter in a bit more detail.

In scenario one, you are driving to a friend's house because you have promised to help her move from one apartment to another across town; she's rented a moving van for the morning, and you're going to help her load and unload her furniture. On your way to her apartment, you spot by the side of the road a wrecked car. Slowing down, you see that the driver is sitting on the ground by the side of the car, bleeding and dazed. You decide that the right thing to do is stop and assist the driver even though it means failing to fulfill your promise to your friend.

In scenario two, as in scenario one, you are driving to a friend's house because you have promised to help her move, and on your way you spot a car stopped by the side of the road. But when you slow down in scenario two, you see that the car has a flat tire. Upon inquiry, you find that the driver is fine, but he is having difficulty fixing the flat. The driver goes on to tell you that he has called a tow truck but that it will be forty-five minutes arriving, and that he will as a result miss an important meeting. You could help the driver with the flat so that he will make his meeting (you are adept at changing tires), but then you will not make it to your friend's house in time to help her load the moving van. So you decide the right thing to do is drive on so that you can fulfill the promise to your friend, even though it means that you will do nothing to help the driver.

The monistic objection implies that all pluralism can accommodate your saying by way of justification for your decisions is: in the first case helping the motorist overrode keeping the promise, and in the second case keeping the promise overrode helping the motorist. But in fact pluralists can accommodate something more. They can accommodate what Beauchamp and Childress call the "justified balancing" of conflicting norms and not simply an "intuitive balancing," which is to say that they can accommodate the giving of "good reasons" for acting "on the overriding norm rather than on the infringed norm" (Beauchamp and Childress 2009, 23).[1]

Specifically, pluralists can cite a general principle about conflict between the duty to keep promises and the duty to lend assistance—a principle such as: generally, the duty to keep a promise morally overrides the duty to lend assistance, except in cases in which the need for assistance is dire. They could then go on to say that although the consequences of not helping the second motorist may have been negative (he would miss his important meeting, which may have been worse for him than it would have been for your friend if you were late showing up to help her move), they were not so dire that they justified breaking the promise to your friend, while the consequences of not helping the first motorist (he might suffer serious injury or death) were so dire that they did justify breaking the promise. We can imagine a similar pair of scenarios in which the conflicting duties are the duty not to lie and the duty not to cause unhappiness. And you might offer by way of justification for choosing to lie in one case and not in the other the general principle that the duty not to lie overrides the duty not to cause unhappiness, except in cases in which the unhappiness that would be caused by telling the truth is dire.

Because this view holds that some duties have a certain kind of general priority over others, it bears a resemblance to Reid's theory, which included "comparison" principles for conflicts between duties, such as the principle that the duty of justice overrides the duty of generosity. But unlike Reid's theory, this view remains pluralist—remains anti-prioritarian—in that it denies that there are exceptionless ordering rules that close entirely the justificatory gap between principles and particular moral judgments when different duties conflict. Whether the negative consequences of keeping a promise are significant enough to justify not keeping the promise is itself a moral question, and this view denies that there are any strict or determinate principles for answering it. Moral justification, on this pluralist view, does not give out at the moment of conflict between two duties. One can pluralistically justify keeping a promise even though the consequences would be better by breaking it, by referring to the idea that one ought to keep promises unless the consequences are dire. But moral justification does give out short of a justification of what makes one set of consequences dire enough, and another set not dire enough, to override a promise.[2] If two people disagree about whether the consequences in a case are sufficiently dire to merit breaking a promise (or a single person is conflicted about the same issue), there may be no principle they (or she) can refer to for resolving their (or her internal) conflict. There may be a moral question here—the question of how dire a set of consequences really is, and whether or not it rises to the level that would justify breaking a promise—that, on this pluralist view, does not admit of a principled answer.

This is the kind of view Ross has in mind when he writes:

Suppose, to simplify the case by abstraction, that the fulfillment of a promise to A would produce 1,000 units of good for him, but that by doing some other act I could produce 1,001 units of good for B, to whom I have made no promise, the other consequences of the two acts being of equal value; should we really think it self-evident that it was our duty to do the second act and not the first? I think not. We should, I fancy, hold that only a much greater disparity of value between the total consequences would justify us in failing to discharge our *prima facie* duty to A. After all, a promise is a promise, and is not to be treated so lightly as a [strictly utilitarian theory] would imply. (Ross 1930, 34–5)

Ross does not deny that the duty to keep a promise can be morally overridden by the duty to promote the good. But he does claim that the good that would be created has to be highly significant for it to be acceptable to break a promise. The nature of promises is such that it takes especially important consequences to override them. There is thus some structure to the relationship between Rossian prima facie duties, with the duty to keep promises for the most part having priority over the duty to promote the good. But this is only "for the most part." The duty to promote the good does sometimes override the duty to keep promises, and there is no invariable and determinate rule that tells us whether or not we are in one of those unusual situations. As Ross puts it, "For the estimation of the comparative stringency of these *prima facie* obligations no [determinate and invariable][3] general rules can, so far as I can see, be laid down. We can only [affirm the somewhat vague and indeterminate rule] that a great deal of stringency belongs to the duties of 'perfect obligation'—the duties of keeping our promises, or repairing wrongs we have done, and of returning the equivalent of services we have received. For the rest, 'the decision rests with perception'" (Ross 1930, 41–2).[4]

This pluralist view is similar to what Michael Moore has called "threshold deontology" (Moore 1997). According to threshold deontology, there are truly non-consequentialist duties—the duty, for instance, not to torture a person even in cases in which the consequences of torturing him would be better than the consequences of not torturing him. This duty not to torture morally overrides the goal of creating better consequences. But if the consequences of not torturing are extraordinarily bad—if the consequences pass some threshold of horribleness—then it may be right to torture. Threshold deontology thus softens the "whatever the consequences" aspect of the strict deontological view of someone like Kant without completely abandoning the deontological intuition that underlies it. As Moore explains, "This aspect of absolutism is often attributed to Kant, who held that though the heavens may fall, justice must be done. Despite my non-consequentialist views of morality, I cannot accept the Kantian line. It just is not true that one should allow a nuclear war rather than killing or torturing an innocent person. It is not even true that one should allow the destruction of a sizable city by a terrorist nuclear device rather than kill or torture an innocent person. To prevent such extraordinary harms extreme actions seem to me to be justified" (Moore 1997, 719). It's not the case that we should decide whether to torture—or whether to lie or to break a promise—based solely on whether doing so will in that particular situation create better consequences than not doing so. The duty not to torture does not collapse into a duty to create the best consequences. Indeed, the duty not to torture overrides the goal of creating the best consequences in almost every circumstance. It's only when the consequences of acting on that duty are really, *really* terrible that the consequentialist goal should win out. As Moore puts it:

A consequentialist is committed by her moral theory to saying that torture of one person is justified whenever it is necessary to prevent the torture of two or more. The [threshold deontological view] is not committed to this proposition. To justify torturing one innocent person requires that there be horrendous consequences attached to not torturing that person—the destruction of an entire city, or, perhaps, of a lifeboat or building full of people.

On this view, in other words, there is a very high threshold of bad consequences that must be threatened before something as awful as torturing an innocent person can be justified. (Moore 1997, 721–2)

Of course, the threshold of bad consequences that has to be passed in order to justify breaking a promise to help a friend move furniture is not as high as the threshold that has to be passed to justify torture. But the general structure of Moore's threshold deontology captures the promise-breaking situation nonetheless. It's not the case that we should decide whether to keep our promises based solely on whether doing so will in each particular situation create better consequences than not doing so. The duty to keep promises does not collapse into the duty to create the best consequences. Indeed, the former duty will override the latter in a large majority of cases we will ever encounter. It's only when the consequences of keeping your promise are dire (albeit less dire than the destruction of a city) that the consequentialist goal should win out.[5]

Similar to the threshold deontological position is Hume's view of the conflict between justice and happiness. Hume thinks that in most typical cases in which justice and the happiness of society conflict, we ought to do what is just. But he also thinks that when the bad consequences of doing the just thing are extremely dire, we ought to do what will best promote happiness. As we have seen, Hume develops several scenarios in which the right thing to do is the just thing even though the unjust thing would produce better consequences. "[A] particular regard to the particular right of one individual citizen," he tells us, "may frequently, considered in itself, be productive of pernicious actions," and yet that right ought nonetheless be protected (E 3.3). Justice can demand, for instance, that we give money to someone even if he is "a vicious man, and deserves the hatred of all mankind," or a miser who "can make no use of" it or "a profligate debauchee" who "wou'd rather receive harm than benefit" from it (T 3.2.1.13, 11, and 14; see also T 3.2.6.9). In such situations, to do what is just will be incompatible with doing what is agreeable and useful, yet doing what is just may still be the all-things-considered right thing to do. Hume also develops scenarios, however, in which the right thing to do is to violate the rules of justice (E 8). One such scenario is during a shipwreck, when it is right for people to use the provisions washed ashore even though they do not belong to them. Another such scenario is during the siege of a city, when it is right for the starving people to break into a silo and eat grain that belongs to an absent land-owner. So what's the difference between the scenarios in which the good consequences of doing the unjust thing do not override the moral force of justice (such as when we should return money to a despicable bigot) and the scenarios in which the good consequences of doing the unjust thing do override the moral force of justice (such as when shipwrecked or besieged individuals make use of goods that do not belong to them)? The difference is that the bad consequences in the second pair of scenarios are very dire—doing the just thing in the second set of scenarios will cross some threshold of extreme badness that doing the just thing in the first set of scenarios will not—and it's only when this occurs that the duty to produce good consequences overrides the duty to be just.[6]

A great advantage of threshold-deontology-type views is that they capture what many people seem to think about moral justification in cases of conflicting duties. I suppose there are some non-consequentialist absolutists, who will never lie or break a promise though the heavens may fall, and perhaps there are some strict consequentialists, who will lie or break a promise whenever they believe the consequences will be even just slightly better than if they don't. But a great many people, it seems to me, think *both* that the duty to keep a promise will not be morally overridden simply because the consequences of not keeping it would be just slightly better *and* that the duty to keep a promise will be overridden if the consequences of keeping it are very significantly worse than the consequences of breaking it. Consider a person who is confronting a conflict between keeping a promise and doing what will create the best consequences. Imagine that she decides she should keep the promise. What would be plausible for her to say by way of justification? It seems to me she might very well say simply: it was a promise. It seems appropriate for her to offer as justification for her decision not to do what will create better consequences simply the fact that she has a duty to keep her promise—which carries with it the implication that, ceteris paribus, promise-keeping overrides creating the best consequences.[7] But now imagine she is in a different situation of conflicting duties and that this time she decides to break her promise in order to create better consequences. What would be plausible for her to offer as a justification for this second decision? Not simply: the results will be better. More plausible, rather, is that she would say something along the lines of: yes, I know I ought to keep a promise, but the consequences of doing so in this case are extremely dire. There is an asymmetry between the typical justification of keeping a promise when the consequences of doing so will be worse and the typical justification of breaking a promise when the consequences of doing so will be better. In the former case we can simply point to the fact that we have made a promise, while in the latter case we feel the need to expand on the especially significant consequences breaking a promise will result in. The former justification requires simply the indication of a promise that is to be kept, while the latter justification requires some indication of the especially dire nature of the consequences that are to be avoided (as opposed to an indication of simply marginally better consequences). And this carries with it the implication that the consequences of keeping a promise have to be extraordinarily bad—that ceteris *not* be paribus—in order for the duty to keep a promise to be overridden.

A number of people have maintained, however, that the notion of a threshold below which better consequences are morally overridden by deontological considerations and above which better consequences morally override deontological considerations is explanatorily empty or hopelessly ad hoc. Alexander (2000) and Ellis (1992) articulate this objection well when they argue that the claim that there is a distinct, codifiable threshold at which consequentialist duties outweigh non-consequentialist ones will inevitably be "paradoxical," "weird," or "counterintuitive"—that the notion that there is a "radical discontinuity" between cases in which consequences fail to override and cases in which they do override is too perniciously arbitrary to be part of a satisfactory moral theory.[8] To support this claim, Alexander and Ellis point to cases just below and just above the threshold. Imagine, for instance, that the threshold for torturing an innocent person is the saving of two hundred lives. Now imagine that a terrorist has planted a bomb that will kill one hundred and ninety-nine people but that we can prevent this if we torture his mother. By hypothesis, it's impermissible (flat-out wrong) to torture his mother. But if one other person is put in harm's way, it now becomes obligatory (flat-out wrong not to). Or imagine that the terrorist's bomb will kill two hundred, the police start torturing the terrorist's mother, and the terrorist then releases one hostage. By doing so, the terrorist has converted the torture of his mother from obligatory to impermissible. In both cases it looks as though the consequence of saving or killing just one person out of two hundred has effected a radical moral change—turning something that had been impermissible into something obligatory (or vice versa). And such a result is both weird and counterintuitive in itself as well as one that any theory other than strict consequentialism doesn't seem to be able to provide a reasonable explanation of.

Ellis and Alexander's objections may cause problems for those who seek to combine threshold deontology with a mind-independent or rationalist view of moral properties. But those objections fail to gain purchase if we accept a Humean sentimentalist account. For the Humean pluralist can make two points that combine to repel the concerns pressed by Ellis and Alexander.[9]

First, the Humean pluralist can hold that the moral question in the kinds of cases under discussion is the contrastive one of: which of two possible acts is morally better than the other? The moral question is not: does this particular act possess the (non-contrastive) property of moral obligatoriness or permissibility or impermissibility? I suppose that it might seem mysterious or weird that an act that saves the lives of one hundred ninety-nine people has the (non-contrastive) property of forbiddenness and not the property of obligatoriness *and* that an act that is exactly the same in every other way but saves the lives of two hundred people has the (non-contrastive) property of obligatoriness and not the property of forbiddenness. But there is nothing at all mysterious or weird about the idea that of these two acts, which are otherwise the same in every way, the one that saves the lives of two hundred is morally *better* than the one that saves the lives of one hundred ninety-nine. Similarly, there is nothing at all mysterious about the idea that of two acts that both involve breaking exactly the same kind of promise (or telling exactly the same kind of lie), the one that produces greater benefit to a third party is morally better than the one that produces less benefit to a third party. (Ellis and Alexander's criticism may seem particularly apt if we focus only on torture-and-killing examples in which there are distinct, quantifiable lives to be saved or lost, which can naturally give rise to the question of exactly how many lives need to be saved before the relevant threshold is reached. But if we don't let ourselves get distracted by extraneous features of certain kinds of examples—if, for instance, we also reflect on cases involving non-quantifiable issues concerning promises, lying, and the like—the criticism loses much of its initial force.) The sentiments in which our moral judgments originate may be suited to deliver judgments about which of a pair of actions is *better*—and those judgments will not be mysterious or weird or arbitrary just because the sentiments underlying them do not give rise to judgments that locate absolute joints between those acts that have a non-contrastive property of forbiddenness and those acts that have a non-contrastive property of obligatoriness. Perhaps some meta-ethical views about the origin of morality carry with them a commitment to actions' either possessing or not possessing some non-contrastive property of obligatoriness or forbiddenness. But Humean sentimentalism fits perfectly well with a contrastive view, one on which our moral judgments are ultimately judgments about which of two courses of action is better or worse.[10]

Of course the difficult choices are not between two actions that are otherwise identical but one saves the lives of two hundred and the other saves the lives of one hundred ninety-nine, or one produces greater benefit for a third party while the other produces less. The difficult choices are whether to do what saves many lives but involves torture or to do what avoids torture but leads to many deaths, or to do what produces benefit but involves lying or to do what avoids lying but leads to harm. In extreme cases—saving millions of lives or saving only one life in the case of torture, preventing the harm of death or the harm of a small inconvenience in the case of lying—it is easy to judge which act is morally better. But what about the cases in the middle, where it is hard to judge? Some may hold that there must exist a sharp line below which the act that involves torture or lying is worse and above which the act that involves torture or lying is better, even if it is not possible for us to determine exactly where that is. Some may be committed to the existence of clean joints in the world between the obligatory and the forbidden. But that is not the way the Humean pluralist has to go. (For this reason, the label of *threshold* deontology can mislead, as it suggests a radical moral discontinuity above and below some point. But this is an extraneous feature of the terminology that should not mislead us into thinking that the position in question is actually committed to such a discontinuity.) Indeed, if morality originates in sentiment, as the Humean maintains, then it makes perfect sense to hold that in the middle there are truly indeterminate cases, cases in which there is no fact of the matter[11] as to which of two acts is better—and this is the second aspect of the Humean pluralist's defense against Ellis and Alexander's criticism.

The sentiments in which our moral judgments originate may not be suited to give rise to distinctions that are finely grained enough to distinguish between every pair of cases we can imagine in which torture is necessary to save lives or in which promise-breaking is necessary to confer benefit. But that does *not* mean that they are unsuited to give rise to moral distinctions between any pair of cases— or indeed, that they are unsuited to give rise to distinctions between the pairs of cases we are most likely to confront in daily life. To see this, consider two other subjects in which (it's at least very plausible to claim) our contrastive judgments are based on sentiments: beauty and personal happiness.

Take two paintings, one by Vermeer and one by Thomas Kincade. It is perfectly clear to you that the Vermeer is more beautiful than the Kincade. There is nothing arbitrary about your drawing that distinction. Now imagine that there is a painting by $Vermeer_2$ that you judge to be slightly less beautiful than the one by $Vermeer_1$, and a painting by $Kincade_2$ that you judge to be slightly more beautiful than the one by $Kincade_1$. Chances are you will judge that the $Vermeer_2$ is more beautiful than the $Kincade_2$. Imagine next that there is a painting by $Vermeer_3$ that is slightly less beautiful than the painting by $Vermeer_2$, and a painting by $Kincade_3$ that is slightly more beautiful than the painting by $Kincade_2$. The chances are still high that you will judge the $Vermeer_3$ to be more beautiful than the $Kincade_3$. But at some (very high) N, you will judge that the $Kincade_N$ is more beautiful than the $Vermeer_N$. That does not imply, however, that for every pair of paintings there must be a fact of the matter as to whether one is more beautiful than the other. $Vermeer_{N-10}$ might be more beautiful than $Kincade_{N-10}$; $Kincade_N$ might be more beautiful than $Vermeer_N$; but it might be indeterminate (and not simply difficult to figure out) whether $Vermeer_{N-5}$ or $Kincade_{N-5}$ is more beautiful. Indeed, if aesthetic value originates in our sentiments, we should expect there to be such indeterminacy—we should not expect you to have an answer to every one of those aesthetic questions. For while our aesthetic sentiments may be developed in a way that gives rise to the distinction between many Vermeers and many Kincades (and thus ground non-arbitrary aesthetic comparative judgments about them), they may very well not be so finely grained that they can or should give rise to distinctions between every pair of paintings we could conceivably encounter. An expert aesthetic judge will be able to judge that a Vermeer has more aesthetic value than a Kincade without necessarily being able to tell us whether a Vermeer has more or less aesthetic value than a Rembrandt.[12] There is nothing in all of this that makes the activity of passing aesthetic judgments on paintings arbitrary or mysterious or weird. And what the Humean pluralist claims is that our activity of moral judgment can have the same kind of non-arbitrary (non-mysterious, non-weird) character, even though there are some indeterminate cases.

The same kind of considerations apply to judgments about your future happiness. Imagine you are deciding between two jobs. The actual work you will do at Job A is more appealing to you, but Job B pays $10 a year more in salary. You have no difficulty deciding to take Job A, as you reasonably believe that you'll be happier doing work that is more appealing to you even if it means making $10 less a year. Now consider you are deciding between Job A and Job B_1, which is the same as Job B but pays $11 a more than Job A. Still you have no difficulty deciding to take Job A; once again, you reasonably believe you'll be happier doing work that is more appealing to you even if it means making $11 less a year. On the other hand, if you are deciding between Job A and Job $B_{100,000}$, which pays $100,000 more than Job A, you will have no difficulty deciding to take Job $B_{100,000}$, as you'll reasonably believe that you'll be happier with $100,000 more a year even if it means doing work that is somewhat less appealing. But there may very well also be some range of Job B's—some B_N to B_{N+M}—at which you are unable to arrive at any clear idea of whether or not you'll be happier taking Job A. You might do your very best to determine all the possible effects of taking one or the other of the two jobs, and yet it still might be indeterminate to you which will make you happier. Indeed, it might be indeterminate not merely because of your limited predictive powers but because there really is no fact of the matter as to which life will be happier for you. In the throes of such decision-making, it might feel as though there's one unique course of action that will make you happier, if only you could figure out what it is. (It might feel like trying to decide which horse to bet on before a race.) But two different lives—one with significantly less money but a more interesting job, the other with significantly more money but a less interesting job—might be quite different from each other and yet not such that you could sensibly judge, even if you had complete knowledge of all contingencies, which is better. The benefits you receive from more money and the benefits you receive from more interesting work might not admit of finely grained enough composition for there to be a fact of the matter as to which of two courses of action is better for you even from a purely self-interested perspective. But that does not imply that your decision to take Job A over Job B, or your decision to take Job $B_{100,000}$ over Job A, is arbitrary. Your reasons for those decisions can be as cogent as anyone could ever hope for. Your sentiments may be well-suited enough to justify a decision about which job to take when confronted with many pairs of possible jobs, even if they are not fine-grained enough to justify a decision about which job to take when confronted with every pair of possible jobs.

Perhaps it will help to imagine a conversation you might have after you have chosen, upon careful deliberation, to take Job C (which has more interesting work) over Job D (which pays $X more). Your companion asks you why you made that choice. "The work at Job C is more interesting than the work at Job D," you tell him. "But," says your companion, "D pays more. Do you mean to tell me that you don't care how much money you make?" "No," you say, "I care about the money. I never said that I didn't. The kind of work I do matters a lot to me, but the money matters too. Actually, if D had come with another $[X+Y], I'm pretty sure I would have taken it even though Job C's work is more interesting." "So $X is not enough to outweigh more interesting work, but $[X+Y] is enough?" "Yeah. I guess so. That's about the size of it." Now suppose that your companion asks the further question: "But why? Why would $[X+Y] be enough money to take Job B, but $X is not enough? What's your principle for that?" And suppose you have no answer to that further question. You gave a reason for choosing C over D—$X is not enough money to outweigh the superiority of C's more interesting work, even if $[X+Y] would have been—but you cannot give another general or principle-based reason for that reason. Would that mean that your entire decision-making about what job to take has been arbitrary? That you haven't made any kind of legitimate judgment at all? No. Your decision may very well have been as reflective and reasonable as anyone could hope for, even if you can't give a reason for the difference the difference between $X and $[X+Y] makes to you. If we take a decision to be non-arbitrary only when every aspect of it can be justified by a general principle, then your decision to take C would be arbitrary. But if we take a decision to be non-arbitrary when it is reflective, reasonable, the result of an exercise of judgment—then your decision could very well be non-arbitrary.

In the aesthetic and personal happiness cases, the agent gives reasons for what she has decided. Her reasons may be such as to run out before they reach an answer for every situation that's principled in the way prioritarianism demands. But this does not vitiate all of her reason-giving. Her not being able to provide a completely principled explanation for every aspect of her decision-making in every possible case does not lead us to conclude that all of her decisions are completely arbitrary, unreflective, impulsive. We may take the job-taker to be making a very reasonable decision even though her reason-giving gives out before achieving the kind of justification demanded by prioritarianism. We may take her to have exhibited as much practical wisdom as one could ever hope for.

Humean pluralism holds that moral decision-making can have the same character as that of the aesthetic judge and the job-taker. An agent's moral decision-making will reflect her sentiments, what she cares about. The agent may care about things that come into conflict with each other, things that demand incompatible courses of action. And the agent's thinking about what to do is guided by what she cares about in a manner that can be captured by general principles, even if those principles are not determinate enough to imply a single answer to the question of what she should do in every case.[13]

If a set of judgments aspires to be fully rational or to scientifically describe the mind-independent natural world, it may make sense to hold those judgments to prioritarian justificatory requirements. If Humean sentimentalism is correct, however, our moral judgments involve sentiments in a way that should forestall those rationalistic or scientific aspirations. If Humean sentimentalism is correct, our moral judgments essentially reflect what we care about when considering character and conduct from a general point of view. There are multiple things that we care about. And it is inappropriate to hold judgments of this sort to the same justificatory requirements as math and science, just as it would be to hold to these requirements our judgments about beauty or happiness.

Monists object that pluralist moral judgment fails to fulfill an essential function of moral judgment, which is to resolve practical quandaries in a principled rather than arbitrary way. If one takes an all-or-nothing view of principledness and arbitrariness—something is either completely principled or completely arbitrary—then perhaps pluralist moral judgment will look to be arbitrary. But there is a fertile middle ground between these two extremes. Moral judgment can be more or less guided by principles, even if there is no one über-principle that is completely determinative for all cases. Pluralist moral judgment can thus fulfill the function of resolving our quandaries up to a point. It doesn't leave us with complete arbitrariness.[14] One of the main reasons we have cars is speed: to get us from point A to point B fast. That doesn't mean that a car that fails to go a hundred and twenty miles an hour is failing to fulfill its function. For we also want from our cars features other than speed, such as safety and economy. Similarly, there are things other than producing principled resolution of moral quandaries that matter to us about moral judgment, such as sensitivity to the particulars of each case and an avoidance of rigid reliance on overly simplistic rules. It may be that we take justificatory finality to be a goal of moral judgment. We may seek the most determinate justification we can come up with for our moral judgments. But that doesn't mean we value justificatory finality enough to make it reasonable to restrict our moral theorizing to monist theories, any more than desiring an automobile because it speeds up the daily commute makes it reasonable to consider for purchase only race cars.

In "Existentialism is a Humanism" Sartre tells the story (a variant of which we'll discuss in Chapter 10) of a student in the Second World War who had to choose between caring for his sick mother or fighting in the French Resistance. Sartre claims that there was no principled moral answer to the question of what the student should have done. Perhaps Sartre is right about that. Maybe the conflicting moral considerations in that case were close enough in strength and different enough in character that one could not have formed the judgment that either course of action was morally overridden by the other. But the possibility of such a situation should not drive us to the conclusion that there is never any justification for choosing one course of action over any other. Sartre is wrong if he thinks the story of the student shows that we can *never* have "behind us nor before us... any means of justification" (Sartre 1956, 353). The student was more justified in either staying with his mother or fighting with the Resistance than he would have been in volunteering to spy for the Nazis, or in running away to a life of dissolute pleasure in Vichy. If by leaving home the student knew he would save thousands of lives and cause merely mild inconvenience to his mother, then he would have been justified in leaving; if he were to have saved one fewer than those thousands of lives and caused very slightly more inconvenience to his mother, he would have still been justified in leaving. If by leaving he knew he would cause his mother great suffering while providing only the most minor help to a trivial cause, then he would have been justified in staying; if by leaving he would have caused his mother slightly less suffering and provided slightly more help to a slightly less trivial cause, he would still have been justified in staying. And our not being able to say where exactly the justificatory balance tips from leaving to staying—indeed, our thinking that in certain cases there is no determinate justificatory answer to the question—does not commit us to holding that the justification in those other cases is ersatz, illusory, or shallow.

9

Moral Justification, Three Prioritarian Views, and Principled Trade-Offs

Some might hold that prioritarianism is demanded by metaphysical considerations. A rationalist such as Samuel Clarke, for instance, would maintain that morality's originating in reason alone implies the impossibility of real conflict between ultimate moral ends. The mathematical structure of the universe can harbor no contradictions, and neither can the moral structure (which has the same metaphysical status). Perhaps some who have meta-ethical reasons for identifying morality with a single good-making property will also reject the possibility of conflict between ultimate moral ends. On certain views, prioritarianism may be an absolute requirement, a side constraint on moral theorizing.

But if Humean sentimentalism is true, there is no reason to take prioritarianism to be a side constraint on moral theorizing. If Humean sentimentalism is true, then our moral theorizing has to answer to our sentimentally grounded moral concerns, to what we care about, and we have no metaphysical assurance that these concerns will all fall into perfect prioritarian place.[1]

Do we care about completely principled moral justification? Would we prefer that all of our ultimate moral ends always pull in the same direction, that moral decision-making never required acting against an ultimate moral end? I believe we do. Do we care about first-order rules and goals that sometimes exert conflicting practical demands? I believe we do that as well. If our purpose is simply to chart the contours of our pre-reflective moral thinking, this is a tension we must admit.[2]

But what if we want to bring to our moral thinking more conceptual coherence? Which commitment—to the formal requirement of completely principled justification, or to a set of ultimate ends that sometimes conflict with each other—should we retain?

In the previous chapter, I tried to show that retaining the pluralist aspect does not entail abandoning moral justification altogether. It does not usher us into utter arbitrariness. It's true that we will have to accept that justification will sometimes give out before we have reached an ultimately adjudicatory principle. At the end of the day, we might be able to say only that the bad consequences in this case are so dire that they override the keeping of a promise, without being able to cite a principle that justifies our judgment of that direness. But that is not the same thing as lacking justification entirely. None of our accomplishments will last forever, but that doesn't mean they aren't real accomplishments. There may be nothing that bestows on our lives eternal meaning, but that doesn't negate the meaning our lives have in the time they are lived. Similarly, that in certain situations we can't give justificatory reasons for every aspect of our judgment does not imply that we can't give justificatory reasons at all. General moral rules and goals can still ground reasons that constitute an infrastructure for individual decision-making and interpersonal coordination.

What are the costs of retaining the prioritarian commitment and jettisoning the pluralist? Two hoary stories supposedly show that the cost of maintaining either of the grand modern prioritarian theories is the abandonment of deeply entrenched first-order moral judgments. The story that supposedly reveals this cost to monistic Kantianism is that of the murderer at the door who asks about the whereabouts of an innocent person you are harboring. Lie to the murderer and the innocent person will be safe. Tell the truth and the person will be killed. Monistic Kantianism supposedly implies that you ought to tell the truth, but that conflicts with what virtually everyone thinks you ought to do. So the question is: which is more costly to give up, the first-order judgment that you ought to lie to the murderer at the door or Kant's formal prioritarian commitment? If there is no antecedent metaphysical or rationally inescapable reason to think morality is monistic, then giving up the formal prioritarian requirement looks to be the way to go. An almost equally well-worn story supposedly shows the untenability of the utilitarian's monistic commitment. A doctor can save the lives of five hospital patients by secretly killing someone else who has checked into the hospital and harvesting her organs. Monistic utilitarianism supposedly implies that you ought to kill the one to save the five, but that conflicts with what virtually everyone thinks you ought to do. So which is more costly to give up: the first-order judgment that the doctor ought not to kill the person or the utilitarian's monistic commitment? Again, if there is no antecedent metaphysical or rationally inescapable reason to think morality is prioritarian, then giving up the monistic requirement looks to be the way to go.

These cases—the Murderer at the Door and the Inhospitable Hospital—should not be taken to show that what utilitarians or Kantians claim to be the ultimate ground of our moral judgments isn't an ultimate ground. They should be taken to show, rather, that what utilitarians or Kantians claim to be the ultimate ground isn't the only or invariably overriding ultimate ground. The Inhospitable Hospital isn't a counterexample to the claim of an ultimate moral concern to maximize welfare; it's a counterexample to the claim that maximizing welfare is the only ultimate or invariably overriding moral concern. The Murderer at the Door isn't a counterexample to the claim of ultimate moral concern to act on universalizable maxims or to treat humanity as an end in itself; it's a counterexample to the claim that that concern is the only ultimate or invariably overriding ultimate one. What these sorts of cases are supposed to reveal is not that we need to give up the bases of utilitarian and Kantian judgments. They are supposed to reveal the strength of our commitment to multiple ultimate moral ends that can come into conflict—a strength that is more powerful than the formal commitment to prioritarianism.

There are two kinds of responses prioritarians give to cases like the Murderer at the Door and the Inhospitable Hospital: the conservationist and the radical. Conservationists argue that in fact their positions do not have the counterintuitive results attributed to them. Radicals argue that their positions do have counterintuitive implications but that accepting those implications is the most coherent response. In this chapter we will look first at two conservationist monistic responses, then at one of the monistic radicals. We will close by examining another position—one that involves principles for all of our moral trade-offs—that might seem to offer a different and more attractive prioritarian alternative.

The major difficulty for monistic conservationists is to develop a position that does not have deeply counterintuitive results and really is monistic. This is a difficulty I don't think can be overcome. I think that in order to conserve the deeply entrenched intuitions they do in fact want to conserve, conservationists end up becoming pluralist after all. I do not have a perfectly general argument to show this. What I will do instead to try to make this contention plausible is argue that it accurately applies to two very well-developed and otherwise compelling conservationist accounts: the non-consequentialist view of Barbara Herman and the consequentialist view of Brad Hooker.[3]

Herman's Kantianism

On Herman's view, there can never be a conflict of moral obligations. This is because in every situation we will ever face, we will have one and only one obligation. Our one and only obligation in a situation is the result of proper practical deliberation on all the morally relevant considerations in that situation. Kant calls these morally relevant considerations "*grounds* of obligation," while Herman calls them "moral facts" (Herman 1993, 167). Say you are in a situation in which you can keep a promise or lend assistance to a friend but cannot do both. On Herman's view, that doing X will fulfill your promise is a moral fact. That doing Y will assist a friend in need is a moral fact. It's also a fact that you cannot do both X and Y. These facts are not in conflict with each other; they're just facts, all of which can be true of the world.

You may, however, experience something like conflict in this situation because you may "adopt a maxim" (or "set yourself") both to keep your promise and to lend assistance, "only to discover" that doing one of those things will make the other impossible. What this experience of conflict (which is not, according to Herman, a conflict of obligations, but rather merely the experience of having formulated an inconsistent maxim) indicates is that you are in a situation "in which deliberation is necessary" (Herman 1993, 167). You ought then to deliberate on the moral facts, your deliberation ought to be "guided by the CI [categorical imperative] procedure," and the result of that deliberation will be your one and only duty (Herman 1993, 168).

Will this CI procedure satisfy the formal monistic requirement we explicated in our earlier discussion of Mill and Kant? It will do so only if it provides more determinate guidance than simply identifying the morally relevant considerations (or moral facts, or grounds of obligation) about which we ought to deliberate. For Humean pluralism can also identify the distinctively moral considerations that ought to play a role in the formation of moral judgment, distinguishing what we approve of from the general point of view from what we desire merely out of selfishness or anger or hunger for revenge (T 3.1.2.4; E 9.6). Where Humean pluralism seems to the monist to fall short is in not being able to provide determinate guidance about how to adjudicate between conflicting moral demands themselves, and so if the CI procedure is going to do better on this score it does need to provide determinate guidance for deliberation about morally relevant considerations that pull in opposite directions.

Herman's discussion of the CI procedure has a negative and a positive aspect. The negative aspect consists of Herman's arguing that previous interpretations of the CI procedure have failed either because the moral conclusions they lead to are unacceptable or because they do not provide any workable moral guidance at all. What Herman calls the "derivation-of-duties model" fails for the first reason, because of its unacceptable results, generating as it does "a rigoristic ethics of duties and standing obligations... [On this interpretation] the CI procedure is taken to be the source of absolute, exceptionless prohibitions. Such a theory is rightly charged with insensitivity to moral complexity and righteous absurdity in requiring... that we keep all promises, tell no lies, regardless of the consequences" (Herman 1993, 133). What Herman calls the "practical and logic interpretations" fail for the second reason, because they do not provide deliberative guidance. These interpretations take the CI procedure to be a test of the moral acceptability of an agent's maxim, but the problem is that they cannot provide a non-arbitrary, non-question-begging way of determining what exactly an agent's maxim is in any particular situation. When we think that an action is morally acceptable, we attribute it to a maxim that we configure so that it passes the CI test; when we think that an action is morally unacceptable, we attribute it to a maxim that we configure so that it does not pass. But all the moral deliberation occurs before we deploy the test, in the configuration of the maxim. If an action we think morally acceptable seems not to pass the CI test, we can redescribe its maxim so that it does pass, but "this begs the questions of demonstrating that a given maxim is or is not permissible. For whether or not the maxim is to be redescribed seems to depend on our understanding its moral status prior to assessment" (Herman 1993, 140). The deep difficulty of these interpretations of the CI procedure is the lack of control on maxim-description. As Herman explains, "How would we determine the correct level of description except as the one that produces the desired moral result?... [A]ny such solution to the problem of erroneous results [i.e. the kind of perniciously rigoristic results that made the derivation-of-duties model unacceptable] undermines the independent authority of the CI procedure" (Herman 1993, 142). So on previous interpretations, the CI procedure implies moral conclusions either too counterintuitive to be acceptable or too indeterminate to be deliberatively effective.

With these negative conclusions of Herman's I am in complete agreement. I think her criticisms of these previous interpretations of the CI procedure do show how they fail to provide a principle that fulfills the formal monistic requirement and is independently acceptable. But I also think that Herman's own positive account of the CI procedure runs into the same problems: to avoid unacceptably counterintuitive results it must abandon the determinacy of moral guidance monism requires.

To see this, consider how Herman's theory handles the case of the Murderer at the Door. Herman seems initially to hold that her theory implies that we ought not to lie to the murderer at the door, as the nonrelative value of the integrity of a rational will makes deceiving someone even to save a life morally impermissible (Herman 1993, 156). But this is the kind of rigoristic, deeply counterintuitive result that led Herman to reject the "derivation-of-duties model." Herman then qualifies her conclusion, however, so that her CI procedure doesn't have as counterintuitive results as it first appeared. Even if it is impermissible to deceive to save a life, "it will not follow that we may never deceive when life is at risk. There is no a priori reason to suppose that no act of deception can accord with necessary respect for rational agency. It depends on the nature of the justifying reasons" (Herman 1993, 156). We might be able to justify deception to a murderer at the door by "arguing that a maxim of deception to repel or prevent aggression has as its object [the murderer's] abandonment of his impermissible maxim. The deception would then be in the service of a morally necessary purpose: a manipulation of a will to bring it into conformity with its own defining principles" (Herman 1993, 157). But now we should wonder whether Herman's CI procedure is any more determinate than the interpretations she dismissed as question-beggingly relying on prior moral judgments in order to formulate maxims to be tested. Surely deception isn't justified to manipulate an individual's will so as to bring it into conformity with its own defining principles *in all cases*. For that would mean we would have a duty to deceive people if by doing so we could keep them from breaking even a very minor promise to others.[4] So when is bringing someone else's will into conformity with its own defining principles a legitimate justification for deception and when is it not? It seems to me that Herman's CI procedure has the same indeterminacy problem in answering this question as Herman herself attributed to the interpretations of Kant that avoided unacceptably counterintuitive results—and, more importantly for our purposes, as monists attributed to pluralism. Herman's CI procedure might serve as a rough guide to deliberating about difficult moral cases, but it does not have the deliberative determinacy to satisfy the monistic requirement any more than pluralism does (see Hill 1992).

After raising the possibility that deception may sometimes be permissible, Herman writes, "As a methodological matter, it is an open question as to what sorts of reasons will rebut a deliberative presumption. It is a substantive claim of Kant's ethics that only a competing deliberative presumption can" (Herman 1993, 157). But so long as the CI procedure leaves the question of what will rebut a deliberative presumption open—so long as it tells us only that one moral consideration *can* override another moral consideration but not when it *does*—adherents of that procedure have no basis for claiming that their view succeeds, while pluralism fails, because the former is, and the latter is not, deliberatively determinate. The monistic requirement of deliberative determinacy is left equally unfulfilled in both cases.[5]

Hooker's Rule-Consequentialism

Let us now turn to a consequentialist conservationism: the rule-consequentialism of Brad Hooker. The rule-consequentialism Hooker develops includes prohibitions on "physically attacking innocent people or their property" and on "taking the property of others, lying, breaking one's promises, and so on" (Hooker 2000a,

17), as well as requirements "to help others" when the cost of helping is low and the benefit is high (Hooker 2000a, 16). Hooker's rule-consequentialism also includes rules allowing you to use your own resources "to favor your own parent, or child, or friend" rather than using them to promote the good of everyone impartially (Hooker 2000a, 17). Hooker's rule-consequentialism, in other words, consists of moral rules that capture very well commonsense morality, just as pluralism does.

The criticism of pluralism with which we have been concerned here is that it provides us with no non-arbitrary way of deciding what to do when those rules conflict with each other. I have argued that pluralism is not afflicted by a pernicious arbitrariness in the way that criticism implies. The question before us now is whether Hooker's rule-consequentialism provides us with any more principled way of deciding what to do when moral rules conflict. My contention is that it does not.

Hooker readily acknowledges that the rules of morality can come into conflict with each other (Hooker 2000a, 89). And he emphatically rejects the idea that such conflict should be resolved by abandoning the rules and doing whatever will produce the best consequences. That act-consequentialist route would provide us with more determinate guidance than pluralism, but it would also lead to profoundly counterintuitive results that Hooker wants to avoid. Hooker also rejects the idea that the rules should have built into them sophisticated exception clauses that would keep them from ever conflicting. This is because the correct moral rules must produce the best consequences when they are internalized, and very complicated rules are difficult and too costly to internalize.[6] As Hooker puts it, "A...misguided idea about how rule-consequentialism would resolve conflicts between rules is that it would build exceptions into the rules so as to keep them from conflicting...The problem with building in exception after exception is that the rules then become harder to learn. More demanding and more complex rules will have higher internalization costs. At some point, the added costs involved in learning more complicated rules will outweigh benefits" (Hooker 2000a, 89–90). The need Hooker discusses here for rules simple enough to internalize fits well with a Humean view, according to which morality grows out of actual psychological principles and our addiction to general rules that do not contain complex specifications.

So how should conflicts between moral rules be adjudicated? What Hooker says is this: "When moral requirements conflict, one should do, as Brandt writes, 'whatever course of action would leave morally well-trained people least dissatisfied'" (Hooker 2000a, 90). Hooker goes on to say that the "best version of rule consequentialism" holds that when "different moral considerations pull against each other," moral right and wrong "cannot be determined except by reference to the dispositions of a virtuous person" (Hooker 2000a, 90–1). This claim of Hooker's seems to me to be eminently sensible—but it is not one that is compatible with rejecting pluralism because pluralism does not provide any method for adjudicating conflict between moral rules. For Hooker's answer is no more determinate than what a pluralist can give. A pluralist can also affirm that when moral requirements conflict the right thing to do is whatever will leave morally well-trained people least dissatisfied. To the extent that Hooker's rule-consequentialism has a "method for determining what is right" when moral rules conflict, it is one that a non-prioritarian can adopt as well (Hooker 2000a, 21).

Other would-be prioritarians run into the same problem as Hooker. Gert et al. (1997) acknowledge that their moral rules can come into conflict with each other. When such conflict occurs, they maintain, the right thing to do is what, "given the morally relevant facts, [an] impartial rational person would publicly allow" (Gert et al. 1997, 46; see also 37). Now it's perfectly reasonable for Gert et al. to hold that correct moral judgments must be impartial and based on a justification one would favor being publicly allowed. But as they themselves acknowledge, those criteria do not ensure determinate guidance about what to do in cases in which moral rules conflict. Two different people, "both fully informed, impartial and rational, who agree that two actions count as the same kind of violation, need not always agree on whether to advocate that this kind of violation be publicly allowed" (Gert et al. 1997, 40; see also 232). And the same kind of disagreement can occur within a single person. One person can be drawn in opposite directions on the question of what to do when the moral rules conflict, and being told that she ought to do what is impartial and what she would favor being publicly allowed might not help her make her own decision any more than it will necessarily resolve all moral disagreements between people. Gert et al.'s impartial and public "framework" may very well facilitate "fruitful moral discussion," and help to "limit the range of morally acceptable behavior" (Gert et al. 1997, 232). But as with moral pluralism in general, it does not close the justificatory gap between conflicting principles and particular moral judgments (see also Gert 2007, 4).[7]

Hooker is very forthcoming about the similarities between his rule-consequentialism and the non-prioritarian pluralist view, which he takes to be exemplified by Ross's position on the content of morality. Like Ross, with whom I too agree, Hooker denies that the moral rules are "lexically ranked," contending that "the correct resolution of a conflict between two duties in one set of circumstances can differ from the correct resolution in other circumstances" (Hooker 2000a, 132). Also like Ross, Hooker thinks that there are some general rules of thumb for resolving conflict between moral rules, such as that duties not to injure or not to lie are "*normally* stronger" than duties to benefit others. These are only general rules of thumb, however, with the qualification *normally* signaling that "if the difference between the size of the injury and the benefit is large enough, the priority is reversed" (Hooker 2000a, 133). As well, Hooker includes a "disaster prevention" rule (Hooker 2000a, 98–9) that coincides with the threshold deontological point Moore and others advanced and which I tried in the previous chapter to appropriate for the Humean pluralist view. In addition, Hooker acknowledges the need for uncodifiable "judgment" in many situations, including in the resolution of conflicts between duties (Hooker 2000a, 106–7).

So in what way does Hooker think his rule-consequentialism superior to pluralism? As Hooker explains it, rule-consequentialism has a "principle underlying the others," a single principle that "ties together" the various general duties (Hooker 2000a, 15–17). Pluralism, in contrast, because it lacks such a principle, leaves us with a mere "unconnected heap" of duties (Hooker 2000a, 21). And of two theories that are otherwise equal, the one that has a unifying principle is superior to the one that doesn't.

We need to ask, however, why a theory with a unifying principle is superior to one without. There are two ways in which such superiority can be attained. But I don't think Hooker's rule-consequentialism achieves either of these over pluralism.

First, a moral theory with a unifying principle could be superior because it provides more practical guidance than a theory without. It could shed more light on how to decide what to do in difficult moral cases. Hooker certainly believes that his rule-consequentialism does better than pluralism on this score, but I think the examination of his theory's way of dealing with conflict between moral rules shows that this is not the case.[8] As we have seen, Hooker's "method" for dealing with situations in which moral principles conflict is to take the course of action that would leave morally well-trained people least dissatisfied, or to do what one thinks a "virtuous person" would be disposed to do. But Hooker gives an agent no further method for determining the dispositions of virtuous or morally well-trained people other than that of trying herself, through reflection and judgment, to determine how such people would deal with the conflict between moral principles—no further method, in other words, than trying herself to determine what is virtuous or moral. Hooker's method thus collapses into the same position pluralists advance on decision-making in cases of moral conflict. But if what Hooker's rule-consequentialism endorses are rules that are pretty much the same as what pluralism endorses, and if Hooker's rule-consequentialism doesn't give more determinate advice about how to resolve conflicts between the moral rules than pluralism does, then Hooker's rule-consequentialism provides no more practical guidance than pluralism does, and so cannot legitimately claim superiority on that score.

But secondly, a theory with a unifying principle could be superior because it is more explanatorily powerful than a theory without. Even if there is no difference between the practical guidance they provide, between two theories that are otherwise equal, we should prefer on purely scientific grounds the one that accounts for the phenomena with one underlying principle over the one that accounts for the phenomena with multiple underlying principles. The first theory satisfies our "brute curiosity" better. It provides us with intrinsically valuable knowledge—knowledge of what ties together the moral principles, even if that "knowledge would have no effect on our practice" (Hooker 2000a, 21–2).

The first thing to say in response to this claim of rule-consequentialism's superiority is that it doesn't lend any support to the monistic objection that we described in Chapter 7. The monistic objection (which I think underlies Kant and Mill's commitment to formal monism) is based on the claim that our view of moral justification commits us to thinking there is one ultimate principle that provides practical prioritarian adjudication of any conflict between other (less than ultimate) moral principles. But the purely explanatory superiority of a theory—superiority in giving us knowledge that has no effect on our practice—does not give it any of the justificatory superiority that Mill and Kant seem to think our concept of moral justification requires.

The second thing to say is that if Humean sentimentalism is true, a theory such as Hooker's that includes a single ultimate normative principle may very well be explanatorily *worse* than a theory that holds that a plurality of moral principles are ultimate. If our moral judgments tracked a priori, rational, or mind-independent properties—if they tracked features akin to the subject-matter of mathematics or the natural sciences—then we would expect morality not to include conflicting ultimate principles. For we do not think that the subjects of mathematics or the natural sciences harbor actual conflict. If a theory of these things implies such conflict, we think that's a problem with the theory, something that a better theory will solve. Even if we assume that morality is based on human sentiment (and not on a priori, rational, or mind-independent properties), a theory that denies ultimate moral conflict will be superior if we also have independent reason, based in the study of human psychology, to believe that we ultimately morally care about only one thing. Hutcheson, for instance, thought that an examination of human psychology showed that we had one and only one ultimate moral concern: the benefit of humanity. So moral sentimentalism, combined with a central Hutchesonian psychological claim, implies that there is a single unifying principle that resolves any (merely apparent) moral conflict. Similarly, some egoists thought that an examination of human psychology showed that we ultimately cared only about our own pleasure and that therefore our own pleasure constituted the single unifying moral principle.

If, however, morality is based on what we humans care about, and if we lack any reason to think that our sentimental nature cannot lead us to have ultimate concern for different and potentially conflicting things, then there is no reason to hold that a theory that includes a single unifying moral principle is explanatorily superior to a theory that does not. The unifying theory would have an explanatory advantage only if we presume that the psychological tendencies that underlie morality are such as to give rise to only one ultimate concern. But Humean accounts counter just that presumption. On Humean accounts, the psychological mechanisms and basic emotions underlying our moral judgments give rise in us to approval of a number of different things. On Hume's own account, the very same psychological mechanisms give rise in us to approval of what makes people happier as well as to approval of the following of rules of justice; to approval of "chastity and modesty" as well as to approval of "extraordinary vigor" in "amorous exploits"; to approval of "sympathetic hearts" who weep easily for others as well as to approval of "reserved" persons of great self-command who exhibit a certain "coldness" of behavior.[9] On the Humean accounts of Haidt, Prinz, and Nichols, morality grows out of several discrete basic emotions, each of which developed to solve certain evolutionary problems. Humean accounts explain our moral concerns as arising not from any pre-ordained normative structure but from a number of psychological tendencies that, while acutely responsive to the significant currents of human life, do not all sprout from a single organizing principle.[10] If we seek wide reflective equilibrium, and if some version of Humean moral psychology is a live option, then a picture of our moral commitments that has at least some of the characteristics of an "unconnected heap" could very well turn out to be superior to a prioritarian picture or one with a single unifying principle.[11]

Of course the best theory should also tell a unified psychological story of the origin of all our moral concerns. But there is no a priori reason to think that the best account of our moral psychology—unified though that scientific account should be—will tell us that we have only one ultimate moral concern. Consider two psychological theories of what you care about in general. Both theories, let's say, tell us that you care about your family, your friends, doing good work, Baroque music, the environment, soccer, etc. Theory 1 holds that there is a plurality of those concerns that are ultimate for you, that you desire several of them for their own sakes. Theory 2 holds that there is one fundamental concern that underlies all the others—that you desire all except one because all those others promote the one. Is Theory 2 superior to Theory 1 because it attributes to you a single unifying principle? Theory 2 will be superior only if we have independent reason for thinking that you are psychologically built to have ultimate concern for only one thing. But if we lack that independent reason—or if, indeed, we think our best psychological account (i.e. the best explanation of how you come to have concerns at all) gives us reason to believe that you are constituted to have multiple ultimate concerns—then Theory 2's attributing to you a single ultimate concern will not be a reason to prefer it to Theory 1. It may in fact be a reason to prefer Theory 1.

Hobbes and Mandeville thought that psychological egoism was explanatorily superior to any alternative psychological theory because it involved only one motivational principle of human action. Hume argued, in contrast, that the phenomena of human behavior are better explained by attributing to humans a number of different ultimate motives (*E*, App. 2). Most philosophers today—those who reject psychological egoism—think Hume was right about this. The psychological story associated with Hobbes and Mandeville does not gain superiority because of the unity of motivation it attributes to us. The best accounts we have of human psychology paint a more multifarious and potentially fractious motivational landscape (which is not to deny that those accounts, as scientific explanations, themselves possess the explanatory virtues of unity and coherence). What Humean moral pluralism holds is that morality originates in human concerns that are, like human motivations more generally, multifarious and potentially fractious.[12]

Kagan's Consequentialism

Let us now turn to a different prioritarian challenge to Humean moral pluralism: the radical monism of Shelly Kagan. In *The Limits of Morality*, Kagan argues for a strict consequentialism, one that implies that if the greater good really would be promoted by, say, a doctor's killing and taking the organs from a patient, then that is what the doctor should do. Kagan is perfectly clear that this result conflicts with moral judgments that are deeply entrenched in commonsense. He writes, "I am *not* merely arguing that although ordinary morality must be given a different foundation than we generally believe, the moderate [i.e. one who makes typical, commonsense moral judgments] is, nonetheless, basically correct about moral practice. Nothing so comforting. Rather, I claim that our moral beliefs and practices need to be drastically revised" (Kagan 1989, 15).

Why does Kagan think we should abandon many of our deeply entrenched first-order judgments and adopt instead a counterintuitive prioritarianism? Because it is only by doing so that we can bring our moral thinking into maximal coherence (Kagan 1989, 11–15). Kagan's prioritarianism does not rely on metaphysical or theological assumptions in the way Clarke and Butler's did. Kagan seeks to show that by the lights of certain commonsense ideas, his radical view is the most coherent to adopt.

We should give this project high degree-of-difficulty points: eschewing any foundational assumptions or claims about the mind-independent structure of reality, Kagan attempts to show that the pressure to bring our own moral commitments into coherence on its own compels us to adopt a radical, deeply counterintuitive view. I think he fails to pull it off, however. To make his arguments for the radical position, Kagan must use just the prioritarian assumption that stands in need of justification.

Consider Kagan's discussion of a situation in which you can prevent two innocent people from being killed by killing one innocent person yourself. We have the intuition that killing the one would be wrong, but Kagan argues that it is more coherent to hold that killing the one is right. That's because, according to Kagan, it is part of moral commonsense that there is a basic agent-neutral duty to "promote the good" (Kagan 1989, 17). Of course it is also part of moral commonsense that there is a basic agent-relative duty not to kill an innocent person. Kagan maintains, however, that there is no convincing, non-question-begging reason to accept as basic the agent-relative duty not to kill (Kagan 1989, 24–32). But of course if the duty truly is basic, then we shouldn't expect there to be any other, deeper reason for accepting it, so its not following from any other principle is not in itself a reason to reject the agent-relative duty as basic. (Kagan offers no reasons for our commitment to the agent-neutral duty to promote the good; that too is supposed to be accepted as basic.) Rather, Kagan's operative reason for rejecting as basic the agent-relative duty not to kill is that it requires that we take a course of action that is incompatible with the course of action demanded by the agent-neutral duty to promote the good, and we cannot give up the agent-neutral duty without doing even greater damage to the coherence of our moral thinking. Maybe Kagan is right in claiming that if we had to give up the basicness of one of the two duties—if prioritarianism were an absolute side constrain on moral theorizing—it would be more coherent to give up the basicness of the agent-relative duty instead of the agent-neutral one. But this argument of Kagan's simply assumes that because the agent-relative duty not to kill and the agent-neutral duty to promote the good imply incompatible actions, the most coherent response is to give up as basic one or the other of them. It simply assumes that prioritarianism is non-negotiable, and that therefore the only choice is between giving up one basic first-order moral duty or the other. Kagan's argument thus overlooks another possibility—the pluralist possibility that the agent-neutral duty to promote the good be taken to be morally basic, that the agent-relative duty not to kill an innocent person also be taken to be morally basic, and that we accept that these two basic duties can come into conflict with each other in ways that are sometimes best resolved one way and sometimes best resolved the other. It's true that this pluralist view requires giving up the prioritarian idea that basic moral duties will never come into conflict with each or are strictly hierarchically ordered. But I submit that our moral thinking in general will gain more coherence by jettisoning that prioritarian idea than by rejecting all of our deeply entrenched moral judgments that are based on the fundamental justificatory force of the agent-relative duty not to kill an innocent person.

The resulting pluralist view has multiple basic principles—multiple points at which moral reasons come to an end—while Kagan's monistic consequentialism has only one. All other things being equal, a view that explains a set of phenomena with one basic principle is explanatorily superior to a view that explains it with multiple basic principles. But between Kagan's monistic consequentialism and Humean pluralism all other things are far from equal. Giving up all those deeply entrenched moral judgments based on the agent-relative duty not to kill is an explanatorily very expensive proposition. Giving up a formal commitment to prioritarianism is relatively cheap.

Kagan writes: "It may be objected that explanations have to come to an end *somewhere*. Perhaps this is so, but it would still be no license to cut off explanation at a superficial level. If a distinction stands isolated, or is at odds with more firmly supported beliefs, we have grounds for rejecting it, despite its intuitive appeal" (Kagan 1989, 14). Now it seems to me that the belief that there is a basic agent-relative duty not to kill is very powerful and deep, not superficial at all—indeed, that it is probably as powerful and deep as the belief that there is basic agent-neutral duty to promote the good, and certainly more powerful and deep than the belief that morality must have a prioritarian structure. If, then, we are trying to develop from the materials of commonsense the most coherent position—if, that is, we are not bound to accept a prior metaphysical, theological, or purely rational assumption that morality must have a prioritarian structure—then what we have "grounds for rejecting" even if it does have some "intuitive appeal" is prioritarianism. Kagan goes on to say, "What I want to suggest is that the distinctions which underlie the moderate's position dangle, and appeal to their intuitive support is no more adequate than such an appeal would be for [a] slaveholder" (Kagan 1989, 14). Kagan takes the upshot of these points to be that the multiple distinct principles of commonsense morality that cannot be brought into explanatory communion with the agent-neutral duty to promote the good—principles that are "isolated" or "dangle," that are basic and thus unsupported by any other principles—ought to be rejected. But if this means that the moral view we eventually arrive at must have only one basic principle, then it simply begs the question against the pluralist. And if it means that Kagan's consequentialism makes better sense of our moral commitments as a whole than pluralism, it's flat-out false. Kagan's prioritarianism does much more violence to how we think about morality than does the rejection of the formal assumption of prioritarianism.

Principled Trade-Offs

Up to this point, I have discussed three ways of being prioritarian, or non-pluralist: holding that there is only one ultimate moral end, holding that there is a plurality of ultimate moral ends but that they never conflict, and holding that there is a plurality of ultimate moral ends that conflict but are strictly lexically ordered. There is, however, another position that also deserves attention, one that is distinct from those three and yet may perhaps be taken to be a kind of prioritarianism nonetheless.[13]

According to this other position, we have multiple ultimate ends that can come into conflict with each other and that do not admit of strict lexical ordering. But each end has a certain deliberative weight, and those weights interact in ways that lead there to be a principled answer to the question of what is right to do when there is such conflict. Let me sketch this idea by first giving a simplistic rendition of it and by then making it more cogent by refinement.

Let us say that you value fulfilling your professional obligations, and that you also value making your friends happy. Of the two, you place a higher value on fulfilling your professional obligations. Fulfilling a professional obligation has for you a value of 10, while taking an opportunity to make a friend happy has a value of 2. This means that if there is a conflict between fulfilling a professional obligation and taking the opportunity to make a friend happy, you have a principled reason to fulfill the professional obligation. It does not mean, however, that professional obligations have strict lexical priority over making friends happy. For if the conflict is between fulfilling a single professional obligation and making ten friends happy, fulfilling the obligation has a value of 10 while making ten friends happy has a value of 20. In such a case, you have a principled reason to make the friends happy (20 > 10). So while there are multiple distinct ends, those ends can come into conflict, and there is no strict lexical ordering of those ends, there is still a principled way of deciding what to do when such conflict occurs.

This rendition is overly simplistic because of its reliance on the assignment of precise cardinal weights prior to decision-making. It's not plausible that we can assign weights of that sort to all of our ends in advance of making decisions in which they conflict—which is what we would need to do in order for the weights to play a justificatory role in our first-personal deliberations.[14] Consider, for instance, the implausibility of the idea that every instance of making a single friend happy or every instance of fulfilling a professional obligation being given one and the same precise cardinal weight. The deliberative weight of making a friend happy is going to vary depending on what kind of happiness it is—curing a friend of cancer is going to have more weight than buying her a cup of coffee—and the same is true of the many different kinds of professional obligations one can have.[15] It seems extremely implausible that we could, a priori, assign cardinal weights to these different acts and to all the other possible instances of making friends happy and fulfilling professional obligations. The easiest way of imagining how that kind of numerical commensuration of independent ends could be accomplished is by supposing that there is a single value (such as hedons or money) to which all other things can be converted. But of course that would be inconsistent with pluralism. The entire thrust of pluralism—and certainly of a Humean pluralism built on the non-fungibility of different kinds of pleasure—is that there is no such single value that can serve as common deliberative coin.

S. I. Benn has shown, however, how we can reframe these sorts of decision-situations so that it still makes sense to speak of principled trade-offs without having to resort to monistic commensuration or cardinal weightings of discrete rules and values. According to Benn, all we need to fund principled trade-offs are ordinal rankings and a commitment to transitivity (Benn 1988, 47–9). Consider the following three professional obligations:

P1. Teaching your scheduled class instead of simply not showing up.
P2. Attending your scheduled office hours instead of simply not showing up.
P3. Getting to a committee meeting on time instead of showing up ten minutes late.

Let us say that you rank these three in the order they have just been presented, with P1 being more important than P2, and P2 being more important than P3. Now consider the following three instances of making a friend happy.

F1. Curing your friend of cancer.
F2. Getting your friend to the airport on time to catch a flight.
F3. Buying your friend a cup of coffee.

Let us say that you rank the Fs in the order just given: F1 > F2 > F3.

Suppose that you are indifferent between P2 and F2. Faced with the choice of missing your office hours in order to get your friend to the airport on time or making your office hours while allowing your friend to miss her flight, you can see no reason to choose one way or another. In this situation there is a moral tie. The right thing for you to do is disjunctive—either P2 or F2. Given your indifference between P2 and F2, and given your ranking of P1 > P2 > P3 and F1 > F2 > F3, you now can cite principled reasons for making other choices when Ps and Fs conflict. The conjunction of P2 = F2 and P1 > P2 constitutes a reason for teaching your scheduled class rather than taking your friend to the airport. The conjunction of P2 = F2 and P2 > P3 constitutes a reason to take your friend to the airport even though it will mean getting to your committee meeting ten minutes late. P2 = F2 and F1 > F2 together constitute a reason to cure your friend of cancer even if it means missing your office hours. P2 = F2 and F2 > F3 constitute a reason to forgo buying your friend a cup of coffee so that you can attend your scheduled office hours.

This kind of reason-giving—which Benn develops in more sophistication than my examples may suggest (see Benn 1988, 43–64)—coheres with sentimentalism. The view that our ultimate ends originate in sentiment speaks against precise cardinal weightings of ultimate ends, but it does not speak against the comparative, ordinal rankings of the Ps and the Fs sketched above, nor against the notion that there are some situations in which we are normatively indifferent between two options. Those kinds of trade-off reasons carry no monistic commitments. The various P and F options do not need to be converted into some commensurable common coin to get this kind of reason-giving up and running.[16] The options just need to be orderable and obey transitivity. As well, this kind of reason-giving allows for conflict between ultimate ends and does not involve strict lexical ordering. The end of fulfilling professionalal obligations sometimes overrides the end of making friends happy (P1 > F3) while the end of making friends happy sometimes overrides the end of fulfilling professional obligations (F1 > P3). We find, then, that this kind of reason-giving cannot be identified with any of the three prioritarian positions I have so far discussed. Is this kind of reason-giving prioritarian? Does it provide principled answers to all our moral questions?

If this reason-giving is simply an after-the-fact explanation of how a person decided, then it is not prioritarian. If we can explain why you made the decisions you did by attributing to you a certain ranking of alternatives, but if those rankings played no conscious role at all in the thought-process you went through when deliberating about what to do, then your decision-making would still have been pluralist. What makes decision-making prioritarian is the use of principles to justify or prescribe certain decisions, to provide normative guidance, not simply the fact that we can explain from the outside why someone decided as she did by citing general psychological propositions about her.

Benn seems to believe, however, that we can and do use indifference points and rankings to justify decision-making—that "indifference maps" can provide normative guidance. I think the following is what he has in mind. Let us say that you are faced with the decision of whether to attend your office hours or take your friend to the airport, and you realize that you are normatively indifferent between those two options. At some later point, you are faced with the decision of whether to teach your class or take your friend to the airport. You recall that you were indifferent between office hours and going to the airport, and you realize that you think teaching your class is more important than attending office hours. You now have a justificatory principle for deciding to teach your class rather than take your friend to the airport: from the deliberative, first-personal perspective, you can justify this decision by citing the indifference point $P_2 = F_2$ and the ranking $P_2 > P_3$. And this kind of principled decision-making could expand considerably (Benn 1988, 63). Perhaps when a person first starts at a job, she finds it difficult to decide how to balance her professional obligations and her concern for her friends; initially, it seems to her that she has to make decisions between conflicting ultimate ends without any principles to guide her. But if she consistently attends to her indifference points and her rankings, over time she will develop ever more principled ways of deciding what to do in more and more situations. Maybe this sort of progression also occurs between raising a first child and raising later ones. With the first, many decisions seem like bare pluralist conflicts between independent ends. But by the second or third child, after one has determined various indifference points and rankings, one develops principles to deploy when such conflicts arise. And this is why decision-making about later children's upbringing can seem easier, less fraught.

Even if some of our decisions involve principled trade-offs of this sort, however, pluralism will still characterize significant aspects of our normative lives. Most conspicuously, our judgments about which bundles of value and rule-following are points of indifference will remain non-prioritarian. The anchor for all the Benn-type trade-off principles is the judgment that in a particular situation there is a normative tie between two conflicting ultimate ends (i.e. the judgment that it is normatively indifferent which of the two ends is acted on). And that judgment outstrips principled guidance, even according to the principled trade-off position we have just been discussing. Benn himself is clear about the need for pluralist judgment when we find ourselves in situations that are new enough that our past decision-making does not provide any determinate answer about what to do. Making these sorts of decisions, Benn says, is a matter of a person's "extending the curves," of "connect[ing] up his value/principle/role-fulfillment curves in regions where he has believed hitherto that trade-offs and subthreshold choices would be impossible" (Benn 1988, 62–3).

It is, moreover, implausible to hold that you can make a few momentous judgments of this sort at some point early in your life (in your twenties, say), and then use principles anchored in those earlier judgments to engage in prioritarian decision-making for the next five or six decades. It may be that mature, high-functioning decision-makers will, as a result of years of experience and thoughtful attention, increasingly rely on principles for trade-off judgments. But we will continue throughout our lives to face situations that are new and complex enough to defy easy placement on an indifference map of our previous decisions. In the example I gave, the situations are ranked along two dimensions—that of professional obligations and friends' happiness. Benn's example of Lucius Junius Brutus is much more fleshed out than mine, but that example also lives in only a two-dimensional normative space (Benn 1988, 50–9). In real life, however, decisions can involve many more dimensions than that. Given such complexity, it is unrealistic to expect all of our future situations to bear a close enough resemblance to past situations to enable us to make fully principled trade-off judgments based on past indifference judgments and clear rankings of alternatives. When we consider situations in which only two dimensions of concern are in play, rankings and a commitment to transitivity might look to be deliberatively very powerful. But in more complex and nuanced situations, the difficulty or indeterminacy of applying rankings of simple action-types to our actual alternatives loosens the deliberative traction rankings and transitivity may have initially have seemed to possess.[17] Indeed, I expect that if pressed to state the trade-off principles we have used to make certain complex decisions, it is more likely that the preference rankings we present would be jerry-rigged to match the particular decisions we came to, rather than our decisions' having been based on any kind of ranking that could have antecedently played a role in our deliberative thinking (just as certain kinds of Kantians decide first that an action is permissible and then later jerry-rig their description of their maxim so that it passes the CI test).

Earlier I said that it was unrealistic to think that we could assign cardinal weightings to our ultimate ends in ways that would provide principled resolutions about what to do in all cases of moral conflict. Benn's indifference maps are not as simplistic as cardinal weightings. It is, however, also unrealistic to expect to be able to draw indifference maps that will be deliberatively efficacious for virtually all of our future decision-making.

The idea of principled trade-offs is, like threshold deontology, one that pluralists can embrace. We have seen that threshold deontology describes a kind of reason-giving that pluralists can accommodate. Once we have the idea of threshold deontology on board, we can see that in cases of moral conflict pluralists are able to do more by way of justifying their decisions than simply say, "In this particular case that end overrides this one, and that's all there is to it." They can also refer to the normative asymmetry of deontological and consequentialist considerations, even if an ineradicable kernel of pluralist judgment (namely, the judgment of when we have reached the threshold beyond which consequentialist considerations override deontological ones) will always remain. Similarly, principled trade-offs can play a role in pluralist justification, further discrediting the view that in cases of moral conflict pluralists immediately slam into a justificatory brick wall. If someone asks a pluralist why on one day she drove her friend to the airport rather than make her committee meeting on time but on another day taught her class even though it meant her friend would miss her flight, the pluralist can do more than simply say, "In the first case the professional obligation overrode the welfare of my friend while in the second case the welfare of my friend overrode the professional obligation, and that's all there is to it." The pluralist can explain that teaching a class is more important than getting to a committee meeting on time, and that this difference goes a long way towards justifying the difference in her behavior on those two different days. She may also point out that driving a friend to the airport is less important than curing her of cancer but more important than buying her a cup of coffee, and these considerations may add further justificatory oomph. (Just as the pluralist may offer these considerations to someone else after the fact, she may also bring them to mind herself when she's trying to decide what to do.) But in her rankings of complex, multi-dimensional alternatives and the judgments of points of indifference, kernals of pluralist judgment will yet remain.

10

Agonizing Decisions and Humean Pluralism

We have seen that in his discussion of highway promises, Adam Smith claims that even in situations in which breaking a promise may be the right thing to do, the promise-breaker should nonetheless feel "some degree of shame" for what he has done. Smith writes:

Fidelity is so necessary a virtue, that we apprehend it in general to be due even to those to whom nothing else is due, and whom we think it lawful to kill and destroy. It is to no purpose that the person who has been guilty of the breach of it, urges that he promised in order to save his life, and that he broke his promise because it was inconsistent with some other respectable duty to keep it. These circumstances may alleviate, but cannot entirely wipe out his dishonour. He appears to have been guilty of an action with which, in the imaginations of men, some degree of shame is inseparably connected. He has broken a promise which he had solemnly averred he would maintain; and his character, if not irretrievably stained and polluted, has at least a ridicule affixed to it, which it will be very difficult entirely to efface; and no man, I imagine, who had gone through an adventure of this kind would be fond of telling the story. (*TMS* 332–3)

Some shame, guilt, and dishonor, Smith tells us here, can attach even to an action that is, all things considered, correct to perform. A moral "stain" or "pollution" can afflict even the performance of the best we can do. This is a point Smith suggests in several other places in *TMS* as well, maintaining that a person who has caused harm to others through no moral fault of his own can nonetheless feel "piacular," in need of atoning for the harm he has caused. Of a person who has "involuntarily deceived," for instance, Smith writes, "Though not guilty, he feels himself to be in the highest degree, what the ancients called, piacular, and is anxious and eager to make every sort of atonement in his power" (*TMS* 338–9, see also 106–7).

In holding that a person who has done the morally best he could nonetheless has reason to feel some kind of guilt or shame, Smith anticipates one of the most common and powerful contemporary arguments for moral pluralism. This argument—which I will call the "agonizing decisions" argument—is our topic in this chapter.

Amy Kane in Hadleyville

The agonizing decisions argument is anchored in a set of phenomena well-illustrated by a critical scene in *High Noon*. In the movie, Grace Kelly plays Amy Kane, the wife of Marshal Will Kane (Gary Cooper). As a Quaker, Amy is opposed to violence of any kind. Indeed, she tells Kane that she will marry him only if he vows to resign as marshal of Hadleyville and put down his guns forever. He agrees. But shortly after the wedding Kane learns that four villains have plans to terrorize the town, and he comes to think it is he who must try to stop them. He picks up his guns in preparation to meet the villains, and in so doing breaks his vow to Amy. Unrelenting in her passivism, Amy decides to leave Will. She boards the noon train out of town. But then she hears gunfire, and, just as the train is about to depart, she gets off and rushes back to town. Meanwhile, Kane is battling the villains. He manages to kill two of them, but the remaining two have him cornered. Then one of them falls.

Amy has picked up a gun and shot him in the back.

We briefly glimpse Amy's face immediately after she has pulled the trigger. She is distraught, stricken. When the camera angle changes to a view from behind, we see her head slowly drop under the weight of what she's done.

What is going on with Amy at that moment? It's possible, I suppose, that she believes she shouldn't have pulled the trigger, that she let her emotions run away with her, that her act has resulted from weakness of will. But I doubt that's it. More likely is that when Amy heard the gunshots she decided—agonizingly—that the right thing for her to do was return to town and help her husband in his desperate fight. But why then is Amy dismayed? If she performed the action she thought was right, shouldn't she feel only satisfaction about what she has done?

If we assume moral monism, Amy's reaction will seem paradoxical or inappropriate. For if there is one and only one basic moral end, then to think that a course of action is the morally right one will be to think that everything of fundamental moral importance supports it. And it would be strange—inappropriate in some way—for someone to feel dismayed about doing something that was in line with everything of fundamental moral importance. If the moral justification of an action ends at a single point, then what could the point be of feeling some degree of "shame," "guilt," or "dishonor" for performing that action?

I don't think we take Amy's reaction to be inappropriate. Far from it. As Grace Kelly plays it, Amy responds to what she has done in just the way we would expect.[1] What would be strange—unconvincing in the movie and jarring in real life— would be Amy's feeling no dismay at all about shooting the man.

This is perfectly explicable, if we assume moral pluralism. If there are multiple potentially conflicting ultimate moral ends, then thinking a course of action is the right one can be consistent with thinking that it conflicts with something of fundamental moral importance. Or to put the point in Humean terminology, since Amy's moral sentiments respond to distinct and sometimes incompatible concerns, there may very well arise situations in which a course of action that she has a feeling of approval towards and ends up following is one that she also has a feeling of disapproval towards. Humean pluralism can thus allow that Amy has decided that in this situation saving Kane from the villains has a fundamental moral importance that overrides the prohibition on killing (that her all-things-considered judgment is based on her approval of killing), while still continuing to believe that there is something fundamentally morally terrible about killing (while still experiencing a feeling of disapproval toward the killing). Similarly, Smith's highway promiser can think that preventing his family from going bankrupt morally overrides keeping his highway promise while still thinking there is a lingering dishonor (or piacularity) to breaking the promise. For the pluralist, there is nothing strange about feeling remorse—about experiencing a negative moral emotion—toward acting against something one takes to be of fundamental moral importance. Indeed, feeling remorse in such a situation is just what we should expect. This is why we take Amy's response to her own action to be not paradoxical but appropriate.

Or so the agonizing decisions argument maintains.

The agonizing decisions argument is an abductive argument. It starts with the claim that there are certain phenomena that are in need of explanation: namely, that people in situations such as Amy can experience remorse about doing what they think is right and that we think it appropriate that they do so. It then maintains that Humean moral pluralism explains these phenomena better than moral monism.

I label the decisions at the heart of this argument "agonizing" in part because of the word's origin. In Ancient Greece, an agon was a contest or struggle between different people (for, say, athletic prizes). The etymology of the word thus contains the notion of conflict between two independent forces, and we can imagine that this pluralist resonance contributes to its aptness as a description of certain kinds of decisions.[2]

The agonizing decisions argument relies on cases like Amy Kane's having four features.[3]

First, Amy is dismayed not merely about what has happened but about what she has done. Amy's reaction is a species of what Williams calls "agent-regret," not merely "bystander-regret" or "situation-regret" (Williams 1981). A bystander witnessing the event might very well be upset by seeing someone gunned down in the street. We might all wish that the situation in Hadleyville had been different. But Amy Kane is experiencing something else. Her reaction to the man's death is bound up with a sense of responsibility for what has happened—a responsibility bystanders and witnesses of regrettable situations do not share.

Second, Amy's dismay is not conjoined with the wish to undo what she has done. Amy believes that, given the circumstances, she has done what she had to do, what she ought to have done. She does not wish to go back in time and do things differently.[4]

Third, Amy's dismay has moral significance. To see this point, imagine a situation in which a person has an essentially first-personal reaction toward something she's done, that reaction is negative, the person does not wish to undo what she has done, and yet the reaction lacks moral significance. The sort of case I have in mind is one in which an agent does something she thinks is called for but finds disgusting. Years ago while hiking through a swamp I had to pull leeches off the cheek of a companion, and thinking about it now still gives me the creeps. Amy Kane might feel disgust about squashing a fat spider even though she thinks the spider needs to be squashed. But the essentially first-personal dismay Amy feels about shooting the man is different. We expect her to be experiencing a negative emotion that is more similar to a pang of conscience than mere squeamishness or disgust. Unlike responses to bad things one has witnessed as a bystander or to one's own spider-squashings, her dismay is not only regretful (in the sense of wishing the situation were different) but also has the phenomenological qualities associated with our reactions to our own wrongdoings. To put the point once again in Humean terminology, her negative reaction is a feeling of disapproval toward her own action—even though she also has a distinct (and, as it turns out, overriding) feeling of approval towards the same action. In what follows I will call this feeling of disapproval—that which makes Amy bow her head after shooting the villain—*remorse*.

Fourth, we may take this remorse to be appropriately felt, even if we agree with the person's judgment about what she ought to have done. We don't think that someone who has a remorseful reaction to doing what she thinks is right in a morally difficult situation is necessarily in the grips of excessive fastidiousness or neurotic irrationality. We think that having this reaction can speak well of the moral character of a person. Indeed, what we would look at askance is the complete absence of such a feeling in a person who had to act in certain kinds of morally difficult situations. Hill makes this point well when he asks us to consider our reaction to an agent in one of these agonizing situations who "said sincerely, not masking deeper feelings: 'There was nothing better to do, as far as I could tell. It's a pity that someone had to do this (or something as bad) and people died. But I am content, even proud, that I wanted to avoid doing anything wrong, and I did. My life is no worse for doing what I did, I have no more reason to feel concern for the people I killed than you do, and, other things being equal, I would happily take up the job of making the hard choice again if someone had to do it.' Something seems missing here: attitudes and feelings we suppose any decent person would have" (Hill 1996, 187). It seems to us that something is missing here because we think remorse is *fitting* to the situation.[5] And the reason we think it fitting is because we think it is evidence that the agent takes to be morally valuable something that she had to act in opposition to, that she not only has a feeling of approval toward the action but a feeling of disapproval toward it as well. We take remorse to be appropriate because we take it to be evidence that the agent places value on a moral consideration in conflict with the moral consideration she acted on. Hill's point that we may approve of this remorse and disapprove of its absence also strengthens the claim (made in the preceding paragraph) that those reactions have moral significance in a way mere squeamishness and disgust do not. We take the presence or absence of this remorse to signal something important about the agent's character. Not so for mere squeamishness or disgust. Your moral assessment of my character would not change on discovering that I had overcome my repugnance toward leeches.

Amy's case thus reveals that the following ideas are consonant with our moral thinking. An agent can face difficult decisions in which there are morally cogent reasons to do x and morally cogent reasons to do y but no possibility of doing both. Even if the agent comes to decide that doing x is right, she may still feel bad about doing it. This bad feeling is an instance of disapproval, possessing a morally significant, remorseful quality—a quality phenomenologically akin to pangs of conscience rather than mere squeamishness or disgust. And we may judge it appropriate for the agent to feel bad in this way. We may take this response not to indicate irrationality, unreasonability, neurosis, or any other psychological shortcoming. To the contrary. We may judge the lack of such a response in agonizing, morally difficult situations to be inappropriate. We may judge the lack of such a response to indicate a moral shortcoming.

The Humean pluralist claims that the best explanation of these thoughts is that commonsense takes there to be a multiplicity of potentially conflicting ultimate moral ends, and that these ends are grounded in the feelings of approval and disapproval we have for distinct things.[6] If commonsense were monistic, we would not judge it appropriate for a person to feel remorseful after having acted in the way she thought was right. Monists can endorse the wish that the world had been different so that it would have been possible to further promote a single ultimate moral end. They can affirm the appropriateness of situation-regret in cases such as Amy's. But they cannot accommodate the appropriateness of an agent's thinking she has done the right thing while also feeling self-disapproval for acting against an ultimate moral end. Humean pluralists, in contrast, can explain our judging that it is appropriate for an agent such as Amy to feel remorse, and they can do so by attributing to us the idea that that remorse indicates that the agent is sensitive to more than one ultimate moral end. The Humean pluralist explanation of our thoughts about an agent such as Amy is that we judge her remorse to be evidence that she takes to be of moral significance not only the consideration that has led her to act in the way she did but also another consideration that she has had to act contrary to.[7]

One way of putting the pluralist point here is that cases like Amy's elucidate the idea that moral conflict sometimes cannot be completely dissolved, even if it can be resolved. If a conflict is dissolved, it disappears. What appeared to be a conflict turns out not to be a real conflict after all. No one on either side is dissatisfied, nothing unrequited. If a conflict is resolved, a satisfactory way of dealing with the opposing forces may have been reached, but everyone may not have gotten exactly what he or she wanted. Conflict resolution doesn't succeed by showing the two sides that they are not really in conflict after all. It takes the conflict as real and then seeks the best way of dealing with it. Monism implies that when a person facing a difficult case comes to think that a certain decision really is the right one, she will no longer experience the situation as involving opposing moral forces but rather take the moral conflict to be dissolved. She will now see what a single fundamental moral force implies. In contrast, pluralism implies that even if someone comes to think that one particular course of action is the right one, she may continue to experience the situation as one that involves conflicting moral forces. One's coming to a conclusion about what one ought to do, on the pluralist view, will not inevitably bring in its wake a dissolution of the experience of moral conflict. The best one may be able to do is resolve the situation, while still leaving something morally unrequited. And it is just this sense of leaving something morally unrequited—the sense of having acted against something morally important, of doing something that she not only approves of but also disapproves of—that makes Amy bow her head. Her action may very well be justified, but that does not mean she has managed to make all of the moral ends meet.[8]

Uncertainty Objection

Monists may object that the negative reactions of people who have had to act on agonizing decisions are merely the shadows of uncertainty, not the residue of a conflict between ultimate moral ends. The situations facing these agents are difficult ones. They might be unsure that the decisions they ended up making were right. And the unpleasant aftertaste of those decisions, according to this objection, signals only their lingering concern about whether they decided incorrectly, not the belief that they acted correctly but in opposition to something of ultimate moral importance. Blackburn suggests this response when he diagnoses the "heavy heart" with which one must make agonizing decisions—"the umbrella of doom" under which one finds oneself acting in these situations—as based on the "fear that with hindsight one will see" that the "alternative [course of action] will prove to have been the right one" (Blackburn 1996, 129).[9]

To assess this monist "uncertainty" objection, we need to distinguish between two kinds of uncertainty—two different ways in which a person may be unsure about whether she has done the right thing. One kind is uncertainty about non-moral facts, and the other is uncertainty (given the non-moral facts) about one's all things considered moral judgment.

The worry uncertainty about the non-moral facts gives rise to is that, since we are making our decisions with only partial information, it is possible that if we had known more we would have realized that we should have decided differently. For this monist objection to work, however, it would have to be the case that whenever one really did know all the non-moral facts and acted as she thought she ought, she would not feel any remorse. Or if she did feel remorse, it would be inappropriate for her to do so. But this view of when remorse is appropriately felt runs directly counter to what I take to be our ideas about people facing agonizing decisions. Amy Kane knows all the relevant facts, and yet she still feels remorseful about what she has done. The difficulty Amy faces is not epistemic.

Even cases that might initially seem more supportive of the monist uncertainty objection turn out to fit better with the pluralist account. Consider, for instance, the story Sartre tells of the student who had to face an agonizing decision (Sartre 1956, 354).

Sartre's Student. The student lived alone with his mother in France during the Second World War. His mother was ill and dependent on the student both materially and emotionally. The boy's father had collaborated with the Germans, and the boy's older brother had been killed in the German offensive of 1940. The student was thus faced with the choice of leaving for England to join the Free French Forces in their fight against the Germans, or of remaining with his mother and helping her to carry on. What should he have done?

I expect most of us, if placed in the student's shoes, would find this situation agonizingly difficult. And the difficulty would not be merely that of trying to steel
oneself to do what one judged to be right. There would also be the prior difficulty
of trying to decide what, in fact, was right to do. It is the difficulty of deciding that
Sartre himself emphasizes. Indeed, Sartre leaves the student in a state of moral
perplexity, which suits his existentialist purposes. But let us move beyond what
Sartre says and imagine that the student does eventually come to a settled judgment about what he ought to do. Let us imagine he decides that the right thing to
do is join the Free French Forces, even though it means abandoning his mother.
When the time comes to act, he does just that.

What attitude do we expect the student to have toward his own conduct? His
reaction would probably be complex, but I believe we would think it appropriate
for him to feel morally significant first-personal dismay about leaving his mother—
to be remorseful. I believe we'd find it troubling if he didn't feel any remorse at all.

Now it may initially seem that Sartre's case is easy pickings for the monist's
uncertainty objection. The student couldn't have known in advance whether his
fighting for the Free French would have any positive effect at all on the anti-Nazi
cause. Perhaps he'd play an instrumental role in a decisive battle. Perhaps his efforts
would be a complete failure or he'd be killed on his first mission. Nor could he have
known for sure how much additional hardship his mother would endure as a result
of his leaving. And, according to the uncertainty objection, it's easy to explain his
lingering dismay about the decision as resulting from this agonizing uncertainty
about what would happen.

But now consider the situation years later. Imagine that the student eventually
comes to realize that the role he played with the Free French was instrumental to
the anti-Nazi cause, helping to save hundreds of lives and greatly advancing the
cause of freedom throughout the world. These results confirm his original judgment that it was right for him to fight. But do we expect his awareness of these
facts to completely dissolve his remorse about abandoning his mother? I doubt we
do. I expect, rather, we think it is still appropriate for the student to feel remorse
about leaving his mother to die alone, even if he also believes that promoting the
anti-Nazi cause was all things considered the right thing for him to do.

The second version of the uncertainty objection holds that the lingering negative reactions agents like Amy Kane and Sartre's student may feel toward their decisions reflect their uncertainty not about the non-moral facts but about whether
(given the non-moral facts) they have come to the correct moral conclusion about
what to do. The idea here is that what concerns the agent is that she may have not
yet found the complete justification (given the non-moral facts) for how she ought
to act, and that if she were to think she had ascertained that complete justification,

her negative reaction would disappear. This objection holds that the experience of a dismaying moral residue indicates only uncertainty about whether one has fully grasped all the moral implications of the different available courses of action, and that it does not indicate the experience of a conflict between different ultimate moral ends. The unpleasant moral aftertaste the agent feels reflects the fear that if she had only put the facts to herself in a new way, if she had only turned the issues over once more, brought to bear on them some new moral light, she would have seen with certainty what ought to be done; and once she had obtained that certainty, there would no longer be any unpleasant aftertaste to her actions. There would no longer be any dismaying moral residue.

In response, pluralists can readily acknowledge that the kind of moral uncertainty described in the preceding paragraph can and often does afflict someone forced to make an agonizing decision. But what the monist has to claim in order to mount an objection to the agonizing decisions argument is that this moral uncertainty absorbs *all* of the moral residue in difficult situations. It has to diagnose the dismay of agents such as Amy Kane and Sartre's student as nothing but concern about whether one has deployed correctly a single moral value—and that thinking one's way to a complete justification for one's actions will reduce that negative reaction to zero. But while there may be some dyed-in-the-wool utilitarians or Kantians who experience agonizing decisions in this way, it does not accurately describe the experience of most people. Consider someone in a situation similar to that of Amy Kane or Sartre's student who, after coming to a decision, said "I'm sure this is the right thing to do, but I still feel guilty about it." The monist objection we are now considering will have to hold that this person is either confused or expressing an inappropriate reaction. But this statement certainly doesn't sound ineluctably confused; it seems as though it could be a perfectly reasonable thing to say. That leaves the proponent of this monist objection no option but to hold that the person who feels morally significant agent-regret about doing what she is sure is right is experiencing something inappropriate—that such a person's attitude toward her own action is something it would be better or more fitting for her not to have. But "I'm sure this is the right thing to do, but I still feel guilty about it" does not seem to constitute a request for help in being disabused of an inappropriate response, nor would we think such a disabusing necessarily called for. To see this, imagine that while the student is not completely sure, he tends to think that he ought to fight for the Free French. And he feels remorseful about what this means for his mother. According to both the pluralist and the monist objection we are now considering, the student's remorse may be appropriate. But the monist objection also implies that if the student were to lose his doubts and come to have certainty that fighting with the Free French was right while continuing to feel remorseful about how his actions affected his mother, that remorse either would shift to something like situation-regret, or would now become inappropriate. But that seems to run plainly counter to commonsense. The student might lose one lingering concern: "Did I do the right thing?" But we expect him to retain another one: "My poor mother!" Indeed, it seems likely that we would find it inappropriate for the student to *stop* feeling bad about leaving his mother just because he came to greater certainty about his action's having been the right one.

Humean pluralism, which holds that our moral ends are based on our senti-ments, explains these experiences of remorse better than a rationalist pluralism such as Price's. According to Price's pluralism, there is a mind-independent truth about what is morally right to do in every situation, and an agent with complete knowledge would be able unerringly to discern what it is. Thus, after pointing out the difficulty of assessing the relative strength of several competing moral require-ments (such as benevolence, justice, and prudence) in particular cases, Price writes, "In reality, before we can be capable of deducing demonstrably, accurately and particularly, the whole rule of *right* in every instance, we must possess uni-versal and unerring knowledge. It must be above the power of any finite under-standing to do this. He only who knows all truth, is acquainted with the whole law of truth in all its importance, perfect and extent" (Price 1787, 286). Price acknowledges that when deciding what to do in a morally complex situation, we may experience trepidation or "painful doubts" (Price 1787, 284). But he takes our unease to be entirely epistemic, based on our uncertainty about whether we are doing the right thing.[10] Our anxiety in such cases is the same as in complicated speculative matters about which we cannot gain certainty. "Truth and right in all circumstances, require one determinate way of acting; but so variously may dif-ferent obligations combine with or oppose each other in particular cases, and so imperfect are our discerning faculties, that it cannot but happen, that we should be frequently in the dark...Nor is this less avoidable, or more to be wondered at, than that in matters of mere speculation, we should be at a loss to know what is true, when the arguments for and against a proposition appear nearly equal" (Price 1787, 282; see also 282–3). Price may be right that in some cases our trepidation is due to uncertainty, akin to speculative doubts. But he's wrong if he thinks that our trepi-dation in every morally fraught situation is like that. In at least some of those cases, it feels more like a conflict between two things we care about and less like a dif-ficult math problem. Moreover, as I've said above, we may continue to feel moral unease about performing a certain act even after we have come to a firm conclu-sion that it is the right thing to do.[11] Price thinks that in making moral judgments we should aspire to come as close as possible to those of the omniscient being who "is acquainted with the whole law of truth in all its importance, perfect and extent."

But it seems unlikely that Price thought such a being's choices would ever cause it to experience agony or remorse.

Humean pluralists can make a different point about moral uncertainty as well. The difficulty of figuring out what's right to do in situations in which all the (non-moral) facts are known is itself most convincingly explained by there being a conflict between different ultimate moral ends. This is one of the most important lessons of Williams' famous story of Jim, who can kill one innocent person or stand by and do nothing while someone else kills twenty (Williams 1973b). It is perfectly clear, given the non-moral facts Williams presents, that Jim's killing the one will have better consequences (barring some very idiosyncratic utility function) than his not killing. So any monistic consequentialism will imply that the decision about whether it is morally right for Jim to kill the one will be as easy as pie. But regardless of whether on full reflection we come to think Jim ought or ought not to kill the one, we will understand and appreciate it if Jim finds the decision very difficult—agonizing, even. The best explanation for our acknowledging the reasonability of Jim's finding this decision difficult is that we think that the (agent-neutral) consideration of what will produce the best consequences is not the only morally relevant feature of the situation. Also relevant is the (agent-relative) consideration of what Jim himself will cause to happen. It's the existence of the two different moral reasons that explains the reasonability of Jim's finding the decision to be unsettlingly difficult—and it's that difficulty that accounts best for his uncertainty about what is right to do.

The aptness of a pluralism-based account of moral uncertainty is also apparent in this more realistic story from Hill (1991, 26).

Hill's Professor. A professor has a student who shows in tutorial conversations signs of deep depression. The student is later found dead, and the circumstances are such that others can easily see his death as accidental. Indeed, the official ruling is that the student's death is accidental, but the professor believes (without being absolutely sure) that it is suicide. A few weeks after the death, the student's mother comes to see the professor. The mother, a devout Roman Catholic, is deeply worried about her son's soul, and she asks the professor whether he has any reason to suspect suicide. Should the professor tell the mother what he really believes or should he assure her that he had no reason to think the boy committed suicide?[12]

Some people may find the decision of whether or not to lie to the mother an easy one. But I think many would expect to find this to be a difficult decision, one that a person could reasonably be uncertain about. What would explain this uncertainty? The pluralist will plausibly claim that it is not uncertainty about how to apply a single moral end, but rather the awareness of conflict between the moral end of easing the mother's pain and the different moral end of telling her the truth.

Can the Remorse Be Generated by Only One Moral End?

A different monist objection holds that agents can have the same reactions as Amy Kane and Sartre's student, those reactions can be appropriate, and yet those agents can be in situations in which there is only one moral end. McConnell suggests this monist reply in his discussion of one of Williams' examples of bad moral luck. In this case, a man we can call Unlucky Bill is driving perfectly safely and yet, through no fault of his own, runs over and kills a young sledder who has completely unexpectedly skidded under his car. "[G]iven the physical arrangement," McConnell writes, "it would have been impossible for Bill to have seen Johnny coming. Bill was not at fault, legally or morally, for Johnny's death. Yet Bill experienced what can only be described as remorse or guilt about his role in this horrible event" (McConnell 1996, 39). Moreover, according to McConnell, this is a situation "in which we will say that an agent's remorse is not inappropriate even though we think that the agent is not warranted in believing that he has done something wrong." We do not need to postulate a multiplicity of ultimate moral ends to explain Bill's negative reaction. His negative reaction can very well result from his sensitivity to only one end—that which is instantiated in the life of Johnny. But if a situation of Bill's type can occur, then the cases of Amy Kane and Sartre's student might also be instances of it, instances of a person's feeling remorse even though she has not been involved in any conflict of moral ends.

The pluralist can respond, however, by pointing to the significant differences between Unlucky Bill, on the one hand, and Amy Kane and Sartre's student, on the other. First and most importantly, neither Amy Kane nor Sartre's student wishes to undo what he or she has done, but Bill clearly does wish to undo what he has done. Amy Kane and Sartre's student thus have a different attitude toward the event they feel remorse about, and it's that difference—their not wishing to undo the event even though they feel remorse about it—that makes those cases evidence for pluralism even though Unlucky Bill's is not. Unlucky Bill, Amy Kane, and Sartre's student might all experience agent-regret. But we can and should distinguish between agent-regret for events one has caused intentionally and voluntarily and does not wish to undo, from agent-regret for events one has caused involuntarily or unintentionally and does wish to undo. While agent-regret of the latter kind does not help make the case for pluralism (as the case of Unlucky Bill shows), agent-regret of the former does.

The pluralist can also respond by contending that we take there to be a *better* fit between the actions of Amy Kane and Sartre's student and their negative reactions than there is between the actions of Unlucky Bill and his "remorse or guilt."

If Bill feels not only situation-regret but also "remorse or guilt," we are likely to suspect that he thinks that there was something that he somehow should have done to prevent Johnny's death. And if we believe that Bill was truly in no position to have acted differently, we will take it to be appropriate to try to move Bill from feeling "remorse or guilt" to feeling only situation-regret. The way in which we might help Bill move toward only situation-regret is by trying to convince him that he could not have done anything differently. For as the Humean would put it, there would be nothing Unlucky Bill did in the situation that reveals in him a motive that would be disapproved of from the general point of view, and thus if we could get Bill to view the situation from the general point of view and in light of all the relevant facts, his self-disapproval should dissipate.

The monist might try to revive the objection by presenting an agonizing case in which moral conflict seems to be generated by only one moral end. Consider this from Marcus, "Under the single principle of promise keeping, I might make two promises in all good faith and reason that they will not conflict, but then they do, as a result of circumstances that were unpredictable and beyond my control" (Marcus 1980, 125). Imagine that I have promised to help A move house, that I have promised to take B to a doctor's appointment, and that events unfold so that it is possible for me to do one of these things but not both. If I keep my promise to one of them, I will appropriately feel remorse that I broke my promise to the other. But, as Marcus's monist objection has it, we do not need a plurality of moral ends in order to explain this reaction. The single moral end of promise-keeping is enough. And this shows that the monist can explain as well as the pluralist the phenomena that are supposed to anchor the agonizing decisions argument.

To see the flaw in this objection, consider that for it to work, the conflict-of-promises case must involve only one ultimate moral end. If the decision in this case involves taking into account more than one ultimate moral end (e.g. if coming to the right decision about which promise to keep involves a sensitivity not only to the moral importance of promise-keeping but also to the moral importance of, say, gratitude, friendship, or the promotion of human welfare), then the case will not serve the monistic cause.

But if the decision in this case involves *only* the moral end of promise-keeping, then it's very hard to see how the agent could come to the conclusion that it is right to keep one of the promises rather than the other. If the moral end of promise-keeping is the *only* relevant moral end, then this case will be a strict moral dilemma, a case in which there are two conflicting moral requirements and neither one of them is overridden (Sinnott-Armstrong 1988). Indeed, this is the kind of case Marcus herself seems to have in mind, as she writes, "All other considerations may balance out. The lives of identical twins are in jeopardy, and, through force of circumstances, I am in a position to save only one" (Marcus 1980, 125). Maybe instances of such perfectly symmetrical moral conflict do occur, but the agonizing decisions argument turns on a different kind of case. At the heart of the agonizing decisions argument is the idea that a person can appropriately feel remorse about doing something she thinks is morally superior to (and not simply as good as) a conflicting alternative. It's the conjunction of the judgment that doing X is morally superior to any alternative *and* the appropriate feeling of remorse that is the phenomenon the agonizing decisions argument contends is best explained by pluralism. That a single moral end can give rise to some cases of strict moral dilemma and that as a result monists may be able to explain how an agent may appropriately feel remorse about not acting on a non-overridden moral requirement does not show that monists can adequately explain how an agent can appropriately feel remorse about acting on a moral requirement that *does* override all alternatives. While pluralists can readily allow that in some cases only one moral end is relevant to difficult decision-making, the point of the agonizing decisions argument is that there are other cases that are best explained only by supposing there is more than one.

A related monist objection comes from Hurka, who claims that the appropriateness of a negative reaction toward doing what one takes to be the morally best course of action does not advance the pluralist cause because monists can accommodate the appropriateness of such a reaction just as easily. Hurka writes:

Imagine, to take the simplest example, that you have a choice between giving five units of pleasure to one person, A, and giving ten units of pleasure to a different person, B. Here the lesser good is not included in the greater good as a proper part; it is not the case that if B enjoys the ten units of pleasure, A will enjoy the five units. Given this, it can surely be rational for you, if you produce the ten units for B, to feel some regret at not having produced the five units for A. There is, on the face of it, only one generic good at issue in your choice, namely, pleasure. But . . . if you have chosen a greater instance of one good for one person over a lesser instance of the same good for another person, you can rationally regret not having produced what would have been better for the second person. (Hurka 1996, 563)

One way for a pluralist to respond to Hurka is to question whether the view he is discussing here really is monistic after all. But Hurka defends his view's being monistic, and I think that defense stands a good chance of succeeding.

What the pluralist can plausibly deny instead is that the agent in Hurka's case both has formed his moral judgment in a monistic way and is appropriately feeling not merely situation-regret but agent-regret of the morally significant kind we have been discussing. It's completely plausible that the agent in this case will wish that A could have been made more happy. But if everything of moral importance in this case boils down to fungible units of pleasure, we will not think the agent should feel remorse for choosing B.[13]

To see the underlying weakness of the objection, consider the important differences between Hurka's case and the cases we've discussed in which remorse for doing what one thinks is right is appropriate. In the cases we've discussed, the difficulty of deciding what is right to do outstrips difficulties in determining the (non-moral) facts. Even if we suppose that Amy Kane and Sartre's student are no longer in any doubt about the facts of their situations, we may still expect them to find the decision about what it is right to do to be agonizing. As I've argued, epistemic uncertainty doesn't account for all of the unpleasant aftertaste of some morally difficult decisions. Now the pluralist can easily explain this lingering aftertaste by pointing to the normative mismatch between the two available courses of action. According to the pluralist, what exerts justificatory force toward Amy Kane's shooting the villain is generically different from what exerts justificatory force toward her not shooting him, just as what exerts justificatory force towards Sartre's student's staying with his mother is generically different from what exerts justificatory force toward the student's joining the Free French. It's this difference—the mismatch between the kinds of things on either side of the justificatory question—that makes it difficult to determine what is right to do.

In Hurka's monistic case there is no normative mismatch. One and the same generic good exerts all the justificatory force on both sides of the question of what ought to be done. In Hurka's case, consequently, if we take all the facts to be fixed, determining what is right to do is easy. If the agent in Hurka's case is confident that one course of action will produce greater moral value than any other, he won't have any difficulty whatsoever determining what is right to do. The moral part of his or her decision-making (unlike Amy Kane's or that of Sartre's student) shouldn't be unsettling in the slightest. This is an easy case, not an agonizing one.

But just because making the decision in Hurka's case does not involve any moral agony, the agent will not think there is any moral remainder or residue after acting in the way he thinks is right. If you think there is no normative mismatch—if you think that the justificatory forces on all sides are generically the same—you will think that the justification for acting in a certain way is precise and clean, leaving no remainder or residue. Even if you think that you had failed to produce certain things of value, you will not think that any justificatory reason has been left to dangle. The lack of normative mismatch will ensure that what normatively underlies your regret at failing to produce certain things of value will be exactly the same thing that underlies the justification of your having done what you did. While there may be things of value that acting in the way you did fails to promote, the justification for acting in that way is based entirely on the same values that explain

188 AGONIZING DECISIONS AND HUMEAN PLURALISM

your wishing those other things had been promoted. The regret you may feel is not regret about not acting in accord with a certain value. It's regret that there couldn't be more of one and the same value.

Hurka's agent bears opportunity costs. Opportunity costs are not pleasant. We wish we could achieve our goals without having to bear them. But if all the relevant costs and benefits in a situation are of a single fungible kind, and if an agent has determined that one course of action in that situation is the most beneficial or least costly, then the agent should not be expected to feel remorse about paying the opportunity costs that course of action involves. If all the relevant costs and benefits are of a single fungible kind, then the agent's feeling no remorse about what he did will give us no reason for thinking that the agent does not fully appreciate something of relevant value. In contrast, we expect Amy Kane and Sartre's student to experience something more than the mere unpleasantness of paying opportunity costs. We expect them to feel remorse because something of moral importance has not been fully compensated for. If they told us that the unfortunate aspects of their actions are fungible *vis-à-vis* the fortunate aspects, we would question whether they had fully appreciated something of fundamental moral importance. It's a Humean pluralist account—which tells us that our moral ends are based on distinct emotions—that explains best why that is so.

Remorse is appropriate only when agents take themselves to have resisted some justificatory pull, to have left some normative itch unscratched. In Hurka's case, the agent will not take himself to have acted in opposition to anything of moral importance, not to have left anything justificatorily unrequited. It's certainly reasonable for this agent to wish that the situation had been different so that he could have made both A and B happy and avoided opportunity costs. But wishing there were no opportunity costs is not the same as experiencing remorse about following a course of action one thinks is right.[14]

Agonizing Decisions and Common Life

The final objection to the agonizing decisions argument is that the cases it is based on are too unusual to serve as probative of commonsense moral thinking. Amy Kane is a fictional character in a life-and-death situation virtually none of us will ever encounter. Sartre's student may have been real, but the circumstances he faced were so extreme that we shouldn't expect our everyday moral ideas to apply to them in any illustrative way. Our moral thinking didn't develop to address cases as unusual as Amy's or the student's. Thus, the picture of our moral thinking intuitions about such cases will produce is likely to be distorted, or stretched beyond its breaking point.

An initial response to this objection is that there are numerous real-life cases we can point to that support the central aspects of the agonizing decisions argument just as well as Amy Kane's and Sartre's student. Hill's Professor is one. Here's another from Marcia (Baron 1988, 263):

Baron's Spouse. A woman is in a marriage that she finds stultifying. She believes that if she leaves her husband, she will be able to grow more as a person. But she is aware that leaving will sever the significant emotional bond she still has with her husband, and that he is likely to suffer pain and depression as a result. Should she stay or should she go?

Hill's Professor and Baron's Spouse both face agonizing decisions. But now let us suppose that they both come to considered conclusions about what they ought to do. The Professor decides the right thing to do is tell the mother he has no reason to think her son committed suicide. The Spouse decides the right thing to do is leave her husband. Even after they have acted in the ways they thought was right, we would still expect them to feel something like remorse about what they've done—to feel dismay of the morally significant, agent-regretful kind. And the Humean pluralist explanation is once again the most apt: we expect them to be remorseful because while they have acted in accord with one moral end, they have also acted in conflict with another, independent moral end (and thus will also feel disapproval toward that course of action).

The cases of the Professor and the Spouse can be taken as representative of broad classes of cases of agonizing decisions that are far from atypical. It's not all that unusual to face situations in which one has to choose between, on the one hand, doing something that will bring a person more happiness or less distress, and, on the other hand, being completely truthful. Nor is it all that unusual to face situations in which one has to choose between one's own self-development and the happiness of others. Because these cases are not all that unusual, there is no reason to think that applying commonsense moral thinking to them will be an exercise in intuition-distortion. These are just the sorts of cases to which our moral thinking has developed, in part, to respond.

Even so, the Professor and the Spouse, no less than Amy Kane and Sartre's student, are in situations in which different moral ends imply strictly incompatible actions. All of these cases involve stark forced choices. And while we do sometimes face decisions like that, they do not dominate our daily lives. There may, thus, be something incomplete—unhealthy, perhaps—about a philosophical diet that consists of nothing but examples of this sort. Anscombe suggests this line of criticism when she says that a person who focuses his moral theorizing on dilemma-like situations in which one is forced to do something one would normally hold to be wrong "shows a corrupt mind" (Anscombe 1956, 40). Hursthouse suggests something similar when she says that "a too great *readiness* to think 'I can't do any-thing but this terrible thing, nothing else is open to me' is a mark of vice, a flawed character" (Hursthouse 1999a, 87).[15]

But when we turn away from stark forced choices to other kinds of agonizing decisions, the case for Humean pluralism becomes even stronger. To see this, con-sider situations in which we are called upon to solve what O'Neill has helpfully termed moral "design problems" (O'Neill 2001).

A design problem is what confronts an architect who seeks to construct a build-ing that is economical, environmentally friendly, and beautiful. In such a situa-tion, the architect is not forced to make a stark choice between different ends. She doesn't have to violate one end completely in order to comply entirely with another. Her design can have elements that are economical, environmentally friendly, and beautiful. She can do things that are in accord with each end. But the architect will almost certainly nonetheless have to make some tough choices, for she will not be able to do everything each of the ends considered solely on its own would lead her to do. If she were to give ultimate trumping power to the value of beauty— if she were to ignore environmental concerns and cost whenever they conflicted with aesthetic considerations—the building would be inefficient and prohibitively expensive. If she were always to choose the cheapest option available, the building would be inefficient and unattractive. So what she must do is try to come up with a satisfactory balance of the three ends.

Design problems differ in two important ways from the forced choices of Amy Kane, Sartre's student, Hill's professor, and Baron's spouse. First, someone facing a design problem is not required to violate one end entirely in order to live up to another end completely. There are likely some things the architect can do that are beautiful, environmentally friendly, and inexpensive; and while she might have to forgo a bit of ecofriendliness (or aesthetics, or expense) in some aspects, she can put some more ecofriendly features in other aspects.

Second, someone facing a design problem is not forced to choose between two and only two stark options. There are many different ways of constructing solu-tions to design problems—many different building plans the architect may con-sider. The relevant mindset here is not that of choosing between two fixed choices that have been thrust upon one but rather that of actively constructing—crea-tively designing—a workable solution for dealing with a complex, multi-faceted problem.

The idea of O'Neil's that I want to embrace is that we face morally significant situations that have features similar to this type of architectural design problem more often than we face stark forced choices. Someone might value family, work, and friends. But it might be impossible for her to promote all of these to the fullest extent. If she did everything possible for her friends, her work and family would get short shrift. If she did everything possible for her family, her work and friends would get short shrift. But that does not mean she will constantly be forced to make stark choices between friends, family, and work. She can construct a life that enables her to realize all three of these things to some extent, even if she cannot realize each of them to the greatest extent imaginable. Nor are there only two options about how to construct such a life. There are many different ways of trying to solve this problem, many different life-designs she can construct.

Does the experience of these sorts of moral design problems fit better with a pluralist view than with a monistic one? I believe it does. To see this, consider the Busy Day—a scenario in which a person, on one particular day, has powerful reasons to spend as much time as possible with her family, and has powerful reasons to spend as much time as possible at work, and has powerful reasons to spend as much time as possible with a friend. Perhaps it is a child's birthday, the day before a major project at work is due, and a day on which a good friend who has helped the person in the past needs help herself. But of course she can't spend the entire day with her family, at work, and with her friend, even if the importance she places on each of these things gives her powerful reasons to do so. So she has to decide how to construct her day so that it is the best it can be. This decision may be difficult for her. But the difficulty here is that of a moral design problem, not a stark forced choice. For first, the person is not required to violate one end entirely in order to promote completely another. She may choose to spend the entire day just with her friend and completely forgo work and family. But she also can choose to spend part of the day doing one thing, another part doing another, and a third part doing a third. She can promote each of these ends to some extent even if she cannot promote all of them to the fullest extent. Second, the person is not forced to choose between only two options. There are many different ways she can choose to plan her day—many different solutions she can construct to deal with the problem of how to spend her time. That situations can have these two features of a moral design problem rather than a stark forced choice becomes even more apparent when we consider that in reality a person usually makes decisions about how to structure her life over a period of weeks, months, or years, and not simply a day, as I have suggested in order to make the exposition of the Busy Day easier.

So now let us say that the person has made what she takes to be the best decision about how to spend her day—a decision that involves spending some time at two of the things (although not as much at either of them as she would if the other concern were not pressing) but not any time at the third. How will she feel about acting on that decision? It seems plausible that she will experience morally significant agent-regret—and not simply the awareness of opportunity costs—about not being able to spend more time with her child/at work/with her friend. It seems plausible that she will feel responsibility for some value-loss, a sense that she has left unsatisfied some desiderata, a sense that she has left undone things that it would have been morally good for her to have done. Even if the person thinks she's done the best she can do under the circumstances, she is still likely to experience a residue of moral unrequitedness.

Would we take the person's sense of value-loss to be appropriate, or to be a sign of fastidiousness, neurosis, self-flagellation? I think we would take it to be appropriate. That the person believes she has failed to satisfy some desiderata can reasonably be taken to be an indication of her proper appreciation of distinct moral ends, and not an indication of morally irrelevant psychological quirks. I suppose we can imagine someone in this situation who feels no sense of loss other than that of having to pay opportunity costs. But I doubt that we take the lack of any remorse in this situation to be more appropriate than the presence of it. Indeed, it seems to me that we may take the person who lacks any first-personal agent-regretful dismay to be inappropriately centered on the cleanliness of her own hands in a way that detracts from her responsiveness to the things of value.

It might be thought that a person will face moral design problems such as I've described only if she has previously made some moral mistakes. According to this line of thinking, if the person had made nothing but impeccable decisions in the past, she would never have found herself in a situation in which she has no choice but to leave some moral desiderata unfulfilled. Even if this were so, it would not speak against a pluralist account. For the pluralist could still plausibly claim that part of what makes past decisions peccable or otherwise is the agent's responsiveness to a multiplicity of ultimate moral ends and her facility at coordinating those ends and predicting their demands. Even if someone finds herself confronted by a moral design problem only because she has made moral mistakes in the past, her feeling remorse about doing what she takes to be the best way of dealing with her situation (and our taking that reaction to be appropriate) will still be evidence for moral pluralism.

But it seems to me that we do *not* take the fact that a person faces a moral design problem to be evidence of her having previously made moral mistakes. It would be easy enough to fill in the details of the Busy Day scenario in such a way that it would be difficult to see how a person could be faulted for finding herself in a situation in which she faces the moral design problem at issue. Perhaps the person who has family, work, and friendship commitments had her original plans upset by events that she could never have been expected to anticipate, such as sudden illness or fluky weather event. Sartre's student cannot be blamed for his mother's frail health, for the Nazi occupation, or for the impossibility of both caring for his mother and going to fight with the Free French. Hill's professor may not have been in position to do anything more than he did do for his depressed student.

There might even be reason to think it morally *un*desirable to structure one's life so that one never faces the type of moral conflict that confronts the person with the Busy Day (or Sartre's student, or Hill's professor). There might be reason to think that a life that has no moral conflict will be attained only at the expense of a responsiveness to things of real moral importance.

The best way to avoid moral conflict is to commit to one and only one ultimate moral end. If a person recognizes as ultimately moral important only, say, family, or work, or friendship, or acting on a certain principle, she will not face the kind of moral conflict I've been talking about here. She might still face difficult decisions about how to live up to an ultimate end—how best to be a parent, or to do her work, or to be a friend, or to apply the principle—and she may have to pay opportunity costs as a result. But she will not face the difficulty of having to balance being the best parent she can be against being the best worker, or being the best friend against acting on a principle. And if this person always acted in accord with what she takes to be the best option, she should never experience remorse. If Sartre's student cared ultimately only about freedom for France, he would not have faced the difficulty of having to decide between ultimate ends (even if he might still have faced difficulties and borne opportunity costs in determining how best to help France) and would not have experienced any remorse after acting as he thought he ought. And if the Busy Day person placed ultimate moral importance only on, say, her family, her decision about how to spend her time would have been easier and should not have occasioned in her any remorse (even if opportunity costs still had to be paid). Such a person would be like an architect who places sole ultimate value on environmental concerns, or on beauty, or on expense. Such an architect may still face many difficult decisions, but they will be decisions about how best to achieve a single goal, not how to balance different goals.

The history of moral philosophy does give us examples of lives such as this, of people like Socrates and Epictetus whose prioritarian value-systems ensured that they would never experience remorse when acting as they thought they ought. There may be people walking among us who have value-systems that similarly insulate them from remorse. In *The Orchid Thief*, Susan Orlean movingly describes her fascination with these types, with people whose overriding concern for one thing simplifies all the decisions they ever have to face. Such people, Orlean writes, "circled their lives around some great desire…a desire that then answered questions for them about how to spend their time and their money and who their friends would be and where they would travel and what they did when they got there" (Orlean 1998, 40–1). By placing ultimate importance on only one thing, such a person can "whittle" her normative world down to a single sharp point (Orlean 1998, 109).

But do we expect these monistic types—these people whose possession of a single ultimate concern insulates them from the experience of remorse—to be leading morally better lives than those who do find themselves confronting moral conflict? I doubt it. I doubt that we take insulation from remorse to be an indication of a morally better life, any more than we think an architect ultimately concerned with only one desideratum is the best one to hire for the construction of our house. We withhold our wholehearted approval from such monistic types not simply because we think they've singled out the wrong ultimate end. We withhold our wholehearted approval because we think there is more than one thing of ultimate importance, and that being disposed never to experience remorse indicates a lack of proper responsiveness to some of those things.

Consider Socrates and Epictetus and their resolutely non-remorseful attitude toward the distress of their families. Or Susan Orlean's orchid thief, John Laroche, a man whose overriding love for the beauty of orchids left no room in his psyche for any agent-regret about anything he did in his botanical pursuits. How attractive yet strange such people seem! Perhaps, like Susan Orlean, we sometimes feel a wistful envy for the moral simplicity of their peculiarly monistic lives. But that simplicity comes at a steep price. These monistic oddballs, regardless of what they single out as ultimately important, must be missing something. The moral simplicity of their lives betokens a lack of appreciation of some of the plurality of valuable ends we take there to be.

Many moral theories have told us to live in accord with a single ultimate commitment, and such theories do promise to show us how to dissolve moral difficulty and inoculate ourselves from remorse. Such theories conflict with ordinary moral thinking. Ordinary moral thinking takes a proper and full responsiveness to moral ends to go hand in hand with a susceptibility to moral agonies—and to the experiences of remorse that may follow in their wake.

Conclusion

No moral view eliminates the need for deliberation and judgment. No one is advocating for an algorithm that enables us to answer moral questions by turning a crank. Humean pluralism tells us something about what we are doing when we are engaged in moral deliberation and judgment: that we are engaged in an activity more akin to deciding how to proceed when there are a number of different things we want to do than to solving a mathematical problem or developing a scientific theory. To take this Humean message on board is not to adopt a procedure about how to make moral decisions. At the same time, it can also be more than simply acceding to a theoretical point without any practical import. It's not as far removed from decision-making as the physics of color-perception is from interior design. How one thinks about one's moral decision-making—whether one takes oneself to be doing something more akin to science and math or to personal negotiation—can influence how one goes about making moral decisions. It can influence the approach one takes to interpersonal and intrapersonal conflict.

Before boarding the train out of Hadleyville, Amy Kane goes to see Helen Ramirez, her husband's ex-lover. To Helen Ramirez, Amy's pacifism makes no sense. She can see only the reasons for Amy to stay and help Will Kane in his struggle. "I don't understand you," she says. "If Kane were my man, I'd never leave him like this. I'd get a gun. I'd fight." We can also imagine a conversation Amy Kane might have had with a more monistically minded Quaker. "You say you understand the reasons never to commit violence," we can imagine this Quaker saying to Amy. "But now you tell me that you feel the pull of a reason to go back and fight by the side of your husband. You're contradicting yourself. To be against violence and also for it: that's self-contradictory." The point of Humean pluralism is that it's not necessarily self-contradictory. We can care about some things in ways that lead us to affirm a moral reason to take one course of action, and we can care about other things in ways that lead us to affirm a moral reason to take another, incompatible course of action. It's only unwarrantedly dichotomous thinking that leads to the insistence that one or the other of those things we care about must be demoted to the realm of the non-moral or erroneous. A state of mind in which you are morally drawn to incompatible courses of action is not self-contradictory. As Herman has aptly put it, to be in such a state is to be in a situation in which "deliberation is necessary"—at least until high noon, when it's time to act.

I said at the beginning of this book that the danger of a mistaken prioritarianism is holding out too long for an unrealistically perfect justification. But prioritarians are prey to the opposite danger as well—of giving up too soon. That you've found a fundamental moral reason to do something is not sufficient for concluding that you ought to do it. There might be a fundamental moral reason not to do it as well. And when someone points to a moral reason to do something incompatible with what you think there is a moral reason to do, she is not necessarily contradicting you. You may both be right. There may be moral reasons on both sides. To recognize that is to recognize, not necessarily a state of contradiction, but a call for deliberation.

Moral judgment—like deciding in general how to live—is an art, not a science.

Notes

Acknowledgements

1. Those less interested in one or the other of the approaches might want to know that the historical material is mainly in Chapters 1–4, discussion of empirically informed moral psychology mainly in Chapter 5, and intuitively supported conceptual arguments mainly in Chapters 7, 8, and 10. I don't know how to categorize Chapter 6.
2. With the notable exception of Joel Feinberg's acknowledgements of Professor Josiah S. Carberry.

Inroduction

1. I will use "end" as a general term to corral all those things that can serve as ultimate moral justifiers. Different philosophers have recognized different kinds of ultimate ends. Clarke's ultimate ends seem to have been mainly principles about action-types. Butler takes principles about action-types to be ultimate ends, but he also seems to think that a character trait or motive can be ultimately justifying. Hutcheson thought the motive of benevolence was the one and only thing we ultimately approve of. Hume's account of moral judgment focuses to a large extent on character traits we ultimately approve of, but he takes obedience to the rules of justice and other "artificial virtues" to be things we ultimately approve of as well; he also explains how our approval of character traits can lead to judgments about which particular actions are justified. Like Hume, Smith thinks we feel ultimate approval for character traits and for certain rules, such as those of justice. In Chs 1–4, I will try to explicate what these historical figures thought, even if the differences between their types of ultimate ends sometimes makes it somewhat difficult to see exactly how their positions speak to each other. I do believe, though, that even though someone like Hume focuses mainly on traits and someone like Clarke focuses mainly on principles concerning action-types (both of which I will categorize as ends), the pluralism of the former is nonetheless in conflict with the prioritarianism of the latter, and I hope eventually to make that clear.
2. As Gaut defines the term, and as I will use it, moral pluralists deny that there are principles to resolve every moral quandary but they do not necessarily deny that there are right solutions to every such quandary. Moral pluralism (so defined) is neutral on the question of whether there are any strict moral dilemmas.
3. Gaut (1993) endorses Davidson's idea that all prioritarian views are in fact monistic, insofar as a hierarchical ordering of principles can be seen as a single large principle. There is something correct about this idea, but there's also something missing, insofar as a view that holds that there are multiple principles implies (*contra* monism) that there is more than one feature of the world that makes things right or good—even if there's also a priority ordering for that multiplicity of features.

4. Yet another kind of multiplism is a view according to which each basic moral end has a certain justificatory weight, so that when they conflict the relative weights determine what the theory recommends. Such a view might seem to capture all the advantages of pluralism while also giving us a prioritarian method for deciding what to do. I discuss this view at the end of Ch. 9 in the section called "Principled trade-offs."

5. We can add to this taxonomy—at the far right of the diagram—the position of moral particularism, which is non-prioritarian and denies the existence of any moral principles at all. For defense of particularism, see McNaughton (1988) and Dancy (2004). For criticism of particularism, see Hooker (2000b) and McKeever and Ridge (2006). For discussion of the various positions on both sides, see Lance and Little (2006) and Timmons (2013, 305–30). In this book, I will not address the issues that separate pluralists from particularists, focusing instead on the issues that separate prioritarians, on the one hand, from pluralists and particularists, on the other. Still, I should say something here about the differences and similarities between Humean pluralism and particularism. So without making any pretense of providing a full discussion of the matter (and with the caution that some of what I'm about to say depends on claims I will only explain later), let me briefly discuss the salient issues. Particularism has explanatory and normative components. The explanatory component is the thesis that are no true moral principles that are needed to explain the deontic status of particular actions. This explanatory thesis can be taken in two different ways. Particularist-explanatory1 is the thesis that no mind-independent principles are needed to explain the deontic status of particular actions. Particularist-explanatory2 is the thesis that no principles of any kind are needed to explain the deontic status of particular actions. Particularist-explanatory1 is a denial of mind-independent moral realism, of which Ross's theory of prima facie duties is a prime example. Humean pluralists agree with particularist-explanatory1; Humeans also deny that there are mind-independent principles that are needed to explain the deontic status of particular actions. What of particularist-explanatory2? There's a sense in which Humean pluralists disagree with it and a sense in which they agree. Humean pluralists seek to explain why humans make the moral judgments they do. This Humean explanation includes general psychological principles, law-like statements about how humans respond to certain kinds of character traits or action-types. If particularist-explanatory2 is taken to be a denial that general psychological principles are needed to explain why humans make the moral judgments they do, then Humeans disagree with it. However, particularist-explanatory2 could instead be taken to allow that general psychological principles are needed to explain why humans make the moral judgments they do, but to deny that in order to explain the deontic status of particular actions we need to refer to moral principles that are independent of any moral judgments humans actually make. This second sense of particularist-explanatory2 would be a denial of the following type of view: an action is right if and only if it produces the highest possible ratio of pleasure to pain in human beings, and that would be true regardless of whether the moral judgments humans actually make have any relation at all to that pleasure criterion. Humean pluralists will agree with this second sense of particularist-explanatory2 (i.e. they will agree with particularists in denying the kind of view described after the colon in the preceding sentence), but that's because Humean pluralists will not countenance the idea of there being a

truth about morality that is entirely independent of the moral judgments humans actually make. If particularists think that particular acts have mind-independent or stance-independent deontic status (i.e. if they think there is a fact of the matter as to an action's deontic status that is entirely independent of human judgment, albeit a fact that is made true not by general principles but by the particulars of the situation), then Humeans will disagree with them in exactly the same way they disagree with the mind-independent realism of Ross. (Blackburn 1984, 1998, has developed an expressivist semantics that explains how Humeans can affirm the normative claim that certain things could be wrong regardless of what anyone thought of them, but I am speaking here of the claim taken in a purely non-normative, explanatory sense.) This points to what I think is a tricky difficulty about bringing Humeanism and particularism into contact with each other: Humeanism is an explanatory thesis about the moral judgments humans actually make, while particularism at least sometimes seems to be an explanatory thesis about what gives particular acts stance-independent (i.e. independent of the judgments humans actually make) deontic status. To put the matter rather crudely: Humeans agree with particularists that mind-independent moral principles should not be included in our most basic ontology, but that's because Humeans think *no* mind-independent moral properties should be included in our most basic ontology (and not because they think the mind-independent non-principled deontic status of particular actions should be included).

The normative component of particularism is the thesis that agents should not rely on moral principles for guidance when deciding what is right to do—that agents will make morally better decisions if they attend to the particulars of each situation rather than use general rules about right-making and wrong-making features. If the principles whose use the particularist is arguing against here are absolutist—never break a promise, no matter what the circumstances; never violate property, no matter what the circumstances—then Humeans are on their side, for Humeanism clearly endorses some instance of promise-breaking and property-violation (as we'll see below). But I don't think there's anything in the Humean view that discourages the use of defeasible or hedged moral principles of the sort developed and defended by McKeever and Ridge (2006, 113–37). Hume's great emphasis on our "addiction to general rules" also suggests that he thought that human minds are built to use principles of that sort, that general rules play a pivotal role in the activity of judging as a whole (see Gill 2006, 214–25). For an updated version of Hume's view of general rules, see Gaus's powerful argument that cultural and biological evolution has led us to use generalizable moral rules in our social lives (Gaus 2011, 112–13 and 122–30). Now the particularist's normative claim is that we shouldn't use principles, even if it turns out that we often do use them. But the Humean pluralist could agree with those who have presented cogent reasons for thinking that agents actually make better decisions when they use principles (see McKeever and Ridge 2006, 196–203; Hooker 2000b, 15–22; Zamzow 2013, 17–44). Moreover, if the moral principles in question are defeasible and hedged, it's unclear how much of a difference there will even be between the agent who uses them and the particularist agent (Timmons 2013, 320–1).

It's important to add, however, that essential to the Humean pluralist position is the claim that different moral principles will come into conflict with each other. There may be some general guidelines we can use when faced with such a situation, such as: benefit to society at large generally overrides benefit to an individual; justice generally overrides benefit. But for the Humean pluralist these guidelines are only rules of thumb, not invariable orderings, which means that we will still need to assess the particulars of situations in which rules conflict. It is this need for non-principled judgment in cases in which moral rules conflict that makes the view pluralist—and this is the critical shared point of Humean pluralism and particularism. I believe that from the first-personal deliberative standpoint, this commonality between particularism and pluralism is more important than the differences between them (especially if, as Timmons suggests, there is vanishingly little difference between a particularist agent and an agent who uses defeasible or hedged principles). From the first-personal justificatory perspective, the difference between non-prioritarians (whether pluralist or particularist) and prioritarians is much more significant than the difference between pluralists and particularists.

6. See Gill 1999, 2008b, 2009a.

Chapter 1

1. See Sommerville 1977, 29–38.
2. For further discussion of views of moral duties in the 18th century, see Heydt (forthcoming).
3. Hutcheson's monistic streak is if anything even more pronounced in his aesthetics, in which he claims that all of our judgments of beauty are based on our positive response to a single quality—namely, uniformity amidst variety (see Hutcheson 1726/2004, 3–82). The more implausible you find this aesthetic claim (and most people do find it pretty implausible) the more credibility you should give to a monistic reading of Hutcheson.
4. "[O]ur moral Sense would most recommend to our Election, as the most perfectly Virtuous [those actions that] appear to have the most universal unlimited Tendency to the greatest and most extensive Happiness of all the rational Agents, to whom our Influence can reach. All Benevolence, even toward a Part, is amiable, when not inconsistent with the Good of the Whole: But this is a smaller Degree of Virtue, unless our Beneficence be restrain'd by want of Power, and not want of Love to the Whole... This Increase of the moral Beauty of Actions, or Dispositions, according to the Number of Persons to whom the good Effects of them extend, may shew us the Reason why Actions which flow from the nearer Attachments of Nature, such as that between the Sexes, and the Love of our Offspring, are not so amiable, nor do they appear so virtuous as Actions of equal Moment of Good towards Persons less attach'd to us. The Reason is plainly this. These strong Instincts are by Nature limited to small Numbers of Mankind, such as our Wives or Children; whereas a Disposition, which would produce a like moment of Good to others, upon no special Attachment, if it was accompany'd with natural Power to accomplish its Intention, would be incredibly more fruitful of great and good Effects to the Whole" (Hutcheson 1726/2004, 126–7; see also Hutcheson 1726/2004, 231–3 and 1728/2002, 8).
5. But Hutcheson would be a motive-utilitarian, not an act- or rule-utilitarian: his view implies that our moral judgments are attuned to the motives we think people act on, and that we approve of a motive to the extent that we think the motive is generally

benevolent. Darwall (1994) argues that Hutcheson is not a meta-ethical utilitarian in that he doesn't think that moral ideas can be reduced to ideas about non-moral states of affairs. Darwall is right about this, but Hutcheson is still fairly thought of as a normatively monistic utilitarian (i.e. a motive-utilitarian about the content of morality) insofar as he thinks morality is based on approval of only one kind of motive—namely, the motive to promote happiness. All our approvals, according to Hutcheson, are responsive to the same benevolent quality.

6. I discuss Hutcheson's anti-egoist project in Gill 2006, 141–55.

7. Butler's criticism of Hutcheson's monistic account of virtue finds a very clear echo in Ross's criticism of G. E. Moore's utilitarian definition of 'right' (Ross 1930, 16–47).

8. I have not found a passage that indicates that Reid had Hutcheson in mind as a target when expounding on the multiplicity of moral principles. But Reid was well aware of the monistic aspects of Hutcheson's view. Indeed, Reid's first publication, "An Essay on Quantity; occasioned by reading a Treatise, in which Simple and Compound Ratios are applied to Virtue and Merit," was a criticism of Hutcheson's proto-utilitarian attempt to quantify benevolence. So it's reasonable to assume that he would have aligned himself with the anti-Hutchesonian multiplist criticisms of Butler, Hume, Price, and Smith.

9. Thanks to Colin Heydt for pointing out to me Price's contribution to this debate.

10. What occurs in the part of this quotation that I have skipped over is a passage that might suggest that Price thought that while human morality is multiplist, divine morality (i.e. morality as God apprehends it) is monistic, with the happiness of all being the single ultimate end. I discuss such a view in the section on Butler in this chapter.

11. This multiplist reading seems to me, in any event, to be the most natural reading of the multiple, distinct moral principles Clarke expounds, such as the following three: "[I]n Mens dealing and conversing one with another; 'tis undeniably more *Fit*, absolutely and in the Nature of the thing itself, [1] that all Men should endeavour to promote the *universal good and welfare of All*; than that all Men should be continually contriving the *ruin and destruction of All*. 'Tis evidently more *Fit*, even *before* all positive Bargains and Compacts, [2] that Men should deal one with another according to the known Rules of *Justice and Equity*; than that every Man for his own present Advantage, should without scruple disappoint the most *reasonable and equitable Expectations* of his Neighbours, and *cheat* and *defraud*, or *spoil by violence*, all others, without restraint. Lastly, 'tis without dispute more *Fit* and reasonable in itself, [3] that I should *preserve the Life* of an innocent Man, that happens at any time to be in my Power; or deliver him from any imminent danger, tho' I have never made any promise so to do; than that I should suffer him to perish, or *take away his Life*, without any reason or provocation at all" (Clarke 1705/1738, 609; I've added the bracketed numbers).

12. Non-conflict pluralism can also be subdivided into modally strong and modally weak versions. Modally strong versions hold that it is impossible for ultimate moral ends to come into conflict, while modally weak versions hold that such conflict is possible but never actually occurs. We should attribute a modally strong version of non-conflict pluralism to Clarke since he assimilates moral ends to principles of math and logic and since he would have taken it to be impossible for such principles to come into conflict.

13. Clarke thus seems to share Hooker's view that moral principles must be "internalizable" (Hooker 2000a, 78–98, 165–74). The need for moral principles to be internalizable implies a significant objection to Richardson's specificationist view (Richardson 1990, 2000): if we continually specify our moral rules so that they are such that we never act in conflict with any of them, they will eventually become so complex that they would be impossible to internalize.

14. In n. 12, I said that non-conflict pluralism can be subdivided into modally strong and modally weak versions, and that Clarke holds to a modally strong version. But we should take Butler (at least in the "Dissertation") to be neutral on the modal question since he wants to remain neutral on the question separating rationalists and sentimentalists. If Butler's view is conjoined with a rationalist meta-ethics such as Clarke's, then the fact that moral ends do not come into conflict would be necessary (and along with this would come Clarke's anti-voluntarist theology). If Butler's view of virtue is conjoined with a sentimentalist meta-ethics, such as Hutcheson's, then the fact that moral ends do not come into conflict would be contingent (and along with this would come Hutcheson's theology, which rationalists like Balguy accused of being voluntarist).

15. Butler's reasons here are similar to Geach's reasons for denying the existence of any true moral dilemmas: God would not command that we do something we are not capable of doing (Geach 1969, 128).

16. We will return to this view in our discussion of Adam Smith. A question worth thinking about is why Butler thought that our commitments to justice, gratitude, and the like couldn't be as mistaken or distorted as our commitment to the general happiness. There are two reasons our judgments about what will best promote the general happiness can go wrong: because of epistemic limitations that lead us to be mistaken about the full effects of our actions, and because of partiality that deceives us into thinking that anything that benefits our side in a contest will benefit all. I suppose Butler might have thought that the non-consequentialist features of justice and gratitude shield us from the first kind of mistake. But why not think that the second kind of mistake can afflict our judgments of, say, justice just as much as it can our judgments of what best promotes the good of humankind?

17. Clarke makes a very similar point when he writes: "[Some] have contended, that all *Difference* of *Good* and *Evil*, and all *Obligations of Morality*, ought to be founded *originally* upon Considerations of *Publick Utility*. And true indeed it is, in the whole; that the *Good of the universal Creation*, does always *coincide* with the *necessary Truth and Reason of Things*. But otherwise, (and separate from *This* Consideration, that *God will certainly cause Truth and Right to terminate in Happiness*;) what is for the *Good of the whole Creation*, in very many Cases, none but an *infinite Understanding* can possible judge" (Clarke 1705/1738, 630). (I think it plausible that Hume had this sort of passage in mind when he wrote section III of the *Enquiry concerning Morals*.) Clarke goes on to argue against anyone who "thinks it *Right* and *Just*, upon account of *Publick Utility*" to lie or break faith in a particular isolated case. It might seem as though in isolated particular cases lying or breaking faith will be most conducive to public utility, but (Clarke argues) we should realize that a full appreciation of all the long-term consequences will reveal that such actions will ultimately do more harm than good. I do not know how to combine Clarke's comments here about public utility with his earlier comments about

the duty to engage in "a constant indeavouring to promote in general, to the utmost of our power, the welfare and happiness of all men" (Clarke 1705/1738, 621).

18. For this reason, I don't think Butler could accept that our apprehension of the moral ends includes ceteris paribus clauses. For Butler believes that God has given us moral ends that are perfectly suited to our epistemic situation. But if our moral ends included ceteris paribus clauses that we could not discharge, those moral ends would be insufficient for providing complete moral justification in some cases (since all we would be able to say by way of justification in such cases is that the *ceteris* are not *paribus*).

Chapter 2

1. It is, however, an oversimplification to say that Humean usefulness to others is the same as Hutchesonian general benevolence, for Hume maintains in the *Treatise* that the others whose happiness we are responsive to when making such judgments are only those in the person's immediate circle, those with whom the person has direct contact, and *not* humanity in general (*T* 3.3.1.18; 3.3.3.2). Then again, in the *Enquiry*, he suggests that we can take into account the effects a person's conduct has on humanity in general (*E* 5.39; 9.5). For penetrating discussion of the question of how far Humean benevolence stretches, see Baier (2004).

2. Swanton has provided an intriguing analysis of the difference between Humean usefulness and agreeability (Swanton 2007, 104).

3. Sayre-McCord is particularly clear about the different purposes different Humean moral ends serve (Sayre-McCord 1996). Roger Crisp has claimed that Sayre-McCord's reading is wrong because Hume believes in a "single overarching standard for evaluating all solutions to problems"—namely, pleasure (Crisp 2005, 171). I believe, however, that Swanton has argued convincingly against Crisp and for Sayre-McCord by showing that Hume's statements about the essential role of pleasure in virtue are meta-ethical, concerning the pleasures of the moral sense at the heart of his response-dependent view of morality—not about the criteria of virtue (Swanton 2007, 106–7).

4. Whenever we speak of the Humean view that our moral judgments are based in our approvals, we should keep in mind that for Hume, correct moral judgments are those that accord with approval we would feel from the general point of view (*T* 3.3.1.14–18 and 3.3.3.2). I will not always mention this important qualification in the text, but it should be taken as implicit.

5. Baier (1991), Sayre-McCord (1996), Dees (1997), Abramson (1999, 2002), and Swanton (1997) have all incisively elucidated aspects of Hume's development of this idea that the principles of natural virtue constitute four independent vectors of moral thought.

6. See also *T* 3.3.1.11; 3.3.1.30; 3.3.2.16; 3.3.5.1; and *E* 2.10; 2.17; 7.11; 7.19; 7.22; 7.29; 8.7; 9.1.

7. When discussing multiplists who did not believe ultimate ends conflict, I noted that this view could come in two different modal versions: those that hold that such conflict is impossible, and those that hold that such conflict is possible but will never actually occur. Multiplists who hold that conflict between ultimate ends will occur also come in two modal flavors: those who hold that it is possible that such conflict would never arise but that in fact it does, and those that hold such conflict necessarily occurs. It's unclear which of these two modal versions we should attribute to Hume. In his description of

the perfect son-in-law, Hume seems to affirm the possibility of all the virtues being harmoniously combined (*E* 9.2), but his discussion of the differences between goodness and greatness seems to fit better with the idea that the virtues cannot all be harmoniously combined (*T* 3.3.4.2).

8. I owe much of what I say here to Abramson (1999).

9. There is a serious puzzle concerning Hume's claims about our moral approval of justice. Hume says that we approve of motives, not actions or mere rule-following (*T* 3.2.1.2–7). But it also seems that he says that we approve of just action or the following of the rules of justice (or at least disapprove of unjust action and the disobedience of the rules of justice), distinct from motives (*T* 3.2.2.23–4). For excellent recent discussion of this puzzle (with reviews of past literature), see Garrett (2007) and Harris (2010). I offer an account of this puzzle in Gill (2006, 321–3). However this puzzle is resolved, it is clear that Hume wants to affirm that we come to approve of instantiations (whether that is taken to include or not to include motive) of justice that are not useful or agreeable to self or others—and that's the only point that's important for my discussion here.

10. For a rich discussion of the differences between the demands of the artificial virtues, see Henley (2011), which adds much to the discussion of Humean conflict pluralism I present here.

11. Baier describes this feature of Hume's view particularly eloquently in "A Catalogue of the Virtues" (Baier 1991, 198–219).

12. For discussion of related issues concerning moral phenomenology, see Gill (2008a, 2009b).

13. As I will discuss in Ch. 5, contemporary sentimentalist pluralists (such as Haidt, Prinz, and Nichols) maintain that we have several different moral emotions at the base of our moral judgments, such as anger, contempt, and compassion, and not just different kinds of approval. This contemporary sentimentalist picture of distinct moral emotions may very well be an improvement on Hume's attempt to base all moral judgments on different flavors of approval.

14. My discussion here of the addiction to general rules is brief; I go into more detail in Gill (1996a).

15. As I mentioned in n. 9, there is a puzzle as to whether Hume thinks every instantiation of an artificial virtue must include a certain kind of motive, or whether Hume would allow that some instantiations of artificial virtue are mere action or rule-following. My reading here is neutral on this question.

16. Hume is explicit in the *Treatise* about how the addiction to general rules plays this explanatory role in our approvals of useless allegiance (*T* 3.2.9.3) and chastity (*T* 3.2.12.7). He is not as explicit about how general rules fill this role in our approvals of useless justice. He does deploy the addiction to general rules in his explanation of our approvals of justice—where he says that the "*general rule* reaches beyond those instances, from which it arose"—but he isn't so clearly speaking there precisely about approvals of useless justice (*T* 3.2.2.23–4). So I am doing a little bit of interpolation when I take Hume's general rules-explanation of useless allegiance and chastity to also apply to his account of justice that fails to benefit society. Korsgaard (1996) has argued that when we realize that our approvals of useless justice are due to our addiction to

general rules we will no longer have normative confidence in them. I believe this criticism of Humean justice is unfounded, as I argue in Gill (1996b).

17. The best psychological explanations for our moral judgments will almost certainly not rely on the same mental mechanisms that Hume proposes. But there is good reason to believe that those explanations will be sentimentalist and pluralist in a way that sides with Hume and against rationalists and monists. For discussion of how recent work in moral psychology supports sentimentalist pluralism, see Gill and Nichols (2008) and Ch. 5.

18. I will discuss Ross's view in Ch. 6.

19. Dees (1997) has done a masterful job of elucidating the kinds of moral ambivalence Hume accounts for, and in this section I mean to endorse and offer additional evidence for Dees's claims. See also Abramson (1999), who discusses how Hume uses his pluralist account of the sources of virtue to provide a powerful explanation of the apparent moral differences between cultures.

20. Hume maintains that moral assessments are of persons' character (T 3.3.1.30). It is unclear, however, what exactly Hume means by character. I will not enter into debate on that question. But I do think it is clear that Hume thinks we form different moral assessments of different qualities that a single person possesses—i.e. that he thinks we may judge a single person to be virtuous in some respects and not virtuous in other respects. If I am right about this, then Korsgaard (1999) is wrong to attribute to Hume the view that our moral assessments are of agents as a whole—i.e. that our moral judgments are always personally global. But defenders of the unity of the virtues thesis— such as Julia Annas—will say that I haven't done Hume any favors, for they will claim that it is wrong to hold (as I say Hume does) that we morally assess persons' qualities piecemeal, one by one. Annas and other unity of the virtues defenders will claim that an accurate understanding of the virtues will reveal their reciprocity—i.e. that a person can possess one virtue only to the extent that she possesses the others. For similar criticism of Hume, see Hursthouse (1999b). Of course if Hume's account of moral ambivalence is compelling as a description of our moral thinking, that would imperil the claim of the unity or reciprocity of the virtues.

21. I think we can and should offer this distinction to the Humean position, but I do not claim that Hume himself was explicit about it. I take myself in this section to be working out implications of Hume's position in ways that he himself did not do much to develop. I will be engaged in a similar task in the next section of this chapter. To use Rosenberg's helpful methodological distinction, I am doing here something closer to "Dionysian" history of philosophy, while in earlier sections I was doing something closer to "Apollonian" history of philosophy (Rosenberg 2005, 2).

22. For discussion of the dispositional aspect of Hume's general points of view, see Radcliffe (1996) and Cohon (1997).

23. I say that this distinction should be part of the Humean account of moral judgment, and I will presently give reasons for thinking this. But I don't claim that the distinction is ever made explicitly in Hume's texts. Hume himself seems to use the words "approval" and "disapproval" to refer both to the different kinds of sentimental responses we might have to a quality (which fill a role in the Humean view similar to what the apprehension of prima facie duties fills in Ross's view) and to the single

response that ends up determining our all-in judgment of it (which fills a Humean role similar to the Rossian apprehension of an actual duty). The distinction I am discussing might be more clearly signaled by calling the first kind of responses "proto-approvals" and "proto-disapprovals," or by calling the second kinds of responses "dispositive approvals" and "dispositive disapprovals." But I will stick with calling the former simply "approvals" and "disapprovals" and the latter an "all-in judgment," which is I think more natural-sounding and closer to Hume's own language.

24. I have argued for this explanatory reading of Hume in Gill (1996b). Of course we still might want to address the question of what things people *should* praise and blame, even if that's not Hume's main project. I discuss the reasons we *should* be prioritarians or pluralists in later chapters. Shaun Nichols and I also discuss the move from explanatory pluralism (i.e. pluralism as a description of what we actually do) to normative pluralism (i.e. pluralism as a normative account of what we should do) at Gill and Nichols 2008, 153–7.

25. The point I make here raises questions about the distinction between aesthetics and morals. Some might hold that an essential feature of morality—and what essentially distinguishes it from aesthetics—is that it has implications for action that make moral ambivalence inherently unstable. According to this way of thinking, we can remain ambivalent in our aesthetic evaluations because they do not have direct implications for how to conduct ourselves, but our ethical evaluations do have these implications and we have to conduct ourselves in one way or another. I doubt, however, that such a sharp distinction between morals and aesthetics could be sustained in the sentimentalist moral views of Hume, Hutcheson, and Shaftesbury, all of whom draw profound connections between beauty and virtue (a point I discuss in Gill 2007). I also expect that in the end an insistence on this kind of morals/aesthetics distinction (i.e. an insistence that our mixed moral evaluations of Harry and Charles be labeled aesthetic rather than moral) would be uninterestingly verbal. It seems to me, moreover, that evaluative ambivalence about things and people is (and ought to be) a significant feature of our moral lives. There are, it is true, some who suffer from dichotomous thinking—who hold that everyone must be placed on one side or the other of a strictly bifurcated moral ledger—but I take them to be aberrant and unfortunate. It is salutary that Humean pluralism does such a good job of accounting for (and, I think, vindicating) the experience of evaluative ambivalence, and that it does so without collapsing this experience into epistemic uncertainty. Hume would probably say that those suffering from dichotomous thinking, which compels one to give everything a single up or down moral verdict, are like the moralists whose religion has so distorted their judgment that they have come to believe that there is a judge who gives everyone a plus or minus for everything he or she does (see *T* 3.3.4.4 and *E* App 4.21).

26. See also Hume's discussion of Beckett (*History* 1.333–4).

27. Price and Ross (in *The Right and the Good*; his view changes in *Foundations of Ethics*, as we'll see at the end of Ch. 6), who are both like Hume in being pluralists but unlike him in holding that morality is mind-independent, do hold that all of our evaluative ambivalence is due merely to epistemic uncertainty—and that there is a mind-independent truth about what ought to be done in every circumstance, even if we cannot always figure out what that is. Price, for instance, maintains that there is demonstrable truth

about what to do in every situation, but that it's "above the power of any finite under-standing to [determine what it is]. He only who knows all truth, is acquainted with the whole law of truth in all its importance, perfection and extent" (Price 1787, 286). "Truth and right in all circumstances," he writes, "require one determine way of acting...but so imperfect are our discerning faculties, that it cannot but happen [in cases in which different obligations conflict with each other], that we should frequently be in the dark" (Price 1787, 282). Price also explicitly compares our inability to infallibly determine what to do in each particular situation to the limitations of our scientific knowledge (in "matters of mere speculation", or "knowledge and assent in general"), where there is nonetheless one true answer (Price 1787, 282 and 289). Similarly, in *The Right and the Good*, Ross says that in situations in which the prima face duties come into conflict, we cannot be as "certain" of what our actual duty is as we can be of any of our prima facie duties (Ross 1930, 30). But that is entirely because of our epistemic limitation. There is a right act—or duty—for me in any particular case, and "if I were omniscient" I would be able to see what it is (Ross 1930, 32). But because I am not omniscient, I must simply make the best guess that I can, and hope that I have the "good fortune" to do what is right, where that rightness is independent of whether or not I manage to light upon it (Ross 1930, 31).

28. An OUP referee has usefully separated out two different questions here: (1) Are there determinate facts about the all-things-considered values of all things, so that (e.g.) Caesar comes out virtuous, not vicious, overall?, and (2) Do things have multiple dimensions of value, so that (e.g.) Caesar can be virtuous in some ways and vicious in others? The point I am making here is that the Humean will give a Yes answer to 2 and a No answer to 1. According to the Humean, those who think there must always be a Yes to 1 are probably suffering from perniciously dichotomous thinking. Why (unless we're all at some point to be measured for wings or horns) must there be one, simple up or down moral verdict passed on everyone?

29. A conflict pluralist denial of an invariable lexical ordering raises issues about value comparability. Two values, x and y, are comparable if either x overrides y or y overrides x. (A different, but less important, question is whether two values are commensura-ble; it's less important because even if two values are incommensurable they may still be comparable; see Benn 1988; Gaus 2011). Two values are incomparable if neither x overrides y nor y overrides x. To understand the conflict pluralist stand on compa-rability, we need to distinguish between abstract ultimate moral values and concrete instantiations of ultimate moral values. At the abstract level, conflict pluralists hold to value incomparability. On the conflict pluralist view, the value of promise-keeping (when we are talking not about any particular, concrete promise but rather the abstract notion of promise-keeping) is neither greater nor lesser than the abstract value of pain prevention (when we are talking not about any particular, concrete instance of pain prevention but rather the abstract notion of pain prevention in general). At the specific, concrete level, however, comparisons can be made. In a particular situation, the value of keeping a certain specific promise might override the value of preventing the pain of certain specific individuals. But in another particular situation, the value of preventing certain person's pain might override the value of keeping a certain specific promise. Conflict pluralists believe value comparisons can be made in concrete situations but

deny that every situation will issue in the same ranking. This view can be analogized to how we would respond to the question: which is more valuable, beauty or usefulness? In some situations beauty is more valuable than usefulness while in other situations the opposite holds. But we cannot meaningfully rank the values of beauty and usefulness when we consider them merely in the abstract.

30. See Ch. 1 nn. 10 and 12.

31. Note the contrast between this statement of Price's and the following quotation from Butler: "Let us compare the nature of man as respecting self, and tending to private good, his own preservation and happiness; and the nature of man as having respect to society, and tending to promote public good, the happiness of that society. These ends do indeed perfectly coincide; and to aim at public and private good are so far from being inconsistent that they mutually promote each other" (Butler 1729b/1983b, 26).

32. Ross does offer an ordering of *goods* to be promoted, with virtue and knowledge being given absolute priority over pleasure (Ross 1930, 149–50) and virtue being given priority over knowledge (Ross 1930, 152–3). See also Ross 1930, 165–6. For discussion of the ways in which Ross's prima facie duties are organized, see McNaughton (1996). I will discuss this kind of view in more detail in Ch. 8.

33. But maybe Price's view is not exactly the same as Ross's. For at times, Price suggests that an infinitely intelligent being would be able to see how all of our duties fit together perfectly, with the implication being that all moral conflict is merely apparent and not real. Our inability to see how we can fulfill every duty in those cases in which we experience moral conflict would thus be akin to our inability to figure out every mathematical problem or infallibly predict the behavior of every physical object. There is a single answer to every mathematical problem and to every question about how physical objects will behave, and if we could understand that answer we would see that there had never really been any conflict between mathematical or physical forces after all. Similarly, there is a single answer as to what is one's duty in every case, and if we could fully understand that answer we would see that. Furthermore, the infinitely intelligent being will see that there never really was a conflict between any mathematical, physical, or moral forces after all (which distinguishes Price's view from Ross's, as Ross thinks that prima facie duties really do come into conflict; on Ross's view, an infinitely intelligent being would be able always to discern the actual duty in every situation, but that would be a discerning of which of two conflicting prima facie duties is decisive, not seeing that the conflict does not really exist). On this Pricean picture of moral conflict, the appearance of moral conflict may be ineluctable for us but does not exist for an infinitely intelligent being.

34. See King (1988) and Abramson (1999).

35. For discussion of Aquinas and Grotius's limiting the scope of need so that justice often does forbid use of another's property, see Fleischacker 2004, 215–16.

36. For discussion of the ways norms compete with each other and evolve, see Nichols (2002, 2010).

37. Joel Feinberg (1980) tells the story of a desperate hiker who breaks into someone else's mountain cabin in order to survive. Feinberg argues that in such a case the hiker's conduct is morally acceptable, but that it nonetheless violates the property rights of the owner of the cabin; this position is in line with the position I am

attributing to Hume and in contrast to the Natural Law position, which holds that if the breaking-in hiker is justified she is not actually violating anyone's rights. As Feinberg tells the story, a compelling reason to think that the hiker violates the owner's right even though she's justified in breaking in is that she would still owe the owner some restitution, which implies that some wrong has been done to the owner (even if it was, all things considered, the right thing for the hiker to do). This style of argument—pointing to the moral harm that's done even in cases in which a person has done the all-things-considered right thing—is one that I use in the last chapter (I will call it the Agonizing Decisions Argument) to argue that commonsense morality is pluralist and not monistic.

38. For fascinating discussion of the ways in which different traits that each serve evolutionary purposes can come into conflict with each other, see Sorensen (1991). Sorensen refers to ch. 10 of Eibl-Eibesfeldt (1975). He gives as an example a bird that has evolved both the trait to remove all red items from its nest *and* the trait to ensure that eggs stay in its nest. What happens when there is a red egg in the nest? It turns out the bird will remove the red egg, and then bring it back into the nest; remove it again, then bring it back again; and so on.

39. See Garrett (2007).

40. The Humean holds that there is a plurality of things we value intrinsically, where "intrinsic" is taken in the sense of being valued for their own sakes and not merely instrumentally. This is consistent with the Humean claim that all value metaphysically depends on human attitudes and the Humean denial of the existence of intrinsic values, where "intrinsic" is taken in the sense of having a mind-independent, non-relational ontological status. For discussion of these two different senses of "intrinsic value," see Korsgaard (1983).

41. One could hold that one moral sentiment includes in its phenomenology an overriding normative authority that the other moral sentiments lack. As I discuss in Gill (2008a), Butler makes phenomenological claims that suggest this line of thought (although Butler is concerned to show that morality has authority over other things, not that one moral principle has authority over another, conflicting moral principle). But I do not see any indication that Hume argues for the phenomenologically grounded authority of any particular moral sentiment over all other moral sentiments.

42. For evidence that Price thinks there is a mind-independent truth as to what ought to be done in each and every circumstance, see Price 1787, 282–9. He maintains there that there is demonstrable truth about what to do in every situation, but that it's "above the power of any finite understanding to [determine what it is]. He only who knows all truth, is acquainted with the whole law of truth in all its importance, perfection and extent" (Price 1787, 286). "Truth and right in all circumstances," he writes, "require one determine way of acting... but so imperfect are our discerning faculties, that it cannot but happen [in cases in which different obligations conflict with each other], that we should frequently be in the dark" (Price 1787, 282). He also explicitly compares our inability to infallibly determine what to do in each particular situation to the limitations of our scientific knowledge (in "matters of mere speculation," or "knowledge and assent in general"), where there is nonetheless one true answer (Price 1787, 282, 289). As I discuss at the end of Ch. 6, Ross changed his mind about this matter, holding in *The*

Right and the Good that one's actual duty is a mind-independent fact but holding in *The Foundations of Ethics* that one's actual duty is (doubly) subjective.

43. I discuss this point in Gill (1996b).

Chapter 3

1. Gaus explains how our moral thinking includes commitments to both consequentialist values and non-consequentialist rules: see Gaus 2011, 140–60.
2. Darwall thinks that Adam Smith's sentimentalism fares better than Hume's, but I will not discuss Darwall's interpretation of Smith's view. See Darwall 2006, 178–80.
3. A more fundamental objection is that the Humean sentimentalism cannot account for reasons at all—that sentiments can never fund normative (as opposed to merely explanatory) reasons for action at all. I will not address that concern here.
4. Darwall thinks that Hume has particular problems explaining our moral obligation to justice (which I will discuss in n. 5), due to his commitment to justice's artificiality and to our approving not of acts but of character traits (Darwall 2006, 188), but I think Darwall's criticism that Hume cannot accommodate certain kinds of non-trade-off judgments, if successful, would target Hume's moral psychology more generally. That the criticism would extend that widely seems to me to be implied by the following from Darwall: "on Hume's official view, as we have seen, voluntary action seeks to bring about some good. This is a source of the contemporary 'Humean' theory of motivation, according to which action always results from desires (which have some apparently good [desirable] state of the world as object). As we noted in the last chapter, however, normative acceptance is irreducibly attitude-of-a-subject-regarding rather than state-of-the-world-regarding" (Darwall 2006, 191).
5. Another version of the non-consequentialist objection is that Hume cannot accommodate our thinking that it is sometimes right to do what is just even though more people would be made happy by doing what is unjust (Darwall 1995, 315 and Korsgaard 1996, 86–9). The best Humean response to this specifically justice-based non-consequentialist objection of which I am aware is Garrett (2007). I have addressed the justice-based non-consequentialist objection to Hume, and have explained why I think it fails, in Gill (1996b and 2006, 333–7). I am assuming here that the justice-based objection can be met—that Hume can explain our approving of a just act even in a case in which more happiness would be created by doing the unjust thing. The different version of the non-consequentialist objection that I will be focusing on is that Hume cannot explain why a person would prefer to perform one act of which she approves herself rather than perform an act of which she disapproves but that spurs other people to perform multiple acts of which she approves.
6. For further discussion of how consequentialists can capture all the seemingly deontological moral phenomena through the use of agent-relative desires, see Dreier (1993) and Portmore (2009). For evidence that commonsense morality opts for consequentialist maximizing in the agent-relative or intrapersonal case but not in the agent-neutral or interpersonal case, see Lopez et al. (2009).
7. Drawing this connection between aesthetics and morals is especially apt in the case of 18th-cent. sentimentalists such as Hume. For connecting beauty and morality was *the*

leading idea of the entire classical sentimentalist project, with Shaftesbury, Hutcheson, Hume, and Smith all placing great emphasis on the similarity, if not the identity, of their accounts of beauty and virtue. See Gill (2007).

8. Bentham's most famous expression of this view is his claim that "the game of pushpin is of equal value with the arts and sciences of music and poetry" in *The Rationale of Reward* (Bentham 1830, 206).

9. Hume's view of pleasure is more akin to Mill's qualitative view than to the quantitative view of Bentham that Mill seeks to distance himself from. Mill's most famous expression of the non-quantitative view comes in his *Utilitarianism* discussion of the higher and lower pleasures (Mill 1861/2002, 7–11).

10. In Ch. 5 I will suggest that contemporary sentimentalists do better than Hume by holding that moral judgments are based in a number of distinct emotions rather than in different versions of the single sentiment of (different flavors of) approval.

11. None of Hume's indirect passions of pride, humility, love, and hatred has a world-to-mind direction of fit. They are not wants, or desires that the world be a certain way. They are evaluations of the way the world is. The same is true of Hume's moral passions of approval and disapproval. Each of these passions, however, either gives rise to or increases certain kinds of desires or wants. For fuller discussion of Hume's belief that the indirect passions are not motives to action, see Ardal 1966, 126; Baier 1986, 53–6; McIntyre (2000); Cohon (2008).

12. Here's what I think explains this difference between pride and love. I typically have much more control over whether or not I can do something to cause me to feel pride for myself than I do over whether or not I can cause other people to do things that will make me feel love for them. And I typically have a much more consistent and powerful desire for my own happiness than I do for the happiness of other people. So it's no surprise that the prospect of feeling pride will have an influence on my will that is more salient or cogent than the prospect of feeling love, and that love's relationship to my desire for my beloved's happiness will be more salient or cogent than pride's effect on my desire for myself to be happy.

13. The idea that aesthetic pleasure is not something that essentially motivates us to do anything to promote our own interests was well-recognized by Shaftesbury, whose account of beauty Hume was well-acquainted with. Shaftesbury puts the point in terms of the "disinterestedness" of aesthetic pleasure. Savile captures well Shaftesbury's point when he says that on Shaftesbury's view aesthetic pleasure is an "unmotivated pleasure. By this I mean no more than that [the pleasure does not] essentially result from the satisfaction of a desire that has occasioned some successfully accomplished action" (Savile 2002, 56). Or as Savile goes on to say, the aesthetic pleasure Shaftesbury "is concerned with is not a response to the awareness that some activity or behavior of ours has achieved any self-benefiting aim we have set ourselves. Were it of such a kind, it would be an interested pleasure, and clearly our aesthetic pleasures are not of that sort" (Savile 2002, 57–8).

14. Are the moral sentiments indirect passions? I don't want to enter into that debate here. All that's important for my purposes is that the moral sentiments are the same as the indirect passions with regard to their relation to motive. For discussion of this issue, see Radcliffe (1996) and Cohon (2008).

15. It's actually more complicated than what I say here: I will approve of the action because I think it is of a kind that is usually generated by a motive that generally produces actions that are pleasurable or useful to the agent or others.

16. Hume also discusses the unusual case of a person who lacks the primary motive to virtue but acts in the way the virtuous would because he realizes he approves of such action (T 3.2.1). For discussion of this case, see Radcliffe (1996).

17. Brown (1988) argues that Hume's motivational argument against the moral rationalists (T 3.1.1.5–11) requires (what she calls an "internalist" view, which is) that moral sentiments (or "moral considerations," or "moral opinions") motivate completely on their own—that Hume's argument against the rationalists will be undermined if moral sentiments motivate only because they have the cooperation of other mental principles. On this basis, Brown maintains that the kind of view of moral motivation I present here (which I call the "prospect view") is insufficient to fund the first premise of Hume's motivational argument against the moral rationalists (i.e. the premise that morals motivate). I myself think that Hume was relying on the prospect view when making the motivational argument, and I think that that view is sufficient for that argument. But I will not argue for that here. (For discussion of these points, see Radcliffe 1996; Abramson 2002; Cohon 2008.) The argument I'm advancing in this chapter against the non-consequentialist objection requires only that according to Humean psychology the moral sentiments can influence the will in the prospective way I describe in this and the following paragraph—and I believe there is ample textual evidence that Hume's account does affirm and offer an explanation of that kind of influence. Even if Brown is right in thinking that Hume's 3.1.1 argument requires that the moral sentiments influence the will in some kind of non-prospective way (which I doubt), that does not affect my claim here that Hume's account also includes a prospective kind of moral motivation that accounts for our non-trade off judgments (and blocks the non-consequentialist objection).

18. Where "love" for Hume can include the relatively weak and impersonal feeling of esteem (T 2.1.5.1; 2.2.2.10; 3.3.4.15).

19. Darwall makes this "wrong kind of reason" objection at Darwall 2006, 94 and 192.

20. Hume's account of how the prospect of self-disapproval motivates an agent to act morally fits well with recent psychological work on the motivational role of anticipations of guilt. This recent work holds that people wish to avoid the unpleasant feeling of guilt, and that this leads them to avoid acting in morally inappropriate ways. As Pelligra explains, "Emotions can exert a strong influence on choice, 'by providing critical feedback regarding both anticipated behavior (feedback in the form of anticipatory shame, guilt, or pride) and actual behavior (feedback in the form of consequential shame, guilt, or pride)' (Tangney, Stuewig & Mashek 2007, 347). These considerations are the building blocks of the so-called 'negative-state relief model' (Baumann, Cialdini & Kenrick, 1981) that posits that people tend to perform actions that are believed to increase positive affect, while reducing any unpleasant emotional state and distress such as feelings of guilt" (Pelligra 2011, 5–6). Nelissen et al. explain the view this way: "So, we argue that the prospect of making inadequate offers elicits anticipated guilt in proposers, which results in more generous offers to avoid an unfair outcome" (2011, 79). Baumeister et al. give the following example: "A person performs a behavior that causes distress to a

friend. The person therefore feels guilty afterwards. The guilt prompts the person to consider what he or she did wrong and how to avoid similar outcomes in the future. The next time a comparable situation arises, there may be a brief twinge of guilty affect that helps the person choose a course of action that will not bring distress to friends (and more guilt to the self)" (2007, 172–3). The plausibility of this picture of the motivational role of anticipations of guilt seems to me to lend strong support to Hume's account of the motivational role of the prospect of self-disapproval and approval.

Chapter 4

1. One might wonder whether Hume and Smith focus more on virtuous character and less on decisions that prompt specific actions than their immediate predecessors, and that it's this difference that explains Hume and Smith's weaker commitment to prioritarianism. Let me briefly make two comments about this. First, if it's a greater attention to virtue that explains Hume and Smith's pluralist aspects, that's still an important result, and reveals a crucial difference between Hume and Smith and their immediate predecessors (such as Clarke and Butler) as well as their immediate successors (such as Kant and Bentham). But secondly, I don't think Hume and Smith's pluralism is due entirely to an emphasis on virtue as opposed to decision-making. They both certainly emphasize virtue, but they also emphatically affirm rules of justice in a manner that could fit with an act-centered approach—and yet they are pluralist even about those rules, holding that while justice sometimes overrides other moral considerations, other moral considerations sometimes override justice.

2. In the passages I am discussing in this and the previous paragraph, Smith is discussing different *virtues*. But Smith also distinguishes between virtue and propriety (*TMS* 1.1.5.7–8). In my discussion of Smith on justice and casuistry, I will try to show that Smith isn't just a pluralist about virtues but is also a pluralist about moral rules, and morality in general

3. Hobbes contended that a person is obligated to pay the ransom he's promised to a highwayman (*Leviathan* 14.27; see also *De Cive* 2.16). Hutcheson took the contrary view: that in such a situation the promise has no moral force whatsoever (*Philosophiae moralis institutio compendiaria* IX; see also *Short Introduction* 2.9.8–9). In his edition of *The Theory of Moral Sentiments*, Hanley helpfully points out that Smith may also have had in mind in his discussion of casuistry Pufendorf, Cicero, Grotius, Augustine, and La Placette (Hanley 2010, 485).

4. It should be noted that Smith also suggests that a morally impeccable person would never be in a position in which it was proper for him to break a promise to a highwayman. For the morally impeccable person would never make such a promise in the first place, even if doing so was the only way to save his life (*TMS* 332). So even though a person may find himself in a situation in which it is not wrong to break a promise, the morally impeccable will never end up in such a situation. (For discussion of the closely related idea that persons can land in moral dilemmas only if they have in the past done something morally incorrect, see Hursthouse 1999a, 63–90.) Perhaps this is evidence that Smith at times took justice to have a kind of priority over all other principles, in that the wholly virtuous person will sacrifice anything (including his life) in order to

avoid being put in a situation in which the morally best option involves injustice. If this were Smith's view (and I don't think it's consistent with everything he says), then he would have a partial ordering of moral ends—with justice having priority. But he would still be a pluralist about conflicts between other sorts of moral ends.

5. As Fleischacker has shown, Smith's view here is not new or radical (Fleischacker 2004, 215–20).

6. The tension between Smith's prioritarianism and pluralism is very similar to—indeed, overlaps to a large extent with—the tension in his work between cultural relativism and universalism, which is wonderfully elucidated in Fleischacker (2005).

7. This dovetails with Smith's claim in his discussion of casuistry that morality is distinct from law.

8. Schliesser has argued that Smith is not an empiricist (Schliesser 2008, 574). But he does allow that for Smith moral judgment is based on the feelings of spectators and that Smith's account of morality is based in empirical features of human nature—and the a posteriori nature of this account is all that is important to the point I am making here. It's worth noting, though, that Schliesser's most important evidence from *TMS* of Smith's non-empiricism is p. 165, which I have claimed is a direct echo of Butler. And I think Schliesser is right to claim that this passage is very difficult to reconcile with an empiricist reading of Smith. But I also think that this difficulty reveals a tension in Smith's thought, not a flaw in reading other parts of *TMS* as empiricist. (Schliesser has recently argued, in correspondence, that at *TMS* 247 Smith might be interpreted as affirming innate moral ideas, in a non-empiricist fashion.)

9. Also indicative of Smith's proto-particularism is his insistence that some virtues, such as charity, gratitude, and being a good friend, are not rule-governed at all (*TMS* 172–4).

10. Griswold provides the most elucidating account of which I am aware of Smith's view of moral rules (Griswold 1999, 181–93). He points out that there is in Smith a tension between the use of rules and a more particularist case-by-case attention to specific cases. Griswold goes on to suggest that Smith thought that moral education involves a working back-and-forth between rules and particulars to develop good judgment and virtuous character. I think Griswold's account of Smith accords best with an overall anti-prioritarian reading, insofar as Griswold explains that Smith thought that it takes judgment even to figure out whether moral rules should be used (Griswold 1999, 188–9).

11. It's possible that some of the claims in the "Influence and authority of general rules" simply do not cohere with other parts of *TMS*, that the entirety of that chapter does not represent Smith's fullest and most mature thinking about morality. In an editors' footnote, Raphael and Macfie point out how similar some of the chapter's passages are to Butler, contend that those passages are inconsistent with Smith's other claims about the sentimental origins of morality, and then hypothesize that those passages "formed part of an early version of Smith's lectures" (*TMS* 164). As I read this hypothesis, the passages in this chapter that are conspicuously Butlerian—and, crucially for our purposes, the passages that imply that the general rules are such that none of them ever ought to be violated—are akin to the early writing on a palimpsest. On this reading, Smith initially thought of the fundamental principles of morality as fitting together in

the way that Butler did. But he eventually came to think of them as potentially breaking apart. On the other hand, Smith's intensive efforts at revising and rewriting *TMS* are reasons to doubt the existence in the 6th and final edition of palimpsest-like passages that Smith no longer endorsed.

12. I do not mean to suggest that Smith left theological thinking behind when he developed the more pluralist aspects of *TMS*. There is a great deal of scholarly debate about the role of theology in the construction of *TMS*, with at least one significant interpretation (Dickey 1986) holding that Smith became more theologically inclined when preparing the final edition of *TMS* rather than less. And indeed, we could read some of the most pluralist-sounding passages in *TMS* in a theologically inflected way, taking Smith's "man within the breast" (*TMS* 227) who exercises particularist judgment—i.e. the aspect of our moral nature that supplies the justificatory deficit left by general principles—to be identified with God's voice inside us, which would bring Smith's impartial spectator theory into direct contact with the Cambridge Platonist's use of Proverbs 20: 27: "The spirit of man is the candle of the Lord."

Chapter 5

1. It seems that psychopaths classified all the rules as moral, but that is probably because they were trying to sound as though they appreciated morality when in fact they lacked understanding of crucial aspects of it (see Blair 1995; Prinz 2007a, 44).

2. See Dwyer (1999), Harman (1999), and Hauser (2006).

3. See Prinz (2007b), Mallon (2008), and Dupoux and Jacob (2007).

4. "According to the version we will develop here, the principle [of double effect] holds that an otherwise prohibited action, such as battery or homicide, which has both good and bad effects may be permissible if the prohibited act itself is not directly intended, the good but not the bad effects are directly intended, the good effects outweigh the bad effects, and no morally preferable alternative is available" (Mikhail 2011, 149).

5. Rousseau is an odd one to include in this list insofar as the *Discourse on the Origin of Inequality* tells a historical, contingent story about the development of moral concepts, and *The Social Contract* tells a story about how our moral concepts can be fundamentally altered.

6. See Gill (2008b, 2009a).

7. This is a significant difference between Hume's view in the *Treatise* and Hutcheson's view, as Hutcheson does want to base morality on original human principles; I discuss this at Gill 2006, 214–25. Hume might have moved closer to Hutcheson's view of morality as based in original principles in the *Enquiry concerning Morals*.

8. The rationalist opponents of Hume I have in mind in this sentence do not include Kant, whose view doesn't include the commitment to mind-independence described here. The main Humean objection to Kantian moral rationalism is that morality depends on contingent features of human nature (in contrast to Kant's position that the morality is based on principles we would affirm even if all the contingent human characteristics were different).

9. Baier (1991) and Sayre-McCord (1996) argue that Hume uses a self-reflexive concept of normativity to justify his view of morality, a position that looks very similar to the reflective equilibrium approach favored by Rawlsians. Indeed, I think Rawls's method

of reflective equilibrium is completely available to Humeans. Rawls himself thought that Hume lacked a notion of practical reason needed for any kind of practical justification, but as I argued in Ch. 3, I think Rawls (along with Balguy, Kant, and Darwall) was wrong about this.

10. That the supposition of a creator God pulled no explanatory weight is one of the most important lessons of Hume's *Dialogues concerning Natural Religion*. It's a point he also made in the section of the *Enquiry concerning Understanding* called "Of a particular providence and a future state."

11. I am deliberately restricting the view I attribute to Hume to that which occurs in the *Treatise*. It is possible that his view changed somewhat in the *Enquiry concerning morals*.

Chapter 6

1. For a helpful account of the different distinctions naturalism-vs-non-naturalism can track, see Ridge (2013). I will be concerned with non-naturalism as a metaphysical or ontological thesis as opposed to a semantic thesis, although these cannot be kept perfectly separate because Ross uses implications of our moral thinking as premises in metaphysical and ontological arguments. For some of the most important arguments against moral non-naturalism, see Bedke (2009), Harman (1977, 1986), Mackie (1977, 15–50), Smith (1994, 18–25), and Street (2006). For some of the most important defenses of moral non-naturalism, see Audi (2004), Enoch (2010), Huemer (2005), Shafer-Landau (2005), and Wielenberg (2010).

2. Ross points to disanalogies between morals and mathematics at 1930, 121–2.

3. Horgan and Timmons (forthcoming) argue that while phenomenological investigations can be very fruitful for many issues, our introspectable phenomenology does not speak conclusively against or in favor of non-naturalism, which means that this debate must be settled by non-phenomenological inference to best explanation. I argue that an individual's moral phenomenology could be infected by her theoretical or meta-ethical commitments in Gill (2008a).

4. Prinz's explanation here of the non-inferential self-evidence of moral judgment relies on specifics of his account, according to which emotions constitute moral judgments. But the general point—that emotion's role in moral judgment accounts for the phenomenology Ross takes to be non-inferential self-evidence—can be (mutatis mutandis) located in the different sentimentalist account of Nichols, according to which emotion's amplification of certain rules explains our experiencing them as obvious.

5. Michael Smith rightly points out that we can be wrong about what we desire (1994, 105–8). We can think we desire something but through discursive reasoning come to see that we really don't desire it; and we can think we don't desire something and through discursive reasoning come to see that we really do desire it. I do not mean to say here that we have infallible non-inferential knowledge of our own desires. My point is just that we usually come to know our desires by non-inferential means—that that is a common phenomenology of desire epistemology.

6. Ross makes the same argument in *Kant's Ethical Theory* when he speaks of "our natural conviction that there is such a thing as duty" and assumes that this conviction includes

the idea that duty is non-natural, independent of everything that "natural science" can tell us (Ross 1954, 87).

7. Mackie famously argued that our concept of morality is pretty much what the non-naturalists thought it was, but that this concept is inexorably in error, as there is nothing in the world that corresponds to non-natural moral properties. Blackburn (1985) argues that there is good reason to doubt that our moral practices are infected by such an error. I have tried to make plausible the idea that the moral thinking of some people is guilty of the error Mackie describes but that the moral thinking of other people is not guilty; see Gill (2008b).

8. In the full passage at 1930, 81 Ross gives us consecutive sentences that start with: "It is surely clear that…," which in itself is enough to arouse suspicion about whether he is really describing something everyone thinks.

9. Ross's picture here differs significantly from the inductive, proto-particularist explanation of our belief in general moral rules that Adam Smith gives at TMS 160. Smith holds that we make all-in moral judgments about particular cases first, and then latter inductively come to believe in certain kinds of general moral reasons. Ross says that we first come to believe in certain instances of (prima facie) moral reasons, and that our all-in moral judgments about particular cases don't play a role in the inductive thinking that leads to general statements of those moral reasons.

10. Ross suggests that deontological duties generally override consequentialist duties unless the consequences in question are extremely serious or dire (1930, 34–5 and 41–2), and this could be taken to be a kind of general principle that bridges prima facie duties and actual duty (I discuss this kind of general principle in the next chapter). But this kind of general principle is not nearly as determinate and fixed as the physical laws. Nor will Ross's principles have the probabilistic character of the laws of quantum physics. One might hold that Ross's principles have the same character as the "soft laws" of scientific disciplines such as psychology (see Horgan and Tienson 1996, 107–44). But acknowledging the softness of laws such as those in psychology does not require us to deny that there are determinate law-like explanations to be had of any natural phenomena. We expect that such answers do exist but that they may be described only by more fundamental scientific laws. When the soft laws of one scientific domain give out before an explanation is reached, we can drop down to a more basic scientific domain and (at least in theory) find answers there. Ross's pluralism, in contrast, implies that there is no objective law-like explanation of morality to be had at any level.

11. I discuss this reluctance in Ch. 10. Another explanation of the uncertainty that Ross takes to be our struggle to discern our mind-independent duty is that we are experiencing the incompatible pulls of two mind-dependent rules; that's how Mikhail and Nichols would explain the phenomenon.

12. It was due to Prichard that Ross changed his mind. For a close discussion of why Prichard held to the subjective understanding and why Ross followed him there, see Dancy (2002).

Chapter 7

1. In this and succeeding chapters, I move more toward discussing the contrast between monism and pluralism, and say less about non-monistic forms of prioritarianism

(such as non-conflict multiplism and ordered conflict multiplism). This is because by the beginning of the 19th century, non-monistic forms of prioritarianism became less and less common—while the grand monistic theories of Kant and the utilitarians grew in stature. It began to seem as though if we wanted to banish ultimate moral conflict, the only way to do so was to commit to only one ultimate moral end. It didn't seem likely that numerous independent ends would always harmonize perfectly, and no strict priority ordering of independent ends seemed plausible. As I tried to show in Chs 1–4, the grappling with multiple ends in Butler, Hume, Reid, Price, and Smith—and, in particular, Hume and Smith's struggle to find their footing along the border between multiplist prioritarianism and moral pluralism—presaged this transition to monism.

2. Bentham also believed that there had to be one and only one fundamental principle of morality, and given that there had to be only one, utility was obviously better than any alternative (Bentham 1823/1907, 1–23). When Mill attacks the "intuitive school of ethics" (Mill 1861/2001, 3) and Bentham attacks those "inclined to think that [their] own approbation, annexed to the idea of an act…is a sufficient foundation for [them] to judge and act upon" (Bentham 1823/1907, 6), they have in mind the kind of non-ordered conflict multiplism I have shown Price to be a prime example of. I have also argued that Hume goes a long way towards non-ordered conflict multiplism, but Mill and Bentham might not have thought the same about him. Bentham, at least, seemed to think Hume was more of a utilitarian monist.

3. Rawls describes Mill's formal argument for monism, and he endorses the general idea that moral theory requires a principled way of adjudicating between competing moral claims, even if the role of intuition can never be wholly eliminated (Rawls 1971, 41).

4. I shouldn't overstate the distinctness of the formal and substantive aspects of Kant's monism. Kant believes that his account of the ultimate end follows necessarily from the concept of morality, so he will hold that a proper understanding will lead us at once to both the formal and substantive aspects. The merger of the formal and substantive aspects of Kant's monism is apparent when, for instance, he writes, "There is therefore only one categorical imperative and it is this: 'Act only on that maxim by which you can at the same time will that it should become a universal law'" (Kant 1785/2002, 222). This is in contrast to Mill, who seems to believe that while the concept of morality requires a single ultimate standard, it is a contingent fact that conduciveness to happiness is that standard. Nonetheless, we can distinguish between Kantian reasons for holding that morality requires a single supreme end and Kantian reasons for holding that the single supreme end is humanity or universalizability. There's a difference between those two types of reasons, even if Kant thought that they were conceptually linked.

5. Richardson (1990, 2000) distinguishes between "intuitive" pluralism, which involves simply barely intuiting which of two conflicting moral principles overrides, and "justified" pluralism, which involves giving reasons for holding that one of two conflicting moral principles overrides. Here I am discussing "intuitive" pluralism. In the next chapter, I will discuss "justified" pluralism. But Richardson argues (as I think any prioritarian should) that in the end even "justified" pluralism falls prey to the concern about justification raised here.

6. Mason is discussing Raz's pluralism in particular, but I think the point she makes captures well the basic concern that led Mill and Kant to formal monism.
7. See Hampton 1986, 97–113.
8. Carol Gilligan's famous arguments in *In a Different Voice* imply that the prioritarian, logic-like, morally hierarchical resolution that Kohlberg endorses is a masculine characteristic, while the more pluralist sensitivity to various different concerns is feminine. Thus "Jack constructs the dilemma as a mathematical equation" that can be solved by the application of clear rules, while "Amy again responds contextually rather than categorically, saying 'it depends' and indicating how choice would be affected by variations in character and circumstance" (Gilligan 1982, 37–8).
9. Eggleston makes the same objection in his discussion of Hooker: "The essential mission of a moral theory, it is widely thought, is to articulate general principles that, in conjunction with specifications of agents' circumstances and options, yield judgments regarding which option an agent, in any given situation ought to choose...[M]oral theories...are supposed to yield determinate verdicts as to which option an agent, in any given situation, ought to choose. Any indeterminacy is a deficiency that, other things being equal, it is desirable to eliminate" (Eggleston 2007, 335).
10. McNaughton (1996) has ably come to the defense of this criticism of Ross.

Chapter 8

1. For criticisms of the balancing of norms, see Richardson (2000) and Gert et al. (1997). I believe the main thrust of criticisms such as these is that ultimately even a "justified balancing" relies on an intuitive—which is to say unjustifiable—preference for one norm over the other in a particular situation. I think that this criticism does get something right: ultimately, a truly pluralist view does have to allow that when norms conflict justification bottoms out in a brute preference for which no further justification can be given. My two-part claim in this and the next chapter is that (1) if Humean sentimentalism is true this kind of bottoming out is just what we should expect and (2) there is nonetheless quite a lot of articulatible, discursively expressible justificatory thinking we can do before we reach the brute preference bottom. As Hume puts it, "The final sentence...which pronounces characters and actions amiable or odious, praiseworthy or blameable...depends on some internal sense or feeling...But in order to pave the way for such a sentiment, and give a proper discernment of its object, it is often necessary, we find, that much reasoning should precede, that nice distinctions be made, just conclusions drawn, distant comparisons formed, complicated relations examined, and general facts fixed and ascertained" (*E* 1.9).
2. See Lance and Little (2004, 2007a, 2007b) on defeasible principles.
3. The material in the square brackets I have added to Ross's quotation.
4. For discussion of the criticism that Ross's view gives us nothing but "an unconnected heap of duties," see McNaughton (1996).
5. A view that might seem to resemble the threshold deontological view is one which includes multiple basic ends but says that there is some way to weight each of them

when they conflict so that the relative weights determine what the theory recommends. I discuss this view in "Principled Trade-Offs" in Ch. 9.

6. As I noted in the previous chapter, Adam Smith adopts a similar position when discussing whether one has a duty to keep one's promise to pay a ransom to a highwayman. If paying the ransom will not cause a great deal of harm, then one will be obligated to do so. But if paying the ransom will cause a great deal of harm, then one's duty is not to pay (*TMS* 331–2).

7. For discussion of ceteris paribus, see Lance and Little (2004, 2007a, 2007b) and McKeever and Ridge (2006).

8. See also Waldron (2011).

9. One common response to Ellis and Alexander's criticisms is to hold that moral boundaries are vague, and that the lack of a clear boundary (such as between baldness and non-baldness, or red and orange) does not make a concept unusable or problematic. This response holds that Ellis and Alexander are failing to appreciate the very general feature of vagueness that characterizes many of our concepts. Ellis addresses this response directly in section VI of his paper (and Alexander quotes and endorses Ellis's response at 908–10 of his paper). Morality, Ellis argues, is different from other vague concepts. The boundary between right and wrong requires a kind of justification that is different from the justification required for the boundary between, say, red and orange. If we all decide to call certain things red and other things orange, then no further justification of the boundary is needed. But, according to Ellis, we need to be able to justify moral boundaries in ways that go beyond simply what we all decide to do (Ellis 1992, 869–70). So even if the change from moral rightness to moral wrongness occurs in a continuous or vague way (so that we don't know if what makes the torture right is the prevention of the killing of forty people or fifty people), there will still be an unacceptable arbitrariness in that change (still an arbitrariness in the difference between forty and fifty) if we can't give any definite reason for it. I believe Ellis's argument here presupposes a non-sentimentalist conception of moral justification. I will be trying to show that if we take a sentimentalist view of morality seriously, the vagueness of moral predicates is not problematic. Ellis says that we have to be able to justify our moral judgments "at the deepest level" (Ellis 1992, 870). The point I try to make is that, if sentimentalism is true, we shouldn't expect or require that moral justification go as deep as Ellis thinks it must.

10. Hume himself emphasizes how contrastive our moral judgments are when he discusses the role of "comparison" in the development of moral and other sentiments. For discussion of comparison and the Humean view of morality, see Gill 2006, 241–61.

11. In the rest of this chapter, I will occasionally speak of there being or not being a "fact of the matter" concerning certain questions of justification. I do not mean that phrase to bring with it any metaphysical baggage. The phrase is a way of expressing the idea of there being a clear or decisive justification (however that is metaphysically construed). I use "fact of the matter" just because it is more colloquial and wieldy.

12. See also Hume's *Essays*, 243–5.

13. For a rich discussion of how our notions of "required" and "forbidden" can be vague in ways that explain difficult (but non-dilemmatic) moral decisions, see Sorensen (1991).

14. I take the point I make here to cohere with what McKeever and Ridge say about "pluralism and explanatory depth" (2006, 189–94). According to McKeever and Ridge, "moral philosophers should look for deeper moral principles which could plausibly serve to unify the seemingly heterogeneous principles culled from common sense" (2006, 189). But this unifying project need not make it all the way to monism in order to be successful. The "deeper principles" that produce explanatory unity may "fall well short of the grandiose ambitions of utilitarianism, but provide illumination of important tracts of moral territory all the same" (2006, 190). "[P]luralistic normative theories" may give us all the explanatory depth that it is appropriate to seek. As McKeever and Ridge put it, "The form of generalism we have been defending does not presuppose a plurality of ultimate moral considerations, but it is compatible with such a plurality" (2006, 190).

Chapter 9

1. For a deeply perceptive and razor-sharp discussion of reasons to forgo the search for a "single supreme principle" of morality, see Wolf (2011).
2. I expect some people are more drawn to a monistic view and some toward a pluralist view. I also expect that in some contexts monism is more predominant, and in other contexts pluralism is more predominant. And there are probably some cases in which it is utterly indeterminate whether the moral discourse carries with it monistic or pluralist commitments. I discuss this kind of variability and indeterminacy in Gill (2008b, 2009a).
3. Wolf (2011) is a convincing account of the problems that afflict Parfit's attempt to develop a prioritarian ethical view.
4. Sinnott-Armstrong (2009) has argued that the obligation to keep promises can be best explained by consequentialism. For a pluralist response to Sinnott-Armstrong, see Gill (2012).
5. Timmons (2006) has developed a similar argument about the indeterminacy of the Kantian view, focusing on the difficulty of fixing on maxims that pass the test of the first formulation of the Categorical Imperative and also produce results that aren't strongly counterintuitive.
6. As I've noted in a previous chapter, the need for moral principles to be internalizable is a reason to reject Richardson's specificationism, as it seems that if we were to continue to specify our moral rules so that they never stated anything that we had to act against, the result would eventually be a set of rules so complex and clause-ridden that they would be impossible to internalize.
7. For a similar assessment of Gert et al. (i.e. that they end up with a view that looks more like Rossian pluralism than their criticism of Beauchamp and Childress's principlism might have led us to expect), see Richardson (2000).
8. For a more comprehensive and, to my mind, convincing account of the practical limitations of Hooker's method for dealing with such conflict, see Eggleston (2007).
9. See *T* 3.2.6.9; *T* 3.2.12.1; *T* 3.3.5.2; D 47; *TMS* 23–4; *TMS* 153.
10. For more on this point, see my earlier discussion of the difference between Hume's naturalistic account of moral commitments and the account assumed in the Natural Law tradition.

11. One might worry that our multiple concerns could be debunked as fetishistic results of our "addiction to general rules," and that once we come to reject those concerns that have unjustifiable origins (i.e. originate in addictive general rules), we will be left with only one fundamental moral concern. So even from a sentimentalist perspective, reflective equilibrium might lead us to monism. In Gill (1996a, 1996b), I explain why Humeans will deny that showing that a concern originates in part from addictive general rules should count as a "debunking." I try to show there why it is plausible to hold that a fully reflective perspective on our concerns will lead us to continue to endorse some of them even though they are partly caused by addictive general rules. A major reason for this is that if we were to expurgate every concern that was partly caused by addictive general rules, we would be left with virtually nothing that resembled our current moral concerns at all. The line between those concerns based on addictive general rules and those not so based will leave virtually everything we currently think of as moral on the wrong side. I should note, though, that Joshua Greene has argued that there is another distinction between the origins of our moral concerns—those that result from automatic valenced representations, and those that result from cognitive neutral representations—that *does* track the distinction between those moral concerns that should survive reflective equilibrium and those that shouldn't (Greene 2008). Greene thus believes that sentimentalist reflective equilibrium will produce a consequentialist monism. Nichols and I examine Greene's arguments and explain why we think they fail in (Gill and Nichols 2008, 157–9). For a fuller critique of Greene's view, see Timmons (2008).

12. In this work, I am emphasizing the multifariousness and unsystematicity of the emotions that underlie our moral judgments, and I am claiming that this multifariousness and unsystematicity explains (and should lead us to expect) the pluralist features of morality. Another route to the same pluralist conclusion—a significant set of considerations that support the pluralist view—is the multifarious and unsystematic historical antecedents of our conception of morality. The way we think about morality has been profoundly influenced by a number of distinct ancient cultures, by European Christianity, by the rise of modern science, by geopolitical events of the last hundred years, by developments in psychology, by art, by popular culture, etc. And once we realize that our moral thinking is a path-dependent historical hodgepodge, we should not be surprised to find that it includes a plurality of fundamental normative commitments that lack the single organizational structure that would ensure a principled resolution for all moral conflicts. This is a point made well by Williams and Falk. Williams says that a consideration that should lead us to expect moral pluralism "is to be found in a fact often neglected by ethical theorists, that our ethical ideas consist of a very complex historical deposit. When we consider this fact, and the relations that this deposit has to our public discourse and our private lives, there seems no reason at all to expect it to take, in any considerable measure, the shape of [what I have been calling a *prioritarian*] theory" (Williams 1995, 189). Falk says, "The concept of morality itself bears the accumulated scars of conceptual evolution. Its multiple associations are a bar to summing it up in any one way" (Falk 1986, 231). In Gill (2009a), I have explored the indeterminacy and variability the complex of historical antecedents has bestowed on our meta-ethical concepts.

13. I wish to thank an OUP referee for bringing this alternative to my attention. I also owe great thanks to Jerry Gaus for patiently helping me to see the importance of this view.

14. As opposed to a merely after-the-fact description of a person's decision-making. That kind of after-of-the-fact description is always possible. As Gaus puts it, "[I]t is in principle possible to devise for any individual a cardinal utility function that integrates" all her normative commitments (Gaus 2011, 158). Indeed, even a particularist should allow that we can formulate a general proposition about what is right to do based on the conjunction of past cases. To be prioritarian, however, a position has to establish principles that an agent can use when making decisions or justifying—i.e. principles that are not merely descriptions of what the agent has done in the past but prescriptions that she can use to make decisions in the future, principles that give prospective normative guidance. My point here is that it is not plausible that we could come up with this kind of *prescriptive* cardinal utility function.

15. Gaus explains how one and the same rule will be given different weights in different situations because of the differences in its "salience" or "impact" (Gaus 2011, 152).

16. For further explication of this kind of non-monistic comparison of different bundles of values and rule-following, see Gaus 2011, 149–56.

17. An OUP referee raised the possibility of "generating comprehensive orderings" of all of our ultimate ends. My point here is that I doubt that it's possible to do this in a way that can justificatorily serve an agent when making first-personal decisions. It will always be possible, after an agent has made her decisions, to generate an ordering (and perhaps even a cardinal weighting) that matches what the agent decided. (As I've already noted, even a particularist should allow that, after the fact, it will be possible to generate a general statement of what is right, composed of a conjunction of past instances of right actions.) But in order to justificatorily serve an agent, an ordering (or weighting) will have to be made in advance of decision-making. And what I am maintaining here is that a fair number of the situations we face are so complex and nuanced that it will be impossible to generate a comprehensive and determinate, prior ordering (let alone a precise cardinal weighting) that an agent will be able to deploy in order to resolve what to do. Pluralist judgment—first-personal deliberations that outstrip principles—will still sometimes be necessary. The OUP referee writes, "The intuitive response to trolley problems seems to be that it's wrong to kill one person to save five lives, but permissible to kill one person to save a billion lives. A view composed of principles for weighing the value of the saved lives and the disvalue of killing one person to determine the rightness of actions will address this nicely." I am maintaining that it's unrealistic to expect us to be able to come up with a weighting that is precise enough to tell us what to do in a nuanced and complex real-world situation in which we might have to make a decision of this sort. Our being able to say in advance that killing one to save two is unacceptable while killing one to save a billion is acceptable is not any basis for confidence that we can say in advance how to weight things in a more complex, nuanced situation. Imagine you are a military commander or war-time political leader who has to decide between killing a certain number of people or letting a greater number of people die. It just seems very implausible to me to that there is any precise weighting that could be developed in advance that you could then simply deploy in order to make the decision. Cases involving killing and letting die, moreover, are ones in which

there are quantifiable numbers of lives involved on either side. It is even less clear how we would assign prior precise weights to all the myriad different kinds of promises one might make (as opposed to the utterly implausible assignation of the same weight to each promise, whether concerning something life-shattering or something minor), or familial duties or professional obligations one might have. The OUP referee writes, "[S]portswriters voting for Most Valuable Player and managers assembling teams have to aggregate [different] dimensions of value to come up with a final assessment of which player is better. Sports statisticians have in recent years developed increasingly sophisticated ways of arriving at total assessments." But sports statisticians are working in an area in which accomplishments are easily quantifiable (in a way many aspects of the moral life are not) and in which there is one quantifiable, easily identifiable, and predominant goal: winning games. In areas in which there are multiple independent, non-quantifiable, and potentially conflicting ends, the techniques of the sports statisticians will not take us very far.

Chapter 10

1. As Michael Smith points out, when we say that we " 'expect" someone to do something we can mean either that we believe she *will* do it or that we believe that she *should* do it" (Smith 1994, 85). I think Amy's response here is what we would "expect" in both senses. But for the argument I present in the rest of this chapter, it is important only that we expect such a response in the sense of thinking the agent *should* have it.

2. Contemporary interest in this argument originated with Bernard Williams (1973a), and the argument has been developed in a number of fruitful ways by various philosophers since then. Blackburn (1996) and Hill (1996) discuss the argument in relation to moral dilemmas, Hursthouse (1999a) in relation to virtue ethics, Wiggins (1978–9) in relation to weakness of will, Foot (1983) in relation to moral realism, Stocker (1990) in relation to particularist meta-ethics, Hurley (1989) in relation to the rationality of decision-making, and Kekes (1995) in relation to moral relativism.

3. Are the agonizing decisions people like Amy Kane face instances of moral dilemmas? It depends what we mean. In ordinary conversation, "dilemma" is often used to describe a situation in which a person faces a morally very difficult decision, a situation in which there are powerful reasons to act in one way and powerful reasons to act in an incompatible way. Philosophers, however, often use "dilemma" to mean something more strict than that; Sinnott-Armstrong has convincingly argued that, on this more philosophical understanding, a dilemma should be understood as a situation in which two moral requirements are in conflict and yet neither of them is overridden (Sinnott-Armstrong 1988). A situation that is a dilemma in the ordinary sense may not be a dilemma in the strict philosophical sense, and that's because a person may eventually come to see that in the difficult moral situation in which she finds herself one of the requirements does override the other. The agonizing decision argument, as I develop it here, is anchored in situations that the agent takes to be a dilemma in the ordinary sense but does *not* take to be a dilemma in Sinnott-Armstrong's strict philosophical sense. As I develop it, this argument turns on the idea that even when an agent thinks one requirement truly does override all others we may still think it appropriate that she feel remorse for acting on that requirement.

4. For astute discussion of the conjunction of agent-regret and the wish *not* to undo what one has done, see Rorty (1980).

5. See D'Arms and Jacobson (2000) for further discussion of how an emotion can be fitting to a situation.

6. We can think of Humean approval and disapproval as stand-ins for positive and negative moral emotions in general, without having to insist that there is just one positive moral emotion (approval) and one negative (disapproval). See Ch. 5's discussion of basic moral emotions in Haidt, Prinz, and Nichols.

7. Approval of remorse in these situations also constitutes a significant reason to prefer pluralism over a specificationist view of moral principles. Specificationists hold that moral principles include specifications—provisos, qualifications, and the like—that are detailed enough to ensure that the principles will never actually imply incompatible actions (see Richardson 1990, 2000). So while the pluralist takes us to think that we sometimes have to break one moral rule in order to conform to another, the specificationist takes us to think that to act morally is to act in conformity with all the moral rules just so long as those rules are suitably specified. Specificationists thus deny that ultimate moral ends will come into conflict not because they think the world has been theologically or rationally arranged to ensure that a plurality of simple basic rules will always converge on the same action but rather because they think that rules contain (or should be revised so as to contain) specifications that are detailed and mutually sensitive enough to ensure that no rule ever manages to step on another duty's toes. In contrast, pluralists contend that ultimate ends can step on each other's toes (and that they ought not to be revised so that this never occurs). Now it might seem to be quite difficult to determine which of these two positions is correct. For both pluralist and specificationist views can explain the difficulty of making certain kinds of moral decisions: pluralists say that the difficulty comes in deciding which rule to violate, while specificationists say the difficulty comes from trying to determine what the full extent of the qualifications of the initially conflicting rules ought to be. But if I think I have acted in accord with all the moral rules, as the specificationist claims I eventually should, why would it be appropriate for me to continue to feel remorse? It seems that if the specificationist were right, when I did what I ultimately thought was the right thing to do I would have no cause to feel what we take it to be appropriate for Amy Kane to feel. For if all these specifications were fully spelled out, we would see that all the moral ends really do fit together perfectly—that there is nothing to feel remorse about. I hasten to add that Richardson claims that his specificationism does a better job than pluralism at explaining how "conflicting norms 'hang around' even after a conflict of norms has been resolved, sometimes giv[ing] rise to what Ross called 'compunction' " (Richardson 1990, 298). But I must confess to not being able to follow his reasoning. What it seems to me his theory can explain is why a new, revised norm that we think we should act on can be similar to an old norm that we have decided not to act on. But that does not explain why we think it might be ethically appropriate to feel remorse for acting on the new, revised norm.

8. Compare to the non-conflict multiplism of Clarke and Butler. It seems that their views imply that remorse for doing the right thing is never appropriate. If what you do is truly in accord with one moral principle, it will also be in accord with every other (even if your limitations make it virtually impossible for you to see this). Most notably, if what

you do is in accord with what we would call a deontological duty (justice, truth-telling, and such), then it will also be the most beneficent, even if you cannot see it right now. So remorse in this situation is, on full reflection, inappropriate.

9. Blackburn is actually talking about moral dilemmas in the strict philosophical sense, while I am talking about morally difficult situations that are not dilemmas in that sense (see n. 3). What Blackburn says about moral dilemmas can be taken to suggest this epistemic objection to the difficult cases argument, but I do not know if Blackburn himself would endorse the objection.

10. At the end of Ch. 6, we saw that Ross distinguished between an "objective" and "subjective" understanding of our actual duty. In *The Right and the Good*, Ross opted for the objective understanding. In *Foundations of Ethics*, he opted for the subjective. Here we find that Price (not surprisingly) opts for the objective.

11. Ross seems to have the same thing in mind when he speaks of a person's feeling "compunction" about violating a prima facie duty even though she is acting on her actual duty (Ross 1930, 28).

12. Hill's case is another revealing example (as was Williams' case of Jim and the Indians) of the difficulty of making some moral decisions that monisms have trouble explaining. We can certainly imagine this case as one in which the ratio of pleasure-to-pain would clearly be better if the professor lies to the woman, and in such an instance a utilitarian would be committed to saying that lying is *obviously* the right course of action—and that it is *easy* to figure that out. We can also see this case as clearly one in which an agent has to choose whether to lie to someone or to tell her the truth, and in such an instance a Kantian (or Kant, anyway) would be committed to saying that telling the truth is *obviously* the right course of action—and that it is *easy* to figure that out. But it's not perfectly and immediately obvious which course of action is right (even if we assume that more happiness will be created by lying). This case (like Jim and the Indians) is one in which we can imagine its being very difficult to determine what ought to be done. And while the monistic views of utilitarianism and Kantianism seem to predict that such difficulty would not arise, the pluralist view that this difficulty is due to the fact that in this case two ultimate moral ends are in conflict is simple and persuasive.

13. I believe the response to Hurka I pursue here is consonant with Mason's astute discussion of "rational regret" in Mason (2011).

14. Monistic utilitarians can endorse, after a fashion, the remorse some feel after doing what they think is right. That remorse, on this utilitarian account, grows out of concerns that when acted on usually promote happiness. In unusual situations, greater happiness can be promoted by acting contrary to those concerns. But it's a good thing that a person feels bad about acting contrary to those concerns even in those unusual situations because that reaction will keep her from acting contrary to those concerns in the more usual cases in which such actions do not best promote happiness. Heeding the reluctance to kill human beings usually best promotes happiness. There are some unusual cases in which killing humans does best promote happiness. But it's better that a person feel bad about killing even in those unusual cases because that will make it more likely that she won't kill in the more usual cases. I take this utilitarian endorsement not to be directly in opposition to the pluralist description of commonsense moral thinking I am advancing here. This utilitarian

endorsement is consistent with the idea that commonsense moral thinking takes there to be a plurality of potentially conflicting ultimate moral ends. It just then goes on to hold that such thoughts are something like a useful illusion—that the single end of happiness is best promoted if ordinary people think like pluralists. I do not agree with the utilitarian view of commonsense pluralism, but I will not take on that issue here.

15. Although Hursthouse isn't hostile to the idea that there are agonizing decisions in which the agent will experience remorse whichever course of action she chooses. Far from it. Hursthouse describes this phenomenon very insightfully in Hursthouse (1999a).

Works Cited

Abramson, Kate (1999). "Hume on Cultural Conflicts of Values," *Philosophical Studies*, 94: 173–87.

Abramson, Kate (2002). "Two Portraits of the Humean Moral Agent," *Pacific Philosophical Quarterly*, 83: 331–4.

Alexander, Larry (2000). "Deontology at the Threshold," *San Diego Law Review*, 37: 893–912.

Anscombe, G. E. M. (1956). "Modern Moral Philosophy," *Philosophy*, 33: 1–19.

Ardal, Pall S. (1966). *Passions and Value in Hume's Treatise*. Edinburgh: Edinburgh University Press.

Attfield, Robin (1987). *A Theory of Value and Obligation*. London: Croom Helm.

Audi, Robert (2004). *The Good in the Right: A Theory of Intuition and Intrinsic Value*. Princeton: Princeton University Press.

Baier, Annette (1986). "The Ambiguous Limits of Desire," in Joel Marks (ed.), *The Ways of Desire*, 39–61. Chicago: Transaction Publishers.

Baier, Annette (1991) *A Progress of Sentiments: Reflections on Hume's Treatise*. Princeton: Princeton University Press.

Baier, Annette (2004). "How Wide is Hume's Circle?" *Hume Studies*, 32: 113–17.

Balguy, John (1991). "The Foundation of Moral Goodness," in D. D. Raphael (ed.), *British Moralists 1650–1800*, i. 389–408. Indianapolis: Hackett Publishing Co.; originally publ. 1728.

Baron, Marcia (1988). "Remorse and Agent-Regret," *Midwest Studies in Philosophy*, 13: 259–81.

Baumann, D. J., Cialdini, R. B., and Kenrick, D. T. (1981). "Altruism as Hedonism: Helping and Self-Gratification as Equivalent Responses," *Journal of Personality and Social Psychology*, 40: 1039–46.

Baumeister, R. F., Vohs, K. D., DeWall, C. N., and Zhang, L. (2007). "How Emotion Shapes Behavior: Feedback, Anticipation, and Reflection, rather than Direct Causation," *Personality and Social Psychology Review*, 11: 167–203.

Beauchamp, Tom L. and Childress, James F. (2009). *Principles of Biomedical Ethics* (6th edn). Oxford: Oxford University Press.

Bedke, Matt (2009). "Intuitive Non-Naturalism Meets Cosmic Coincidence," *Pacific Philosophical Quarterly*, 90: s188–s209.

Benn, Stanley I. (1988). *A Theory of Freedom*. Cambridge: Cambridge University Press.

Bentham, Jeremy (1823/1907). *An Introduction to the Principles of Morals and Legislation*. Oxford: Clarendon Press.

Bentham, Jeremy (1830). *The Rationale of Reward*. London: Robert Heward.

Berthoz, S., Armony, J. L., Blair, R. J. R., and Dolan, R. J. (2002). "An fMRI Study of Intentional and Unintentional (Embarrassing) Violations of Social Norms," *Brain*, 125: 1696–1708.

Blackburn, Simon (1984). *Spreading the Word: Groundings in the Philosophy of Language.* Oxford: Oxford University Press.

Blackburn, Simon (1985). "Errors and the Phenomenology of Value," in *Essays in Quasi-Realism,* 149–65. Oxford: Oxford University Press.

Blackburn, Simon (1996). "Dilemmas: Dithering, Plumbing, and Grief," in H. E. Mason (ed.), *Moral Dilemmas and Moral Theory,* 127–39. Oxford: Oxford University Press.

Blackburn, Simon (1998). *Ruling Passions: A Theory of Practical Reasoning.* Oxford: Oxford University Press.

Blair, R. J. R. (1995). "A Cognitive Developmental Approach to Morality: Investigating the Psychopath," *Cognition,* 57: 1–29.

Blair, R. J. R., Jones, L., Clark, F., and Smith, M. (1997). "The Psychopathic Individual: A Lack of Responsiveness to Distress Cues?" *Psychophysiology,* 34: 192–8.

Brown, Charlotte (1988). "Is Hume an Internalist?" *Journal of the History of Philosophy,* 26: 69–87.

Burnet, Gilbert, and Hutcheson, Francis (1725/1971). "Letters between the late Mr. Gilbert Burnet, and Mr. Hutcheson, concerning the true Foundation of Virtue or Moral Goodness," in B. Peach (ed.), *Illustrations on the Moral Sense.* Cambridge, MA: Belknap Press.

Butler, Joseph (1729/1983a). "Upon the Love of Our Neighbor," in *Five Sermons,* ed. Stephen Darwall, 57–68. Indianapolis: Hackett Publishing.

Butler, Joseph (1729/1983b). "Upon Human Nature," in *Five Sermons,* ed. Stephen Darwall, 25–33. Indianapolis: Hackett Publishing.

Butler, Joseph (1736/1983). "Dissertation upon the Nature of Virtue," in *Five Sermons,* ed. Stephen Darwall, 69–75. Indianapolis: Hackett Publishing.

Carmichael, Gershom (1724/2002). *Natural Rights on the Threshold of the Scottish Enlightenment: The Writings of Gershom Carmichael,* ed. James Moore and Michael Silverthorne. Indianapolis: Liberty Fund.

Clarke, Samuel (1705/1738). "A Discourse concerning the Unchangeable Obligations of Natural Religion," in *The Works of Samuel Clarke,* ii, ed. John Clarke. London: John and Paul Knapton.

Cohon, Rachel (1997). "The Common Point of View in Hume's Ethics," *Philosophy and Phenomenological Research,* 57: 827–50.

Cohon, Rachel (2008). "Hume's Indirect Passions," in E. Radcliffe (ed.), *A Companion to Hume,* 159–84. Oxford: Blackwell.

Crisp, Roger (2005). "Hume on Virtue, Utility, and Morality," in S. Gardiner (ed.), *Virtue Ethics, Old and New,* 159–78. Ithaca, NY: Cornell University Press.

Dancy, Jonathan (2002). "Prichard on Duty and Ignorance of Fact," in P. J. Stratton-Lake (ed.), *Ethical Intuitionism,* 229–47. Oxford: Oxford University Press.

Dancy, Jonathan (2004). *Ethics without Principles.* Oxford: Clarendon Press.

D'Arms, Justin, and Jacobson, Daniel (2000). "The Moralistic Fallacy: On the 'Appropriateness' of Emotion," *Philosophy and Phenomenological Research,* 61: 65–90.

Darwall, Stephen (1994). "Hume and the Invention of Utilitarianism," in M. A. Stewart and J. P. Wright (eds), *Hume and Hume's Connexions,* 58–82. Philadelphia: Penn State University Press.

Darwall, Stephen (1995). *The British Moralists and the Internal "Ought."* Cambridge: Cambridge University Press.

Darwall, Stephen (2006). *The Second-Person Standpoint.* Cambridge, MA: Harvard University Press.

Dees, Richard (1997). "Hume on the Characters of Virtue," *Journal of the History of Philosophy,* 35: 45–64.

Dickey, Laurence (1986). "Historicizing the 'Adam Smith Problem': Conceptual, Historiographical, and Textual Issues," *Journal of Modern History,* 58: 579–609.

Dreier, J. (1993). "Structures of Normative Theories," *The Monist,* 76: 22–40.

Driver, Julia, "The History of Utilitarianism," in Edward N. Zalta (ed.), *The Stanford Encyclopedia of Philosophy* (Summer 2009 edn): <http://plato.stanford.edu/archives/sum2009/entries/utilitarianism-history/>.

Dupoux, Emmanuel, and Jacob, Pierre (2007). "Universal Moral Grammar: A Critical Appraisal," *Trends in Cognitive Science,* 11: 372–8.

Dworkin, Ronald (2001). "Do Liberal Values Conflict?" in M. Lilla, R. Dworkin, and R. B. Silvers (eds), *The Legacy of Isaiah Berlin,* 73–90. New York: New York Review of Books.

Dwyer, Susan (1999). "Moral Competence," in K. Murasugi and R. Stainton (eds), *Philosophy and Linguistics,* 169–90. Boulder, CO: Westview Press.

Eggleston, Ben (2007). "Conflicts of Rules in Hooker's Rule-Consequentialism," *Canadian Journal of Philosophy,* 37: 329–49.

Eibl-Eibesfeldt, Irenaus (1975). *Ethnology,* tr. Erick Klinghammer. New York: Holt, Rinehart & Winston.

Ellis, Anthony (1992). "Deontology, Incommensurability and the Arbitrary," *Philosophy and Phenomenological Research,* 52: 855–75.

Enoch, D. (2010). "The Epistemological Challenge to Metanormative Realism: How Best to Understand it, and How to Cope with it," *Philosophical Studies,* 148: 413–37.

Falk, W. D. (1986). *Ought, Reasons, and Morality.* Ithaca, NY: Cornell University Press.

Feinberg, Joel (1980). "Voluntary Euthanasia and the Inalienable Right to Life," in *Rights, Justice, and the Bounds of Liberty,* 221–51. Princeton: Princeton University Press.

Fleischacker, Samuel (2004). *On Adam Smith's Wealth of Nations.* Princeton: Princeton University Press.

Fleischacker, Samuel (2005). "Smith und der Kulturelativismus," in C. Fricke and H.-P. Schütt (eds), *Adam Smith als Moralphilosoph,* 100–27. Berlin: Walter de Gruyter.

Foot, Philippa (1983). "Moral Realism and Moral Dilemma," *Journal of Philosophy,* 80: 379–98.

Garrett, Don (2007). "The First Motive to Justice: Hume's Circle Argument Squared," *Hume Studies,* 33: 257–88.

Gaus, Gerald (2011). *The Order of Public Reason.* Cambridge: Cambridge University Press.

Gaut, Berys (1993). "Moral Pluralism," *Philosophical Papers,* 22: 17–40.

Geach, Peter (1969). *God and the Soul.* London: Routledge & Kegan Paul.

Gert, Bernard (2007). *Common Morality: Deciding What to Do.* Oxford: Oxford University Press.

Gert, B., Culver, C., and Clouser, K. (1997). *Bioethics: A Return to Fundamentals.* Oxford: Oxford University Press.

Gill, Michael B. (1996a). "Fantastick Associations and Addictive General Rules: A Fundamental Difference between Hutcheson and Hume," *Hume Studies*, 22: 23–48.

Gill, Michael B. (1996b). "A Philosopher in his Closet: Reflexivity and Justification in Hume's Moral Theory," *Canadian Journal of Philosophy*, 26: 231–56.

Gill, Michael B. (1999). "Relativism and the Concept of Morality," *Journal of Value Inquiry*, 33: 171–82.

Gill, Michael B. (2006). *The British Moralists on Human Nature and the Birth of Secular Ethics*. Cambridge: Cambridge University Press.

Gill, Michael B. (2007). "Moral Rationalism vs. Moral Sentimentalism: Is Morality More Like Math or Beauty?" *Philosophy Compass*, 2: 16–30.

Gill, Michael B. (2008a). "Variability and Moral Phenomenology," *Phenomenology and the Cognitive Sciences*, 7: 99–113.

Gill, Michael B. (2008b). "Meta-Ethical Variability, Incoherence, and Error," in W. Sinnott-Armstrong (ed.), *Moral Psychology*, ii. *The Cognitive Science of Morality*, 387–402. Cambridge, MA: MIT Press.

Gill, Michael B. (2009a). "Indeterminacy and Variability in Meta-Ethics," *Philosophical Studies*, 145: 215–34.

Gill, Michael B. (2009b). "Moral Phenomenology in Hutcheson and Hume," *Journal of the History of Philosophy*, 46: 569–94.

Gill, Michael B. (2012). "The Non-Consequentialist Force of Promises: A Reply to Sinnott-Armstrong," *Analysis*, 72: 506–13.

Gill, Michael B. and Nichols, Shaun (2008). "Sentimentalist Pluralism: Moral Psychology and Philosophical Ethics," *Philosophical Issues*, 18: 142–63.

Gilligan, Carol (1982). *In a Different Voice*. Cambridge, MA: Harvard University Press.

Greene, Joshua (2008). "The Secret Joke of Kant's Soul," in W. Sinnott-Armstrong (ed.), *Moral Psychology*, iii. *The Neuroscience of Morality: Emotion, Disease, and Development*, 35–80. Cambridge, MA: MIT Press.

Griswold, Charles (1999). *Adam Smith and the Virtues of Enlightenment*. Cambridge: Cambridge University Press.

Haidt, Jonathan (2001). "The Emotional Dog and its Rational Tail: A Social Intuitionist Approach to Moral Judgment," *Psychological Review*, 108: 814–23.

Haidt, Jonathan, and Bjorklund, Fredrik (2008). "Social Intuitionists Answer Six Questions about Moral Psychology," in W. Sinnott-Armstrong (ed.), *Moral Psychology*, ii. *The Cognitive Science of Morality*, 181–217. Cambridge, MA: MIT Press.

Haidt, Jonathan, and Graham, Jesse (2007). "When Morality Opposes Justice: Conservatives Have Moral Intuitions that Liberals May Not Recognize," *Social Justice Research*, 20: 98–116.

Hampton, Jean (1986). *Hobbes and the Social Contract Tradition*. Cambridge: Cambridge University Press.

Hanley, Ryan (2010). Introduction and notes to Adam Smith's *Theory of Moral Sentiments*. London: Penguin Classics.

Harman, G. (1977). *The Nature of Morality: An Introduction to Ethics*. Oxford: Oxford University Press.

Harman, G. (1986). "Moral Explanations of Natural Facts: Can Moral Claims Be Tested Against Moral Reality?" in N. Gillespie (ed.), *Spindel Conference: Moral Realism, Southern Journal of Philosophy*, suppl. 24: 57–68.

Harman, Gilbert (1999). "Moral Philosophy and Linguistics," in K. Brinkmann (ed.), *Proceedings of the 20th World Congress of Philosophy*, i. *Ethics*, 107–15. Bowling Green, OH: Philosophy Documentation Center.

Harris, James (2010). "Hume on the Moral Obligation to Justice," *Hume Studies*, 36: 25–50.

Hauser, Mark (2006). *Moral Minds: How Nature Designed a Universal Sense of Right and Wrong*. New York: Harper Collins/Ecco.

Henley, Kenneth (2011). "Character Naturalized: Hume Distinction between Artificial and Natural Virtues and the Rejection of Traditional Virtue Ethics," *Southwest Philosophy Review*, 27: 73–81.

Heydt, Colin (forthcoming). "Hume's Innovative Taxonomy of the Virtue," in Jacqueline Taylor (ed.), *Reading Hume on the Principles of Morals: Essays on the Second Enquiry*. Oxford: Oxford University Press.

Herman, Barbara (1993). *The Practice of Moral Judgment*. Cambridge, MA: Harvard University Press.

Hill, Thomas (1991). "Autonomy and Benevolent Lies," in *Autonomy and Self-Respect*, 25–42. Cambridge: Cambridge University Press.

Hill, Thomas (1992). "Kantian Pluralism," *Ethics*, 102: 743–62.

Hill, Thomas (1996). "Moral Dilemmas, Gaps, and Residues," in H. E. Mason (ed.), *Moral Dilemmas and Moral Theory*, 167–98. Oxford: Oxford University Press.

Hill, Thomas (2002). Introduction to and commentary on Kant's *Groundwork of the Metaphysics of Morals*, tr. Arnulf Zweig. Oxford: Oxford University Press.

Hobbes, Thomas (1651/1994). *Leviathan*, ed. Edwin Curley. Indianapolis: Hackett Publishing.

Hoffman, M. L. (1983) "Affective and Cognitive Processes in Moral Internalization," in E. T. Higgins, D. N. Ruble, and W. W. Hartup (eds), *Social Cognition and Social Development: A Sociocultural Perspective*, 236–74. Cambridge: Cambridge University Press.

Hooker, Brad (2000a). *Ideal Code, Real World: a Rule Consequentialist Theory of Morality*. Oxford: Oxford University Press.

Hooker, Brad (2000b). "Moral Particularism—Wrong and Bad," in Brad Hooker and Margaret Little (eds), *Moral Particularism*, 1–23. Oxford: Oxford University Press.

Horgan, Terence and Tienson, John (1996). *Connectionism and the Philosophy of Psychology*. Cambridge, MA: MIT Press.

Horgan, Terence and Timmons, Mark (forthcoming). *Illuminating Reasons: An Essay in Moral Phenomenology*. Oxford: Oxford University Press.

Huebner, B., Dwyer, S., and Hauser, M. (2008). "The Role of Emotion in Moral Psychology," *Trends in Cognitive Sciences*, 13: 1–6.

Huemer, Michael (2005). *Ethical Intuitionism*. Basingstoke: Palgrave Macmillan.

Hume, David (1739–40/2002). *A Treatise of Human Nature*, ed. David Fate Norton and Mary J. Norton. Oxford: Oxford University Press. Cited as *T*, with the numerals following denoting book, part, section, and paragraph.

Hume, David (1751/2006). *An Enquiry concerning the Principles of Morals.* Edited by Tom L. Beauchamp. Oxford: Oxford University Press. Cited as *E*, with the numerals following denoting section and paragraph. The appendices from the *Enquiry* are referred to as "App," with the numerals following denoting appendix number and paragraph.

Hume, David (1932). *The Letters of David Hume*, ed. J. Y. T. Greig, i. Oxford: Oxford University Press. Cited as *Letters.*

Hume, David (1983). *The History of England* (based on 1778 edn). Indianapolis: Liberty Fund. Cited as *History*, with numerals following denoting volume and page.

Hume, David (1987). *Essays, Moral, Political, and Literary,* ed. Eugene F. Miller. Indianapolis: Liberty Fund. Cited as *Essays.*

Hume, David (1998b). "A Dialogue," in *An Enquiry concerning the Principles of Morals*, ed. Tom L. Beauchamp. Oxford: Oxford University Press. Cited as D, with numeral following denoting paragraph.

Hurka, Thomas (1996). "Monism, Pluralism, and Rational Regret," *Ethics*, 106: 55–75.

Hurley, Susan (1989). *Personality and Polity*. Oxford: Oxford University Press.

Hursthouse, Rosalind (1999a). "Resolvable Dilemmas" and "Irresolvable and Tragic Dilemmas," in *On Virtue Ethics*, 43–90. Oxford: Oxford University Press.

Hursthouse, Rosalind (1999b). "Virtue Ethics and Human Nature," *Hume Studies*, 25: 67–82.

Hutcheson, Francis (1726/2004). *An Inquiry into the Original of our Ideas of Beauty and Virtue* (2nd edn), ed. Wolfgang Leidhold. Indianapolis: Liberty Fund.

Hutcheson, Francis (1728/2002). *An Essay on the Nature and Conduct of the Passions and Affections; with Illustrations on the Moral Sense*, ed. Aaron Garrett. Indianapolis: Liberty Fund.

Joseph, H. W. B. (1933). *Some Problems in Ethics*. Oxford: Oxford University Press.

Kagan, Shelly (1989). *The Limits of Morality*. Oxford: Oxford University Press.

Kant, Immanuel (1785/2002). *Groundwork for the Metaphysics of Morals*, tr. Arnulf Zweig, ed. Thomas E. Hill, Jr. and Arnulf Zweig. Oxford: Oxford University Press.

Kant, Immanuel (1797/1991). *The Metaphysics of Morals,* tr. and ed. Mary Gregor. Cambridge: Cambridge University Press.

Kekes, John (1995). *The Morality of Pluralism*. Princeton: Princeton University Press.

King, James (1988). "Hume on Artificial Lives," *Hume Studies*, 14: 53–92.

Kohlberg, Lawrence (1981). *The Philosophy of Moral Development: Moral Stages and the Idea of Justice*. New York: Harper & Row.

Korsgaard, Christine (1983). "Two Distinctions in Goodness," *Philosophical Review*, 92: 169–95.

Korsgaard, Christine (1996). *The Sources of Normativity*. Cambridge: Cambridge University Press.

Korsgaard, Christine (1999). "The General Point of View: Love and Moral Approval in Hume's Ethics," *Hume Studies*, 25: 3–42.

Lance, Mark and Little, Margaret (2004). "Defeasibility and the Normative Grasp of Context," *Erkenntnis*, 435–55.

Lance, Mark and Little, Margaret (2006). "Defending Moral Particularism," in J. Dreier (ed.), *Contemporary Debates in Moral Theory*, 305–21. Boston: Blackwell.

Lance, Mark and Little, Margaret (2007a). "Where the Laws are," in R. Shafer-Landau (ed.), *Oxford Studies in Metaethics*, ii. 149–71. Oxford: Oxford University Press.

Lance, Mark and Little, Margaret (2007b). "From Particularism to Defeasibility," in M. Lance, M. Potrc, and V. Strahovnik (eds), *Challenging Moral Particularism*, 53–74. London: Routledge.

Leibniz, G. W. (1704/1996). *New Essays on Human Understanding*, ed. P. Rmenant and J. Bennett. Cambridge: Cambridge University Press.

Locke, John (1991/1689). *An Essay concerning Human Understanding*, ed. P. H. Nidditch. Oxford: Clarendon Press.

Lopez, T., Zamzow, J., Gil, M., and Nichols, S. (2009). "Side Constraints and the Structure of Commonsense Ethics," *Philosophical Perspectives*, 32: 305–19.

McConnell, Terrance (1996). "Moral Residue and Dilemmas," in H. E. Mason (ed.), *Moral Dilemmas and Moral Theory*, 36–47. Oxford: Oxford University Press.

MacIntyre, Alisdair (1988). *Whose Justice? Which Rationality?* Notre Dame, IN: University of Notre Dame Press.

McIntyre, Jane (2000). "Hume's Passions: Direct and Indirect," *Hume Studies*, 26: 77–86.

McKeever, Sean, and Ridge, Michael (2006). *Principled Ethics: Generalism as a Regulative Ideal*. Oxford: Oxford University Press.

Mackie, J. L. (1977). *Ethics. Inventing Right and Wrong*. Harmondsworth: Penguin Books.

McNaughton, David (1988). *Moral Vision: An Introduction to Ethics*. Oxford: Blackwell.

McNaughton, David (1995). "An Unconnected Heap of Duties?" *Philosophical Quarterly*, 46: 433–47.

Mallon, Ron (2008). "Reviving Rawls's Linguistic Analogy Inside and Out," in W. Sinnott-Armstrong (ed.), *Moral Psychology*, ii. *The Cognitive Science of Morality*, 145–56. Cambridge, MA: MIT Press.

Marcus, Ruth Barcan (1980). "Moral Dilemmas and Consistency," *Journal of Philosophy*, 77: 121–36.

Mason, Elinor, "Value Pluralism", in Edward N. Zalta (ed.), The Stanford Encyclopedia of Philosophy (Fall 2011 edn.): <http://plato.stanford.edu/archives/fall2011/entries/value-pluralism/>.

Mikhail, John (2007). "Universal Moral Grammar: Theory, Evidence and the Future," *Trends in Cognitive Science*, 11: 143–52.

Mikhail, John (2011). *Elements of Moral Cognition: Rawls's Linguistic Analogy and the Cognitive Science of Moral and Legal Judgment*. Cambridge: Cambridge University Press.

Mill, John Stuart (1861/2001). *Utilitarianism*, ed. George Sher. Indianapolis: Hackett Publishing Co.

Mill, John Stuart (1843/1904). *A System of Logic Ratiocinative and Inductive* (8th edn). New York and London: Harper & Brothers Publishers.

Moll, J., De Oliveirra-Souza, R., and Eslinger, P. J. (2003). "Morals and the Human Brain: A Working Model," *Neuroreport*, 14: 299–305.

Moore, Michael S. (1997). "Torture and the Balance of Evils," in *Placing Blame: A General Theory of the Criminal Law*, 669–736. Oxford: Oxford University Press.

Nelissen, R. M. A., Leliveld, M. C., van Dijk, E., and Zeelenberg, M. (2011). "Fear and Guilt in Proposers: Using Emotions to Explain Offers in Ultimatum Bargaining," *European Journal of Social Psychology*, 41: 78–85.

Nichols, Shaun (2002). "On the Genealogy of Norms: A Case for the Role of Emotion in Cultural Evolution," *Philosophy of Science*, 69: 234–55.

Nichols, Shaun (2004). *Sentimental Rules: On the Natural Foundations of Moral Judgment*. Oxford: Oxford University Press.

Nichols, Shaun (2005). "Innateness and Moral Psychology," in P. Carruthers, S. Laurence, and S. Stich (eds), *The Innate Mind: Structure and Content*, 353–69. New York: Oxford University Press.

Nichols, Shaun (2008). "Sentimentalism Naturalized," in W. Sinnott-Armstrong (ed.), *Moral Psychology, ii. The Cognitive Science of Morality*: 255–74. Cambridge, MA: MIT Press.

Nichols, Shaun (2010). "Emotions, Norms, and the Genealogy of Fairness," *Politics, Philosophy and Economics*, 9: 275–96.

O'Neill, Onora (2001). "Practical Principles and Practical Judgment," *Hastings Center Report*, 31: 15–23.

Orlean, Susan (1998). *The Orchid Thief: A True Story of Beauty and Obsession*. New York: Random House Publishing.

Otteson, James (forthcoming). "Adam Smith on Justice, Social Justice, and Ultimate Justice."

Pelligra, V. (2011). "Empathy, Guilt-Aversion, and Patterns of Reciprocity," *Journal of Neuroscience, Psychology, and Economics*, 4: 161–73.

Portmore, Douglas (2009). "Consequentializing," *Philosophy Compass*, 4: 329–47.

Price, Richard (1787). *A Review of the Principal Questions in Morals*. London: T. Cadell in the Strand.

Prinz, Jesse (2006). "The Emotional Basis of Moral Judgments," *Philosophical Explorations*, 9: 29–43.

Prinz, Jesse (2007a). *The Emotional Construction of Morals*. Oxford: Oxford University Press.

Prinz, Jesse (2007b). "Is Morality Innate?" in W. Sinnott-Armstrong (ed.), *Moral Psychology, i. Evolution of Morals*, 367–406. Cambridge, MA: MIT Press.

Prinz, Jesse and Nichols, Shaun (2010). "Moral Emotions," in J. Doris and the Moral Psychology Research Group (eds), *The Moral Psychology Handbook*, 111–46. Oxford: Oxford University Press.

Radcliffe, Elizabeth (1994). "Hume on Motivating Sentiments, the General Point of View, and the Inculcation of 'Morality,'" *Hume Studies*, 20: 37–58.

Radcliffe, Elizabeth (1996). "How does the Humean Sense of Duty Motivate?" *Journal of the History of Philosophy*, 34: 383–407.

Reid, Thomas (1983). *Inquiry and Essays*, ed. R. E. Beanblossom and K. Lehrer. Indianapolis: Hackett Publishing.

Rawls, John (1971). *A Theory of Justice*. Cambridge, MA: Harvard University Press.

Rawls, John (2000). *Lectures on the History of Moral Philosophy*. Cambridge, MA: Harvard University Press.

Richardson, Henry (1990). "Specifying Norms as a Way to Resolve Concrete Ethical Problems," *Philosophy and Public Affairs*, 19: 279–310.

Richardson, Henry (2000). "Specifying, Balancing, and Interpreting Bioethical Principles," *Journal of Medicine and Philosophy*, 25: 285–307.

Ridge, Michael, "Moral Non-Naturalism," in Edward N. Zalta (ed.), *The Stanford Encyclopedia of Philosophy* (Fall 2013 edn): <http://plato.stanford.edu/archives/fall2013/entries/moral-non-naturalism/>.

Rorty, Amelie (1980). "Agent-Regret," in Amelie Rorty (ed.), *Explaining Emotions*, 489–506. Berkeley, CA: University of California Press.

Rosenberg, Jay (2005). *Accessing Kant: A Relaxed Introduction to the Critique of Pure Reason*. Oxford: Oxford University Press.

Ross, W. D. (1930). *The Right and the Good*. Oxford: Oxford University Press.

Ross, W. D. (1939). *The Foundations of Ethics*. Oxford: Oxford University Press.

Ross, W. D. (1954). *Kant's Ethical Theory*. Oxford: Oxford University Press.

Rozin, P., Lowery, L., Imada, S., and Haidt, J. (1999). "The CAD Triad Hypothesis: A Mapping between Three Moral Emotions (Contempt, Anger, Disgust) and Three Moral Codes (Community, Autonomy, Divinity)," *Journal of Personality and Social Psychology*, 76: 574–86.

Sanfey, A. G., Rilling, J. K., Aronson, J. A., Nystrom, L. E., and Cohen, J. D. (2003). "The Neural Basis of Economic Decision-Making in the Ultimatum Game," *Science*, 300: 1755–8.

Sartre, Jean-Paul (1956). "Existentialism is a Humanism," in Walter Kaufman (ed.), *Existentialism from Dostoevsky to Sartre*, 345–68. Cleveland, OH: World Publishing, Meridian Books.

Savile, Anthony (2002). "Aesthetic Experience in Shaftesbury," *Proceedings of the Aristotelian Society*, 76: 55–74.

Sayre-McCord, Geoffrey (1996). "Hume and the Bauhaus Theory of Ethics," *Midwest Studies in Philosophy*, 20: 280–98.

Schliesser, Eric (2008). "Review of D. D. Raphael's *The Impartial Spectator*," *Ethics*, 118: 569–75.

Schnall, S., Haidt, J., and Clore, G. L. (2005). "Disgust as Embodied Moral Judgment," unpublished manuscript, Department of Psychology, University of Virginia.

Seung, T. K. and Bonevac, D. (1992). "Plural Values and Indeterminate Rankings," *Ethics*, 102: 799–813.

Shafer-Landau, Russ (2005). *Moral Realism: A Defence*. Oxford: Oxford University Press.

Shweder, R. A., Much, N. C., Mahapatra, M., and Park, L. (1997). "The 'Big Three' of Morality (Autonomy, Community, and Divinity), and the 'Big Three' Explanations of Suffering," in A Brandt and P. Rozin (eds), *Morality and Health*, 119–69. New York: Routledge

Sidgwick, Henry (1907). *The Methods of Ethics*. London: Macmillan & Co.

Singer, Peter (1972). "Famine, Affluence, and Morality," *Philosophy and Public Affairs*, 1: 229–43.

Sinnott-Armstrong, Walter (1988). *Moral Dilemmas*. Oxford: Blackwell Publishing.

Sinnott-Armstrong, Walter (2009). "How Strong is This Obligation: An Argument for Consequentialism from Concomitant Variation," *Analysis*, 69: 438–42.

Smith, Adam (1759/1984). *The Theory of Moral Sentiments*. Indianapolis: Liberty Fund.

Smith, Adam (1776/1976). *An Inquiry into the Nature and Causes of the Wealth of Nations*, ed. R. H. Campbell, A. H. Skinner, and W. B. Todd. Oxford: Oxford University Press.

Smith, Adam (1978). *Lectures on Jurisprudence*, ed. R. L. Meek, D. D. Raphael, and P. G. Stein. Oxford: Oxford University Press.

Smith, Michael (1994). *The Moral Problem*. Oxford: Blackwell Publishing.

Sommerville, C. John (1977). *Popular Religion in Restoration England*. Gainesville, FL: University Presses of Florida.

Sorensen, Roy A. (1991). "Moral Dilemmas, Thought Experiments, and Conflict Vagueness," *Philosophical Studies*, 63: 291–308.

Stocker, Michael (1990). *Plural and Conflicting Values*. Oxford: Oxford University Press.

Street, Sharon (2006). "A Darwinian Dilemma for Realist Theories of Value," *Philosophical Studies*, 127: 109–66.

Swanton, Christine (2007). "Can Hume Be Read as a Virtue Ethicist?" *Hume Studies*, 33: 91–113.

Tangney, J. P., Steuwig, J., and Mashek, D. J. (2007). "Moral Emotions and Moral Behavior," *Annual Review of Psychology*, 58: 345–72.

Timmons, Mark (2006). "The Categorical Imperative and Universalizability," in C. Horn and D. Schoenecker (eds), *Kant's Groundwork of the Metaphysics of Morals: New Interpretations*, 158–99. Berlin and New York: de Gruyter.

Timmons, Mark (2008). "Toward a Sentimentalist Deontology," in W. Sinnott-Armstrong (ed.), *Moral Psychology, iii. The Neuroscience of Morality: Emotion, Disease, and Development*, 93–104. Cambridge, MA: MIT Press.

Timmons, Mark (2013). *Moral Theory: An Introduction* (2nd edn). Lanham, MD: Rowman & Littlefield Publishers.

Unger, Peter (1996). *Living High and Letting Die: Our Illusion of Innocence*. Oxford: Oxford University Press.

Waldron, Jeremy (2011). *What are Moral Absolutes Like?* Public Law Research Paper, 11-62. Available at SSRN: <http://ssrn.com/abstract=1906850 or http://dx.doi.org/10.2139/ssrn.1906850>.

Wheatley, T., and Haidt, J. (2005). "Hypnotically Induced Disgust Makes Moral Judgments More Severe," *Psychological Science*, 16: 780–4.

Whichcote, Benjamin (1751). *The Works, in Four Volumes*. Aberdeen: J. Chalmers.

The Whole Duty of Man (1704). London: Norton & Pawlet.

Wielenberg, Erik J. (2010). "On the Evolutionary Debunking of Morality," *Ethics*, 120: 441–64.

Wiggins, David (1978-9). "Weakness of Will, Commensurability, and the Objects of Deliberation and Desire," *Proceedings of the Aristotelian Society*, 79: 251–77.

Williams, Bernard (1973a). "Ethical Consistency," in *Problems of the Self*, 166–86. Cambridge: Cambridge University Press.

Williams, Bernard (1973b). "A Critique of Utilitarianism," in *Utilitarianism: For and Against* (with J. C. C. Smart), 77–150. Cambridge: Cambridge University Press.

Williams, Bernard (1981). "Moral Luck," in *Moral Luck*, 20–39. Cambridge: Cambridge University Press.

Williams, Bernard (1995). *Making Sense of Humanity*. Cambridge: Cambridge University Press.

Wolf, Susan (1992). "Two Levels of Pluralism," *Ethics*, 102: 785–98.

Wolf, Susan (2011). "Hiking the Range," in Derek Parfit, *On What Matters*, 33–57. Oxford: Oxford University Press.

Zamzow, Jennifer (2013). "*Moral Decision-Making: How the Normative and Empirical Can Inform Our Prescriptive Accounts*," Doctoral Dissertation, Department of Philosophy, University of Arizona.

Index